Exit Through the Fireplace

Many of today's leading actors and directors began their careers in the far less exalted world of local rep. In this nostalgic and often hilarious book Kate Dunn draws on theatre people's first-hand experiences to trace the great days of this renowned British institution.

Not very long ago every provincial town had its own repertory theatre. Productions were usually done on a shoestring, so great ingenuity was required from the lowly and ill-paid assistant stage managers, who often had to double as actors too. Bernard Cribbins remembers having to take charge of a prop goat which he brought to work on the bus with him; Phyllida Law recalls 'being in costume, prompting, lying on the floor to work the dimmer board which had great big handles that you pushed up and down with your feet'. Theatrical digs could also be somewhat unusual – at one the landlady's dead father was discovered in a coffin under the bed.

At theatres like the Birmingham Rep, the Liverpool Playhouse and the Bristol Old Vic standards were high, and provincial theatres gave a kick start to many careers. Derek Jacobi, Alan Ayckbourn and Peter Hall all describe how they learned their craft in local rep. In *Exit Through the Fireplace* Kate Dunn brings together the experiences of the famous and of the less well-known – actors, writers, directors, designers and those who made up the audience – to give an irresistible account of a great theatrical tradition.

KATE DUNN comes from a theatrical family that spans four generations. Her great-grandfather Arthur Whitby played all the comic roles in one of the earliest repertory companies. Her grandfather, the actor and playwright Hugh Williams, began his career at the renowned Liverpool Playhouse, and her uncle Simon Williams worked in rep before achieving fame in the television series *Upstairs Downstairs*. Kate obtained a degree in English and Drama at Manchester University before embarking on a theatrical career herself in which she has had extensive experience in rep.

Exit Through the Fireplace

The Great Days of Rep

Kate Dunn

Foreword by Richard Attenborough

John Murray
Albemarle Street, London

A catalogue record for this book is available from the British Library

ISBN 0-7195-5481 0

Typeset in Baskerville by Servis Filmsetting Ltd, Manchester
Printed and bound in Great Britain by
St Edmundsbury Press Ltd, Bury St Edmunds, Suffolk

For Lily
(and her parents)

Contents

Contents

Illustrations

(between pages 178 and 179)

The author and publisher wish to thank the following for permission to reproduce illustrations: Plate 1, Hilary Mason; 2, 3 and 13, The Raymond Mander and Joe Mitchenson Theatre Collection; 4, 15, 16 and 18, Penny Arkwright; 5 and 6, The Theatre Collection, Bristol University; 7 and 17, Charles Simon; 8, 9, 12 and 20, Vilma Hollingbery; 10, Prue Dunn; 11, Wolsey Theatre, Ipswich; 14, Bernard Cribbins; 19, Dennis Ramsden.

Foreword

I AM DELIGHTED to welcome this cogent testament to the contribution made by a very special kind of theatre to the entertainment and culture of our nation.

Throughout this century, repertory theatre has provided a crucial focus for communities, large and small, and an invaluable source of training for members of the acting profession. My own career began in this way at the Intimate Theatre in Palmer's Green and at the much-lamented old 'Q' Theatre by Kew Bridge.

The actors, actresses, stage managers, directors and producers who owe their start to rep are legion. Many have gone on to achieve international renown in television and cinema as well. Part of this book's fascination is the large number who have kindly contributed their recollections, providing us with a series of first-hand accounts, which must become a valuable and enduring part of theatre history.

The narrative is bursting with stories which conjure up the enormous excitement of putting on a new play every week, the panic to be ready on time, the first-night nerves, the inevitable disasters and the sense of triumph when excellent performances were achieved against all the odds.

A great number of these vivid and amusing insights into life back-stage – so endearingly familiar to those of us who lived and laughed through similar plights – will be a revelation to younger members of the profession. Many will never know the agonies of rehearsing in an incredibly short space of time, while preparing their own costume and begging props and furniture from local shops. For them the highs of the first night may never be contrasted with the sort of low you experience when a door handle comes off in your hand and you are obliged to exit through the fireplace!

All the members of our profession, both eminent and less well known, who have contributed to this colourful and funny book are united by a feeling of affection for the theatres and companies which granted them their experience and training. They bring to life all the dedication, hard work and camaraderie that went into entertaining and enriching local audiences for almost a hundred years.

As a result, *Exit Through the Fireplace* is a splendid tribute to an unsung national asset and a powerful evocation of the magic of living drama. With the modern rival temptations of cinema, television and video, it is also a sobering and timely reminder of a vigorous and important art form that is all but lost to future generations.

Richard Attenborough

Acknowledgements

I AM PROFOUNDLY indebted to all the actors, actresses, directors and stage managers who told me the wonderful stories about the golden age of repertory theatre which make up this book. I talked to more than two hundred people and all of them were unstinting in giving me their time, their enthusiasm and very often lunch as well. This is an opportunity for me to thank them all, for without their help this book could never have been written. I would in particular like to single out the late Daniel Massey, whose death has been announced as I am writing this. He spoke to me with such eloquence and fire about the importance of rep to the theatre as a whole that I am sure, if enough people shared his passionate commitment to the movement, there would not be such a large question mark hanging over its future.

I would also like to thank the many people who expressed interest in my project but whose schedules ultimately proved to be too full for us to arrange to have a conversation.

The Actor's Charitable Trust, the Authors' Foundation, the K. Blundell Trust and the Equity Trust Fund have been sympathetic and generous in supporting me through the long period of researching the contents of this book and I am deeply grateful to them for their benevolence.

Lynn Spur, Tony Jackson and Nigel Seale of *Spotlight* have all been most generous in helping me to glean information and material and, in doing so, have taken from my shoulders some of the pressure of what has seemed at times like an enormous undertaking. I would also like to thank Chris Robinson and Sarah Morris of the Bristol University Theatre Collection, Nicola Watt at Samuel French's, Anne Wigzell, Pat Marmont, Margaretta Scott, Jonathan Dockar Drysdale, Avril

Angers, Angela Pleasence, Glynn Sweet, Alexa Povey, Allan Watkins, Katerina Obeng-Boateng, Sarah Whitlock, Steve Cameron and Peter, Kathryn, Sam, Ben and Alice Lloyd for their many and various contributions.

Finally, my love and thanks for the back-up they have given me over several busy years go to Caroline Knox, Sarah Molloy, Anna Mason, Heather Lawler, Kate Darnborough, Latifa Strong and of course my Aunt Loo. I would like to thank Jenny Mitchell, Gill McLoughlin and Maryon Shearman for their moral support, Barrie Hinksman for his loving kindness and my mother and my father for their limitless care. Last of all I would like to give a big hug to my son Jack for being tolerant and understanding when my work has intruded on our lives together.

Introduction

'*Repertory shall be deemed to cover performances at a place of entertainment at which the same management is presenting or intends to present plays for a period of not less than six consecutive weeks with approximately the same company of Artists and / or nucleus of a working cast.*'

Esher Standard Contract for Repertory Season at
Provincial and London Suburban Theatres

THERE HAS BEEN much lamentation over the state of repertory theatres in Great Britain in recent years. These regional companies were once centres of dramatic excellence, the foundation on which our world-renowned theatre tradition was built. It is possible that factors other than the purely economic, most importantly the advent of cinema and television, have contributed to the demise of this once-flourishing source of popular culture. Whatever the causes, the fact remains that in recent decades theatres have closed, these beautiful buildings have been demolished or put to other uses and those that survive do so because they have been obliged to limit their repertoire to only the most popular types of play – thrillers and farces.

This has not always been the case. Playwrights such as George Bernard Shaw, J.M. Synge and John Galsworthy often had their work first staged by repertory companies during the heyday of the repertory movement, which sprang up at the turn of the century and flourished well into the 1960s. Every sizeable town had its local theatre, staffed by a group of actors engaged for a year or more, producing plays on a weekly, fortnightly or three-weekly basis. The heart of the movement still beats strongly, with hundreds of actors enthusiastically engaged in quality work up and down the country, but as long as funding remains tight, the survival of this unique art form is under threat. Although largely a twentieth-century phenomenon, the origins of repertory theatre extend back over many centuries to when bands of strolling players formed themselves into what were known as circuit companies, which toured so regularly round a particular region that special buildings were erected to accommodate them on their visits. These were the early provincial theatres. In the mid-nineteenth century the circuit companies gave way to stock companies, which were housed in a specific theatre, where they put on a different bill of entertainment every night. However, these stock companies were unable to compete with the touring companies, which began to spring up in the late nineteenth century as the railway network spread around the country, facilitating travel.

The term repertory theatre was first coined during the season at the Royal Court Theatre in London between 1904 and 1907, which was presented by John Vedrenne and Harley Granville-Barker. These two producers emphasized the importance of the play, rather than of individual actors, thus fostering a feeling of teamwork among the company they assembled. They premièred five plays by George Bernard Shaw, as well as new work by John Galsworthy and Harley Granville-Barker himself; other writers in their repertoire included Euripides, Henrik Ibsen, W.B. Yeats and Gerhart Hauptmann.

A real impetus was given to the repertory movement by Annie Horniman, who founded the famous Abbey Theatre in Dublin in 1903. She fostered talent by drawing regularly on a pool of actors and writers, amongst them J.M. Synge, so that a recognizable house style emerged – another feature of the repertory movement. She became responsible for the first repertory company in mainland Britain when she bought the Gaiety Theatre in Manchester in 1908 and established a company there. She described her enterprise as, 'purely a dramatic venture on honest commercial lines'. The idea was becoming popular and in the next five years similar projects were started in Glasgow, Liverpool and Birmingham. The inspiration and the finance for the last came from Sir Barry Jackson, who declared that his intention at the Birmingham Rep was 'to enlarge and increase the aesthetic sense of the public; to give living authors an opportunity of seeing their works performed and to learn something from revivals of the classics; to serve an art instead of making that art serve a commercial purpose'. Not all these lofty ideals found expression in the numerous reps which started to spring up, but the notion of resident companies which served a local audience caught on rapidly and before long there were more than a hundred such theatres in the country.

The spread of the repertory movement was helped by the formation of the Council for the Encouragement of Music and the Arts (CEMA) in 1939 as the Second World War started. Because London was vulnerable to attack by Germany, a policy of decentralization was pursued, with the result that theatres far away from the capital were encouraged.

When the war was over the Arts Council was set up to take over the responsibilities of CEMA. During four years as Arts Minister for the Labour government, Jennie Lee placed great emphasis on the importance of regional theatre, and in the 1960s and 1970s subsidies were made available and an ambitious programme of theatre building was embarked upon. The twenty years after the war are arguably the finest that the repertory movement has seen, encompassing the establishment of Joan Littlewood's Theatre Workshop first in Manchester and from 1953 in Stratford East; the founding of the Studio Theatre Company by Stephen Joseph in 1955; the work of George Devine with the English Stage Company at the Royal Court Theatre in London; the building of the first postwar theatre, the Belgrade in Coventry and the subsequent establishment of its renowned Theatre in Education Team and the flowering of John Neville's company in Nottingham in the 1960s. The darkness of subsequent decades has been illuminated by companies like the Royal Exchange in Manchester and Alan Ayckbourn's in Scarborough, but the recent history of the movement is characterized not by growth but by decline. For this reason it is vitally important that a record of the best and worst of repertory theatre is made while there are enough surviving examples for it still to have relevance and while practitioners remain who can remember both the golden and the dark ages.

Exit through the Fireplace does not set out to be a comprehensive history of the repertory tradition, since there are already many fine books on the subject. What it offers is first-hand testimony from hundreds of actors, actresses, directors, producers and stage managers who worked in companies from the 1920s until the present day. Its scope is defined by what the participants have to say, so inevitably there will be gaps which may seem frustrating to the theatre historian, but I hope the particular insights and experiences which the members of the profession were kind enough to share with me will more than compensate for any omissions.

In this introduction I have tried to place the anecdotes which follow in a context, to suggest briefly the historical development of the repertory movement. Rep had its own special significance for the people who worked in many companies the length and breadth of the land. Sir Peter Hall says, 'My ideal, my idea of paradise, is a pleasant town and a pleasant theatre and a small group of actors working together.' Countless other professionals shared the same vision and were prepared to work for very little money under strenuous circumstances in far-flung corners of the country in order to realize this collective dream. Almost everybody thinks that the effort was worth it. Derek Fowlds admits, 'There was a feeling that no other life existed outside the stage door.' The dedication felt by actors to the work they were doing is made plain by Alan Bennion: 'There was something evangelical about it. You were providing live entertainment at cut prices, it was rather like doing good works.' Belinda Lang says, 'Rep was a bit like wartime, I think of it as my time in the army,' while Evangeline Banks's experience of it was subtly different. 'Being in rep was rather like going to a very nice boarding school.' Richard Briers remains amazed by what performers used to accomplish. 'Now the prospect of all the work we did renders me speechless. These days when I finish a show I go straight home to bed, then you didn't want to leave the theatre, you wanted to sleep under the stage. We lived in it and for it.'

The importance to an actor of having some experience in rep was widely recognized, as Jonathan Cecil explains. 'If I went along to an audition they would say, "What have you done in rep?" Even at television castings they would say, "Have you done repertory?" Television was not thought of. I remember being quite excited because one television popped up after another, and a director friend of mine saying, "Well, television is what actors do when they can't get theatre work, to fill in. You mustn't think of it as a way of life, because you won't get anywhere."'

In the interests of balance and credibility it is important to note that not everybody eulogizes about their time in repertory. Suzanne Bertish says, 'Being in the provinces in the mid-Seventies was pretty bleak', and Stephanie Cole points out, 'Shows used to go on slightly under-rehearsed and things would go wrong. I remember doing one awful old drawing-room comedy or farce or something – we did do an awful lot of crap, it's all very well, "Oh, the good old days", but believe me we did stuff that now would never see the light of day and quite right too.' Her opinion is shared by Russell Dixon. 'The romanticism about rep is not justified. It's hard work. There were no golden days of rep. It was about coping and making do.' In spite of these dissonant notes, Richard Johnson probably speaks for the majority of those who worked in the provinces when he observes, 'I know it's a cliché, but it was one of the happiest times in my life. We were a group of people who were all in it together, we were working terribly hard and we were dependent on each other. Bugger the world, we were it.'

Jonathan Cecil is concerned that, 'On the whole there's an awful lot of stories which I think give the younger generation of actors the impression that it used to be like the local amateurs or the Home and Colonial Light Opera Company; that it was nothing but things going wrong all the time, people losing their lines. What amazes me is how high the standard was in general.'

My particular intention in collecting these stories about rep is not to dismiss the movement as merely something humorous or quaint, no more than the sum of its weaknesses, but to draw attention to its unique strengths at a time when they are most needed to fend off the threat of its demise. The service that repertory companies gave to their local communities is irreplaceable, a fact which Sir Peter Hall recognizes when he says, 'Even at its leanest and meanest I think theatre is like a beautiful cooked dinner or a hand-made piece of furniture or clothing, it is made for you, and you tonight, and you only. It's very special.' We let it perish at our peril.

Kate Dunn
Bristol, 1998

1

Starting in Rep

'I'm not leaving until you give me a job.'

Vilma Hollingbery

FOR MANY PEOPLE the easiest route into the acting profession was through securing a job in a repertory theatre. A great number of aspiring actors considered the training offered by these provincial outfits to be either more helpful or more affordable than the formal approach adoped by drama schools, and so passed up the opportunity to attend the Royal Academy of Dramatic Art and its rival establishments in favour of a good stint in a regional company. It was generally recognized that experience in rep provided a grounding in the theatre second to none. Even companies such as the J. Arthur Rank Organization, which made films, recognized its benefit, as Elspet Gray recalls. 'I got a contract with Rank Films and they got all the young pretty things to attend the Rank Charm School because they wanted to build a bevy of young starlets to take to Hollywood. Part of your training there was to be sent down to the Worthing Rep. People in those days believed that theatre training was the best thing for us.'

Since 1929 the practices of the acting profession have been governed by its trade union, British Actors' Equity. From its inception until the Conservative government under Margaret Thatcher abolished restrictive practices, Equity operated a closed shop. This meant that an actor could not get a job until he had his Equity Card, even though he needed a card to get the job in the first place. Theatrical agent Patricia Marmont describes how the system operated. 'There used to be a restriction from Equity whereby people could only get their card by getting their first job in a repertory company. They couldn't do tele-vision first, they couldn't work in the West End first or do Number One tours first [Number One tours were sent to the major touring venues].' This catch twenty-two was designed to protect the interests of existing members and to test the mettle of prospective ones. Although tele-vision companies, West End and touring managements were barred from issuing Equity cards, as it was deemed that they offered insufficient training for new members, every repertory company was allowed to give out two cards a year and the competition for them was understandably fierce. For this reason people went to enormous lengths when trying to secure their vitally important First Job, and no one more so than Maureen Lipman. She wrote to the director Giles Havergal, who in 1967 was running the Palace Theatre in Watford. Newly graduated from the London School of Music and Drama, she was looking for work. She told Havergal that a television documentary film unit wanted to make a feature about a young drama student setting out on her first job and that they had asked her to be in it. What she needed now was to find the job and could he help? Havergal obliged and offered her the part of Nancy in *The Knack*. The line about the film company was a complete fiction, a brilliant device for gaining employment. Maureen Lipman approached the first morning of rehearsals with some trepidation and several wild ideas about ringing round friends to ask if they could turn up with cameras and extraneous equipment. In the end she decided to brazen it out and turned up at rehearsals for ten o'clock sharp, saying, 'Are they here yet? Have they arrived?' The matter was not referred to again. Later, when she asked Havergal what he'd thought, he said that the whole thing had been transparent but he had wanted her anyway.

While some people resorted to such elaborate fictions to secure employment, others had to pay for the privilege of getting their toe in the theatrical door. In a tradition that was certainly operating as late as the 1950s when Vilma Hollingbery started out, newcomers were expected to pay their prospective employers a lump sum in the form of a premium, which would then be doled back to them as a weekly wage. She remembers, 'When I was eighteen I walked into the Boltons Theatre in South Kensington and said, "I'm not leaving until you give me a job." I'd read in *The Stage* that they wanted students for fifty pounds. I didn't realize that the fifty pounds was the premium you paid them and then they paid it back to you as salary. I thought they would be giving me fifty pounds. I don't know how I lived. If I sold programmes for part of the time I could earn thirty shillings, which just about paid my fares and one meal a day, which was usually a little tin of soup cooked under the stage. I lived on nothing really, but I seemed to survive.'

Richard Pasco had a similar beginning. He says that, from a very early age, 'I used to haunt the stage doors, not to see actors I hasten to add, but to see if by any chance the dock doors were open at the back, so I could see down on to the stage. In the summer evenings they often were to let the air in, so you could see down into this magic world backstage. I used to go home and reproduce what I saw on a model theatre that I had.' After a childhood absorbed in re-creating theatre sets at home, Pasco was determined to work in the business professionally as an adult. He too was charged what amounted to an admission fee.

'I started at the "Q" Theatre. My father paid a hundred guineas for me to do a nine-month season as an apprentice. I was a pot boy because my job really was sweeping the stage, washing the teacups, even cleaning out the gents' loos on occasion. It was the job that Dirk Bogarde had four years prior to me. I learned so much.'

The rates at Aylesbury were considerably less than the hundred guineas charged by the 'Q' Theatre, but Hilary Mason still had to borrow the money necessary as a premium to be student assistant stage manager for ten weeks in Buckinghamshire. 'I handed my twenty-five pounds over to the leading lady, who was sitting in the ticket office clad in a brassière and a pair of khaki shorts. It was a very hot day. It was 6 June 1939 – not a good year to start a career. They seized my twenty-five pounds with alacrity because they were all very poor and I played ten wonderful parts. I played Queen Victoria from eighteen to eighty and stage-managed the play as well. At the end of my ten weeks they did take me on and they paid me three pounds a week.'

Other actors found the financial arrangements rather less formal, although Robin Bailey was taken aback at being asked to part with a percentage of his first wage. He describes his theatrical blooding: 'I did a lot of amateur plays in the church hall and eventually the director that they were employing on a paid basis (paid not very much I'm sure, but he was paid – occasionally he played tiny parts at the Theatre

Royal in Nottingham with a repertory company run by Harry Hanson, who ran a chain of very successful repertory companies, twice nightly, once weekly), one week this man whose name, magically, was Weston Wade, couldn't do the part he was being offered and he said that if I would like to do it he thought he could persuade the director to let me and would I be interested. Well! Would I be interested! This was what I wanted to do, to be in the theatre, I was going to be paid a pound for the week of twelve performances – one and eightpence a performance! It was in 1938. I was delighted, but a little startled when Weston Wade, who had a motor car and a trilby hat and gloves and all those things, was a proper grown-up person and I was a lad, and he said, "In view of the circumstances I wonder if you might see your way to letting me have ten shillings of that." It was unbelievable! Looking back it was unbelievable, but I gladly did. That was my real beginning.'

An actor's willingness to part with hard cash was one factor which made securing the vital first job easier; another was the extent of his wardrobe. Under the terms of what was known as the Standard Esher Contract, which both the actor and the company signed when employment was offered, performers were obliged to provide their own clothes for all productions except those requiring period dress, for which the management would hire or make costumes. Producers and directors were always on the lookout for actors who had a limitless supply of different things to wear, a point that Belinda Lang played on when she begged Jack Watling, who was running the theatre at Frinton, to cast her in a play by Noël Coward. 'I was desperate to play Amanda in *Private Lives* and I said to Jack, "You must cast me as Amanda, it's ludicrous not to, I have all the clothes," which won him completely, because that was the thing, getting props and costumes.'

Geoffrey Hastings, who was the director of the rep at Colwyn Bay, was similarly influenced by Leslie Lawton. 'I went down to London for an audition and he said, "We're looking for a juvenile. Have you got two suits and a dinner jacket?" So I lied and said, "Yes," and he said, "Fine, you start rehearsing in six weeks." I had to borrow some money from my dad to go and buy two suits and a dinner jacket. That was weekly rep; in twenty weeks I played eighteen leads and I was very bad in seventeen of them, but I learnt a great deal.'

For those who were unable to pay their way into a rep company or use the size of their wardrobes as a passport into work, there was a simple but radical solution: to set up their own company. Phillip Manikum was one of the first actors recruited by the director Terry Hands when he set up the Everyman Theatre in Liverpool. Phillip recalls rehearsing in the morning and spending the afternoons stippling the walls of the gents' lavatory so that the decorating would be finished in time for the opening night. Gabrielle Drake joined the company soon after it opened and remembers those precarious early days. 'We did it on a shoestring, we did matinées every day and we only did evening shows on Monday, Tuesday and Wednesday because on Thursday, Friday and Saturday there was a night club down below us.'

Jill Gascoine was involved in a venture which turned out to be vital in establishing a permanent theatre in Leicester; hers was a company to which the current Haymarket Theatre is indebted. She tells the story. 'In about 1960 an actor called Joe Goodwin was my partner and with him and Bill Hayes and Ken Loach we decided to open our own repertory company. I'd made quite a bit of money doing cabaret and a St Trinian's film and it was wonderful, because although I'd put up some of the money they insisted I did stage-managing and small parts. We started the rep in Leicester in an old church hall. We wanted to do plays that were not commercial rubbish, we were very high minded in those days in the Sixties. The actors who we chose were on the Equity minimum, which was seven pounds ten a week. It was pretty hairy, we literally did build it ourselves. We used to sleep in the theatre on the drapes and we made our own scenery. Later, the Phoenix Theatre was built on our design. I think we opened with *Antigone*, a wonderful, wonderful play, but it emptied the theatre and we had about five pounds in the bank. After the first production the Arts Council coughed up some money and the local council and the University helped us. The *Manchester Guardian* gave us a couple of good reviews and people started to take us seriously.'

Although the company did not last in that form, it paved the way for the Phoenix Theatre in Leicester, which ultimately led to the creation of the existing Haymarket company. Jill Gascoine remembers a recent trip to the city. 'Years later I went to see my husband in a play at the Leicester Haymarket and I was sitting in the audience and someone tapped me on the back. I turned round and he said, "It's Jill Gascoine, isn't it? I wonder if everyone here knows that we're sitting here because of you lot. Welcome back to Leicester, some of us don't forget." I was so touched.'

Bernard Cribbins also helped to found a company, which was the forerunner of what is now a jewel in the crown of regional theatre. 'We began a theatre in Manchester, which was again a rep theatre, doing fortnightly, called the Piccolo Players, it was actually the basis for the Royal Exchange Company. Frank Dunlop was there as director with Casper Wrede and James Maxwell. Eric Thompson was in the company. I helped to build the stage above the Conservative Club in Chorlton cum Hardy. I literally built it. I built the stage and hung all the drapes and built rostra for seats. Dame Peggy Ashcroft came and opened the place.'

Another venture that began in this do-it-yourself fashion, but which was ultimately less successful than either the Liverpool, Manchester or Leicester projects is described by Eileen Atkins. 'I trained at the Guildhall and a few of us got together and found out that the Women's Institute hall in Perranporth, where Peter Bull used to run a rep with Pamela Brown, was vacant again. We ran it like a co-op, it was pretty disastrous, but we did some good shows. I would never join Ian McKellen's Actors Company because Perranporth put me off for ever. I can't stand everybody chipping in. Everybody quarrelled. We didn't have enough money to stay in digs, so we took the local school hall and we slept on camp beds, the women in one classroom and men in the other. The only place to wash was in the loos on the other side of the playground. It was very, very hard going, but on the other hand one also had a marvellous time. There was only one dressing-room and I remember we all had our surfboards lined up outside it because the surfing in Perranporth was wonderful. We would go down on the beach with a flag advertising the night's show, in fact we did very good business. We did a summer season in Perranporth for three years running.'

Not only did Eileen Atkins survive the dissensions and quarrels of running a co-operative company for all that time, she was also a graduate of another peripheral form of theatre group, which also provided a route into the profession for many hard-pressed actors: the Butlin's Repertory Company. 'I worked in the rep at Butlin's. You always tried out the new plays on the end of the pier at Brighton. One of the productions we did was *The Paragon*. All the plays were cut to an hour, that was the longest anyone could sit it out in the audience. If you hadn't finished when the hour was up, a huge bell rang to tell them to go on to the next thing, which was bingo or pony racing. It was marvellous training for not letting the play spread, you had to stick to what you'd rehearsed. When the bell rang people just walked out, whether you'd finished the play or not.'

M.C. Hart, who went on to direct for the BBC, was also a veteran of a season on the Palace Pier in Brighton. He remembers that when the wind was blowing in a certain direction the cloth covering the floor on stage would billow up and all the actors would have to rush over and stand on it to hold it in place. From Brighton he went to the Butlin's camp at Pwllheli, where they had no sound system at all. 'If you wanted a sound effect you had to telephone Radio Butlin's and say, "Now." Once in the middle of *Dial M for Murder* we got the sound of jumping beans.'

Anna Carteret also started out in the business courtesy of Butlin's, but this time at their Skegness holiday camp, where she did three different plays a week, playing the juvenile lead and stage-managing at the same time. Philip Voss was not a protégé of Butlin's; he started his career at the end of a pier. 'My very first job was in rep at Bognor Regis on the pier. We did comedies like *Doctor in the House* in the theatre upstairs and the theatre downstairs did nude shows. We could lift up a hatch and see Marilyn Most in all her mottled flesh, standing still in those days, in 1958.' There were many managements other than Butlin's existing on the fringes of the mainstream regional theatre. Doreen Andrew encountered one in 1946 up in Scarborough, run by a man called Harold G. Roberts. 'I went up to do a play called *Quiet Weekend* and I think they could tell at once that I'd had little or no experience and they sort of put up with me. I can remember the director saying, "That's a laugh line, ducky, come down to the footlights and give it to us." I was also warned by a member of the company not to breathe the word Equity, otherwise I would be out on my ear.'

In their bid to get started, actors were willing to put up with salaries which, if they existed at all, were small, with hard working conditions that often went beyond the rules laid down by the union and with performing and stage-managing at the same time. It is reckoned that 80 per cent of Equity members are unemployed at any given moment, so the competition for jobs is such that if one person demurs another will quickly take their place. There was a brief period when this was not the case. During the Second World War, with so many men away fighting at the Front, there was a tremendous shortage of male actors. A few remained, those who were too young or too old for active service. Companies the length and breadth of the land were very keen to lay their hands on men.

Alec McCowen benefited from this. 'My first job was when I was still at RADA during the long vacation. I remember going to the Westminster Library in Leicester Square – I suppose I couldn't even afford to buy a copy of *The Stage* – and I went through the Wanted ads. It was in the middle of the war and there was quite a lot of employment to be had and I picked out an ad requesting Stage Manager and Character Juvenile needed for small north-country weekly rep. I wrote off to a lady called Amy Viner offering my services, explaining it could only be a holiday job, but they were so desperate for men at that time that she engaged me for three pounds a week, which was pretty good, and I think she wrote in the letter, "I will not be sending you a contract unless you request it."' McCowen ended up spending a year in Macclesfield.

John Warner found employment in the south-west. 'I wrote off answering stage adverts for leading men because it was during the war and they were very short of leading men and I put down as my experience Rose May in *Ruddigore*, Portia in *The Merchant of Venice*, Caitiff in *Trial by Jury* and couldn't understand why nobody wanted me! So I lowered my sights and answered an advert for a student assistant stage manager at the Little Theatre in Bristol, which was run by Peggy Ann Wood. That was in 1941 and they'd just had that terrible blitz in Bristol and her husband was in the fire service, I think, so she was running the theatre. I wrote off to her and got a letter back saying, yes, would I come to an interview. I arrived very late and she said, "Young man, you're very late, where have you been?" and I said, "I've been waiting at the station," and she said, "What, at Temple Meads?" and I said "Yes." "Why were you waiting at Temple Meads?" I said, "Because your letter said, 'Looking forward to meeting you'." Why she employed this idiot child I can't think. I was engaged for no money at all for six weeks to see how we got on, literally no money, none at all. Then I was accepted, my salary went up to fifteen shillings a week, so I opened my post office savings account. My digs were fifteen shillings a week all in. When my salary went up to a pound a week, I wrote home and said, "I don't need money any more from home because I'm going to be able to save five shillings a week."'

There are never as many employment opportunities for women as there are for men, as fewer female parts are written and there are more people chasing them. Soon after the war the actress Maria Charles launched herself at the theatre, but found that she was in for a rude awakening. 'I thought, "The world is waiting for me." But actually the world wasn't waiting for me, so I looked in *The Stage*. I didn't have an agent and I went to every single audition and in those days you queued up for auditions and I queued up at an office in Cambridge Circus. *The Stage* said, "Juvenile wanted for Oldham Rep". I was seen by an agent called Miriam Warner, who was a very famous old-type agent, she was a real toughie, and when I got there I was greeted by a hundred ladies and there was a spiral staircase going up to the top floor and it was so cold we stood on newspapers and we stood all day.'

While Maria Charles was obliged to queue endlessly with myriad other hopefuls, Michael Kilgarriff had an altogether less orthodox experience auditioning for his first job in rep. 'I auditioned for the Charles Denville players at the YMCA in Liverpool. He wore the old homburg hat and the long overcoat. My audition was at about seven-fifteen and when I mentioned I played the piano, he said, "Let me hear you." I sat at the piano and started to play, with visions of him starring me in some musical. I played and played until I realized I was playing the audience in. Denville was greeting everyone like long-lost friends. During the first interval he was there chatting to people, and in the third act he came on as the Sergeant. The play was *See How They Run* and he didn't know a line, he kept clapping his hands together and saying, "Now what shall we do?"'

A lucky few were not subjected to the ordeal of auditioning. Tom Conti made an effortless entry into the profession before he had even finished as a student. 'The first rep experience I had was at Dundee in Scotland, at the end of my first year in drama school, in the vac between the first and second year. I was called by Dundee Rep, who were desperate for an actor to play a part in a whodunnit. This was at Edinburgh Festival time and all the actors in Scotland were engaged at the festival and they couldn't afford the fare to bring an actor from England, so they phoned in desperation the drama school I attended, called the Royal Scottish Academy of Music and said, "Is there anyone you think might be capable of doing this?" and they said, "Oh well there's a new young actor called Tom Conti and we think maybe you should have a word with him." So they called me and I said, "Oh yes, well, I'd be delighted," thinking to myself, "My God, how thrilling." '

Equally thrilling and almost as seamless was Edward Jewesbury's initiation. 'I went to RADA in 1936–7 and we had a public show in which we did extracts from *Fanny's First Play*, which Harcourt Williams directed. Bernard Shaw was quite interested in it all and came to one or two of the rehearsals, which was wonderful. He actually gave us some advice. He was a friend of Harcourt Williams and also of Barry Jackson. Shaw and Barry Jackson were at the public show and I got what was known as a scholarship to the Birmingham Rep through Shaw and Barry Jackson between them.'

Liza Goddard got started without trying at all! 'I very first worked at Farnham when I was a baby. I played the infant Queen Elizabeth in *The Merry Wives of Windsor*, aged six months. My father was stage manager and my mother was playing small parts. They kept me in a dressing-room in a carrycot when I wasn't on stage.' She pipped Elizabeth Counsell to the post by three and a half years. The latter was four when she made her first public appearance at her father's theatre in Windsor. She was allowed to appear in a dress rehearsal of *Cinderella* and afterwards announced, 'Buttons sang flat,' which apparently he did.

Bernard Cribbins remembers that a young person's existence in the theatre could be harsh. 'When I was a child it really was slave labour, because I used to work a seventy-hour week and I used to get fifteen shillings for it. I became an actor by accident, really, because the local producer at the Oldham Rep spotted me in a school drama festival and asked me to play little boys' parts when they came along. When I left school at thirteen I was offered a job and that was it.'

Although Dorothy Tutin was not a child when she began her career, the first part she played was that of a young boy. 'My first job was at Bristol, it was three-weekly rep and I played a boy, Lucius, in *Julius Caesar*. I was very young, I was about nineteen and it was a time I shall never forget. I fell in love with Bristol and I learnt an enormous amount from my fellow actors. They were highly intelligent and they knew about music and art and I used to sit and listen to them talking, not about acting, strangely enough, but about philosophy and things like that. It was my education, apart from anything else.'

Derek Nimmo's arrival in the business was decided for him by somebody else. 'The secretary of the family firm in which I was working saw me in an amateur play and thought I'd be better off in the theatre rather than giving indifferent shorthand notes so without telling me she wrote off to three companies, one in Southport (a man called Donald Bodley was director there), one in York and, more particularly, one in Bolton – the Lawrence Williamson Players. Lawrence Williamson himself replied and said I should go to audition for Jack Austen, the director. I don't think I really wanted to go into the theatre at that point, but I got on the train and went to this repertory company and I auditioned and they offered me a job at four pounds a week, which was rather less than I was getting and my father was deeply miffed that I proved to be a wastrel so early on in my life.'

Some actors found the hardest part was securing the job in the first place, but for others their first day at work was both testing and full of surprises. Brian Cox remembers, 'My first job in rep was in Dundee, where I was taken on as a general factotum and I used to mop the stage and take the box-office money to the bank. The first day I arrived at the theatre, there was this fight going on. One of the actors was beating hell out of the stage manager. I think they were recovering from a drunken binge the night before and it had gone slightly wrong. It was very funny. Everybody called each other "Darling" and I thought that was amazing, nobody had ever called me darling.'

There were no fights to worry about for Sheila Reid, but a crisis of catastrophic proportions unfolded when she went to Scotland at the start of her first job. 'We arrived at Perth for the first day on the Sunday train and we were all having coffee in the one local place that was open, and suddenly there were flames roaring into the sky and I looked up and said, "It would be a joke if that was the theatre," and it was! We spent our first night in Perth trying to douse the fire with a chain of buckets.' In true theatrical tradition the show went on, as did the life of poverty and hardship that most actors have to put up with when they are starting out in the profession. Throughout her time in Perth, 'Money was exceedingly tight and I used to hit the chocolate machine in the bus station on the way home in case any sixpences fell out. Sometimes they did! Sometimes a bar of chocolate fell out!'

In spite of the shortage of money, most people were so delighted to find an opening in theatre that they were more than happy to do whatever was asked of them. Phyllida Law was taken on by the Bristol Old Vic, where she not only played any small parts which came her way, but was also a wardrobe assistant, which involved finding, cleaning and maintaining the cast's costumes. On top of this she was asked to paint the scenery. Alan Ayckbourn's beginnings were also lowly. 'My first job was a season at the Edinburgh Festival, where I polished Donald Wolfit's furniture.' Jean Boht sums up the humble position of actors at the outset of their careers and the dedication with which they carried out the menial tasks allotted to them. 'At twenty-six I must have been the oldest student in the business, but nobody worked harder. I loved every corner of the Liverpool Playhouse. I was not allowed to address an artiste by their Christian name whilst in the theatre; never to enter the green room except to address an artiste or make a cup of tea or call them for an entrance. There was no intercom system to the dressing-rooms or green room, so artistes had to be called by the student and I had to sit in the prompt corner next to the stage manager on the book during all the performances ready to make the calls for the entrances.'

For those beginners lucky enough to secure a part in a production, their first appearance must often have seemed a let down. 'The first play I was in was a farcical thriller called *Meet a Body*,' Rosemary Leach recalls. 'At the end of the first act I appeared, or rather one arm appeared as the leading actor opened a hall chest. Curtain. At the end of the second act I staggered on under a blood-stained sheet. Curtain. At the end of the third act I came on and said, "They've gone to the Green Man at . . ." and someone put a chloroform pad over my face!'

In spite of the difficulty in starting out, lack of money, the permanent insecurity of employment and the punishing regime that many people endured, once they had realized their ambition to become actors, most of these fledgling professionals were swept up by the peculiar magic exerted by the theatre. Tony O'Callaghan felt a sense of elation. 'My first job was in Cheltenham. I remember getting to the theatre first thing in the morning before anyone else had turned up and just the cleaning people were there. Cheltenham is such a beautiful theatre. I remember walking on to the stage and the house lights were

on and it was just wonderful. I thought, "Ahhh, this is it, I've arrived." '
For Nancy Mansfield, starting out three decades earlier, the thrill was
just as strong. 'I remember being paid at the end of my first week, in a
play called *Bird in Hand* by John Drinkwater at Lichfield, I got six
pounds and I didn't want to take it. I said, "I don't think I should have
that – it's all been so lovely. I don't expect money as well." '

2

The Role of Stage Management

'One and a goat to Rose Bank.'

Bernard Cribbins

IT IS A fact universally acknowledged that in the theatre pecking order assistant stage managers are at the bottom of the pile. A large percentage of actors started their careers in rep in this humblest of capacities. Derek Nimmo, speaking from grim experience, observes, 'The ASM was literally the lowest form of life and had to do everything from sweeping the stage to tidying up the dressing-rooms to making the tea.' Peggy Mount agrees, 'Assistant stage manager sounds wonderful but you were just a dogsbody. I even scrubbed the stage,' while Juliette Mander puts it more succinctly, 'A hierarchy existed where stage management were considered to be not-bring-outable in public. You were all right if you were an actor, but stage management couldn't read or write or even wear a dress and they were all lesbian anyway and not presentable.' Deborah Grant was made to feel like a member of a sub-species. 'The hierarchy in a company was simply dreadful, nobody spoke to the ASMs, I had to follow the leading actresses around with chairs and ashtrays, I don't think they ever spoke to me.' This must have come as a considerable shock to her, as she admits, 'I came out of the Central School of Speech and Drama with all the arrogance of "Here I go, I'm a huge star," and there I was grovelling about, literally scrubbing floors and clearing out cupboards and dressing-rooms.'

Like many others whose greenness is apparent when they first start work, Deborah Grant says she was 'the scapegoat of all the jokes from the old professionals, like asking me to go and get the key to the grid'.

(This is the area at the top of the theatre fly tower or 'Flies', where the lights are hung from metal bars. Needless to say it is not kept locked!) Similar tricks were played on Liz Crowther, who remembers, 'As a novice you get sent to look for things that don't exist like the key to the grid or a black gel for the lights,' and Liza Goddard suffered from the same kind of teasing. 'I remember on my first day I was sent off to find a left-handed spanner.' Simon Williams didn't need anyone to take advantage of his naïveté, he was baffled enough as it was. On his first day as acting ASM at Worthing he was told that during the interval he must get the iron in – this being the term for the metal safety curtain that divides the backstage area from the front of house. Later on the stage manager found him standing with the ironing board in the middle of the stage.

Brigid Panet was just as ignorant when, during her holidays from the Central School of Speech and Drama, she worked as an ASM in Salisbury. The stage manager and the electrician, who were a married couple, walked out after a row with the management and Bridget ended up running the entire show herself. However, as some of these accounts demonstrate, a willingness to be pitched into the deep end at very short notice is a prerequisite for anyone contemplating a career in rep theatre.

Clive Francis arrived at the Penguin Players in Bexhill-on-Sea, where he had been employed as what was known as acting ASM. This meant he had to be general dogsbody backstage and also play small parts in the productions. He was raring to go and his hopes must have been dashed when the director said, 'I know you want to be an actor, but I'm not going to let you anywhere near a script for at least six months, I'm going to make life as miserable for you as I can. If at the end you still want to be an actor then you're going to do it.' The same ground rules were laid down for Julian Fellowes when he was offered a contract at Northampton, which, he says, 'was run by Willard Stoker, a wonderful old man who had done quite well with the Liverpool Playhouse. Before I joined he told me I wouldn't play any parts for the first season I was there. I was slightly downcast, but anyway I arrived on the date appointed and the chap said, "You'd better drop off your things before we take you on to rehearsal," and I said, "I don't think I have to go to rehearsal at this stage, do I?" and he said, "What do you mean? You've got four parts to play and you open on Monday!"'

During his time at Weston-Super-Mare, Bernard Cribbins found he was stage-managing and playing not only small parts but leading roles as well. As he observes with dry understatement, 'Playing Stanley in *A Streetcar Named Desire* and stage-managing at the same time was quite something.' Often there were clashes and confusions between the dual roles of actor and ASM. Angela Thorne remembers, 'I took over from the leading lady who was playing Miss Marple in *Murder at the Vicarage*. I remember rushing on at the interval because I had to set the props, and then going to get ready because I was the first character on in the second act and the curtain went up early one night and I was caught setting the props in my Miss Marple costume.'

Sir Alan Ayckbourn recalls an embarrassing situation. 'I remember playing a South Sea servant in a play called *South Sea Bubble* by Noël Coward, wearing a sarong and completely covered with brown make-up from head to toe and rather self-consciously climbing the fly-gallery ladder in my sarong to operate the flies up there.'

Sometimes an acting ASM could be working quite happily in one part of his job specification, only to be catapulted with very little warning into the other. Sir Alan Ayckbourn again: 'I remember going on at short notice. I was in the scenic workshop at Worthing painting away, an obscure ASM, and somebody ran up and said, "Alan, can you come down a minute, they want to see you in the theatre." This was on a Saturday afternoon. I was drawn to one side by the producer and the stage manager and they said, "Look, a very grave situation has arisen. We had the run-through this morning and the juvenile actor ran out of the theatre, he's had some sort of breakdown and we open on Monday and we want you to take over." They gave me the script and I went home and I sat up all Sunday learning it, with my landlady running the lines, and I went in on Monday morning and they took me through it and in the afternoon I went through it with the company. I went on on Monday night and I thought, "This is it, the dressing-room with the star on," and at the end of the opening night, at the curtain call, the leading lady Elizabeth Spriggs hugged me and said, "Well done, you've saved us all!" The manager bought me a drink in the bar afterwards and he said, "Oh Alan, I've got some good news, we've got a proper actor coming down tomorrow." And I was back in the workshop! I thought, "Well, this is the reality of showbiz." But I carried on playing small parts, which was nice, usually covered in scenic paint.'

The ease with which people could move from behind the scenes to centre stage is now a thing of the past. With the development of high-technology equipment such as computerized lighting systems and hydraulically operated stage machinery, stage management has become an increasingly specialized field, for which particular training is now offered by the drama schools. This means that there is less and less cross-fertilization between backstage activities and performing, a fact which Sir Alan Ayckbourn laments. 'The nice thing about it was that on the whole it wasn't compartmentalized. I think with the rise of the stage management union, as it were, nowadays you couldn't have an acting ASM. Stage management think that's terrible – they're not properly trained and they don't know how to set things and do things. In my day you worked in all departments, which for me was wonderful. I worked in the scenic workshop, on the lighting board, I did whatever was going, wherever there was a shortfall of manpower I would be. You were allowed the whole run of the theatre with proper supervision and a few raspberries from the professionals when you buggered it up a bit.'

Between the two World Wars, decades before this demarcation became pronounced, Beryl Cooke was taken on as ASM at the theatre in Harrogate, but hankered to be allowed to act as well. When she asked if she could perhaps play some small parts, she was sacked for her presumption. Judy Campbell and the two other ASMs who worked with her at Coventry before the Second World War shared their acting and stage-managing responsibilities between them. 'We each spent one act doing the book [sitting in the prompt corner and giving all the cues necessary for the show to run] and the rest of the time we did other duties.' So much for continuity.

Vilma Hollingbery remembers that, rather than being allotted an act at a time to run the show, she sat tight for the whole evening with occasional breaks. 'When you were an acting ASM you were often on the book; when it was time for you to act in a scene, someone would take your place on the book while you went out on stage, then you would go back on the book when your scene was finished.'

Being 'on the book' was an onerous responsibility, which started during rehearsals. The first duty of an ASM on arriving at the rehearsal room was to make a rough mock-up of the scenery or set. Jenny Seagrove says, 'I remember having to mark out the floor for rehearsals or help mark it out.' This consisted of sticking strips of coloured tape on the floor to show where scenic flats containing doors, windows and fireplaces would be so the actors could judge the distance of their moves. As rehearsals got under way, the ASM on the book would mark down in the book or script all the moves as they were decided, so a complete technical record of the performance would be made. At a later point lighting and sound cues were added to the book and during a show the ASM would ensure that all the special effects were synchronized to the action. If she had time while all these demands were being made on her, she would also prompt the actors when they dried or forgot their lines. For this reason, the place where she sits during a performance, which is the corner of the stage nearest the audience on the actors' left, is always known as prompt corner and is usually the hottest seat in the house.

Even the most efficient ASM can be floored when something unexpected happens, as Julia Chambers explains. 'We were doing a production of *French Without Tears* at the Little Theatre in Bristol and one of the actors was about to give a soliloquy before the curtain came in for the interval. I had everything on standby, the lights, the music, and my fingers were poised to give the "go" at the end of his speech. There was an almighty bang, I jumped and my fingers hit the buttons. The music went, the house lights came on and the curtain came in just as he was starting to speak. A bomb had gone off in Park Street behind the theatre, but it sounded as if it was in the building itself. Everybody was frightened except this actor, who stormed over to me and said, "Don't ever do that to me again!"'

Stage managers coped with their responsibilities with varying degrees of success. John Warner says, 'Beryl Bainbridge was our ASM at Liverpool and she was always writing poetry when she was on the book so you never got a prompt properly.' Actors at the Penguin Players when Clive Francis was in the prompt corner had an even tougher time of it. 'They put me on the book for quite a while and in those days I used to have a pronounced stammer. One thing no actor in the Penguin Players ever did when I was on the book was to forget their lines, because if they did they looked in the corner and saw this poor bloke going blue trying to belch these words out of his mouth.' The general chaos of trying to do several things at once has stuck in Belinda Lang's mind. 'At Frinton when I was stage-managing I can remember standing in the wings balancing the book between my chestbone and the wall, doing the lights with one hand and something else with the other.' The same is true for Phyllida Law. 'I remember being in costume, prompting, lying on the floor using my feet to work the dimmer board (to vary the intensity of the lights on stage). It had great big handles on that you pushed up and down and I worked them with my feet.' Martin Duncan tells frenetic tales. 'At Lincoln I played Rosencrantz in *Hamlet* while being on the book – crazy things. One of the craziest was *The Wizard of Oz*: not only was I on the book for it, which was very complicated, I also had a part in it playing the witch's henchman. I played him like Frankenstein with a big built-up forehead and a bolt through my neck, in a dinner jacket, sitting doing the book. I played the double bass and the director wanted me to play the double bass, but I couldn't get in and out of the orchestra pit in time, so I sat with my double bass in the prompt corner, playing the numbers, cueing the show and then rushing on. It was absolutely mad.'

Computerized lighting and sound systems have taken some of the madness out of running a show, but in days gone by things were far less sophisticated. Before they were phased out, some of the ancient lighting systems were positively dangerous. Richenda Carey remembers, 'The last old lighting board in the country was at Derby. There were gigantic levers that you pulled down. We had to wear plimsolls and rubber gloves to avoid getting electric shocks.' Although in theory they were simple enough to be foot-operated, the mechanical nature of the old boards meant that it was easy to make mistakes, as Liz Crowther found to her cost. 'We had a funny old lighting board with about three master switches on it, rather than being all computerized. You had to snap out a cue on one of the masters, having brought up something else that would take its place, and I remember blacking out the whole theatre once when someone turned a table lamp off.'

Some of the other effects could also only be achieved by hand, as Sir Alan Ayckbourn discovered. 'We were doing a play called *River Breeze*, which is all about a family who live by a river. The gimmick of it was that their windows looked out over the river and occasionally, courtesy of a sort of truck with some rope tied on, people would be seen rowing past on the river – the stage manager in a boater and blazer. They would go past regularly on this same truck, but in apparently different vehicles. I said – this is the ASM talking – "The trouble with that lighting is that you ought to be able to see the river reflecting on the roof, on the false ceiling." The director said, "Yes, yes, I don't know how we do that," and I said, "What you need is a mirror in a tin bath of water, then shine a lamp on it." The director said, "Yeah? Yeah? Then what?" "Then it would sparkle." "Not unless the water was in constant motion." I said, "Well you could find a way to do that," and the director said, "Yeah, you need someone sitting there shaking it," and I said, "Yee-aah . . ." and I spent the entire play, except for one scene where they drew the curtains, thank God, shaking this tin bath full of mirror and I thought, "That will teach you to make smart suggestions."'

The arrangements for sound effects were equally crude, as Deborah Grant remembers. 'My boyfriend at the time had left the Central School to do weekly rep. There were five people in the company, he was playing all the juvenile leads and doing the sound operation at the same time, which meant that if a sound cue came up he had for some obscure reason to disappear off the stage to press a knob and then come back on again. "Oh I think I hear a car coming," and vanish! "Vroooom!" I can't imagine how we all got away with it.' Phyllida Law describes how the system worked. 'A panotrope was a turntable for the old seventy-eights. You could put cans [headphones] on and listen to the music. I marked these records, would you believe it, with tailor's chalk, so I knew where to put the needle on to start the supposedly atmospheric music.' Clive Francis could have benefited from some tailor's chalk. 'I used to sit there with the sound effects, you had one or two LPs and on these were all the sound effects and in the dimness of the corner you had to try and set your needle at the right place. I was forever getting this wrong. I remember once we did a play called *The Two Mrs Carrolls*. The play finishes with the star saying, "Oh to hell with all of you, I'm going to leap into my Ferrari and I'm going to race off to Monte Carlo and I'm going to play the wheel!" and off he went and slammed the door, and I'm there with my needle trying to get the sound of the Ferrari. He made this wonderful exit and there was the sound of a coach and horses! Then a terrible scratch as the needle was wrenched to the right position.' On another occasion he had all the audience jumping to their feet. 'I remember playing the National Anthem once by mistake instead of another piece of music in the middle of a show and all of the audience stood up.' Philip Voss recalls a production of *Death of a Salesman* in Colchester. 'On the Saturday night the stage manager was drunk – there was a lot of drinking in those days – and when Willy Loman crashes the car there should have been the sound effect of a car crashing, and suddenly there was the sound of wedding bells.'

Mindful of the possible pitfalls inherent in using the panotrope, Jean Boht took extra precautions on a sensitive occasion at the Liverpool Playhouse. '*The Hostage*, in which everyone appeared including myself as Miss Gilchrist (who is hardly off the stage at all), was like a six-ring circus. That was the year that President Kennedy was assassinated and at the Saturday matinée it was decided that the company would remain on stage and the American national anthem would be played. I dashed off at the final curtain, Mr Hamilton-Moore announced the news to the audience and asked them to stand with the company to honour his memory. I found the track on the album we possessed of ALL national anthems and it went well. At the evening performance, however, it was decided that it was a bit risky to use the record as we might get the Brazilian or some other anthem by mistake, so the Stars and Stripes was put on tape for safety. At the end of the show I dashed off yet again, the announcement was made, I switched on the tape machine and horror of horrors the damn thing got caught up in itself and the anthem ground its way at quarter-speed over the auditorium. By some miracle I had switched on the record at the same time and banged the needle down, praying it was the right track. JFK up there in the heavens decided to smile on me as I was only doing my best, after all, and our honour was saved.'

If the panotrope could not always be relied upon, there were methods dating back centuries which proved dependable. Alec McCowen says, 'If there was rain in the play, the old-fashioned way of making rain was peas on a drum, and you would stand in the wings making very good rain as these peas went round and round. There would be two electrical sticks to make the lightning, which would be quite frightening. You'd put them together and there'd be a great flash of lightning. I seemed to do several plays in which there were storms and rain.' The Bristol Old Vic still has its eighteenth-century thunder run, a wooden chute along which cannon balls were rolled to create the effect of a thunder clap.

Nowadays the play is relayed to the dressing-rooms by a tannoy system, so members of the cast can judge how a performance is progressing and hear when they are called to the side of the stage ready to make their entrances. In the era of dimmers and panotropes there were no tannoys and calling the actors was another duty which devolved to the hapless ASM. This was another responsibility of the young Alec McCowen. 'When I was stage managing and acting at the same time I'd be making up and then literally I had to go and call the half-hour, there were no tannoy systems. I had to go round all the dressing-rooms calling the half, the quarter, the five, beginners.' (These are calls made to the actors, which mark off the passing of time before Act One Beginners is announced and the opening actors assemble on stage.)

The placing of props is equally important. These must be set in such a way that they are comfortably accessible to the actor when he needs them – a pencil put at the wrong side of a desk can have a devastatingly destabilizing effect on a performer, especially if a bit of business is dependent on a particular prop being in a specific position. Alec McCowen was well trained in this art. At York he was tutored by 'a demon stage manager called Norman Hoult, who really worked me like stink, taught me a hell of a lot, made me a very good stage manager. He taught me how to set cups and saucers so that the handle of the cup was conveniently placed and how to set a telephone so that the actor didn't get tangled in the wires, or at the interval to empty the ashtrays and a host of little things like that.' John Warner was lucky enough to have the same kind of grounding. 'We had a marvellous stage manager called Marie Edwin, who was a real martinet. I learnt more from her than anybody. If you set a glass there instead of there! You had to plump the cushions and empty the ashtrays before every act, and dust. And of course polish the brasses and the silver and sweep the stage and make the tea and all those sorts of thing.' Patricia Brake benefited from a similar education. 'You learn lots of little things like not making hot tea for the actors to drink on stage because they won't be able to get through the scene with it. When I was at Bristol the stage manager went and checked the props on stage before the performance and thought everything was there, good. But he'd actually left off the main piece of furniture, which was a sofa that everyone sat on and where the gun was hidden behind a cushion.'

The Bristol stage manager was not alone in leaving something vital off the stage. Clive Francis says, 'I was always forgetting to set props on the stage so I was forever handing props to actors as they went on, saying, "Would you mind putting this over there?" Once I even had to hand the murder weapon to the policeman who was going on and had to discover it in a drawer. It was a dagger and he had to secrete it in his raincoat pocket and sneak it into the drawer when no one was looking. I don't think any actor ever went on stage without having to take something on with him.'

Just what a dreadful situation this negligence can place a poor actor in was brought home to Belinda Lang. 'I'd forgotten to set a prop and, when I went on at the interval to clear the stage, I went to where the prop should have been, at a desk, where the actor concerned had dried repeatedly because the prop wasn't there, and he'd scribbled a note on the piece of paper on the desk – "I wish I was dead" – and I remember suddenly feeling the crushing weight of responsibility.'

However, the job also had its perks. Peter McEnery remembers, 'As ASM I was in charge of dishing out the cigarettes that actors smoked on stage. Generally they would take a couple of puffs and put them out. I would take great delight in going round the ashtrays and collecting all these cigarettes, which then kept me going for the whole week.' Setting the props which were used by cast members during a performance was one aspect of a wider responsibility to dress the set. The basic scenery, in the form of canvas flats, was designed and painted by the scenic artist, but all the furniture, decor and ornamentation had to be found by the ASM. This was time-consuming and had to be tackled in the most pragmatic way possible. Clive Francis again: 'As an ASM you would look at the little plan (always found at the back of the script issued by Samuel French's Acting Editions) and say, "French windows there, desk over there, bowl of fruit on the desk." You had to do that because you were working so fast.'

However, sometimes things became more complicated, as Deborah Grant found out. 'I do remember one point at five o'clock in the morning in Bristol being told to make the drawing-room curtains and being given hundreds of yards of velvet, which I was dispatched with to somewhere up in the attics with a sewing machine. I was completely at a loss, I don't think I'd ever made a curtain in my life. For *You Never Can Tell*, which has a dinner scene later on in the play, there was a sort of balcony-terrace thing looking out over the sea with beautiful lights and a palm court orchestra playing somewhere in the distance.

It was all supposed to be terribly glamorous. I was dispatched to make stars, old milk bottle tops or something to hang on long pieces of black cotton of different lengths, and these were to hang on a beam in front of the black curtain and would catch the light and look like stars. It sounds ludicrous! I spent hours doing this, getting my stars at different lengths and spacing them all very carefully so that when the bar went up, there they would hang beautifully. What happened on the first performance was up went the bar and all the stars swung together and twiddled round each other and hung in rather nasty clumps.' In a similar vein, Liza Goddard recalls that during her time as ASM at the old Castle Theatre in Farnham she had to stick two hundred and fifty roses made out of different materials on to a gauze front cloth for a production of *Beauty and the Beast*. For Simon Williams a vital tool of the trade was the staple gun. 'Everything was done with a staple gun – curtains up, carpets down, even hems on costumes.' Tricks learnt as an ASM can last a lifetime, as Liza Goddard, again, says, 'Still today I stick braid round my chairs with Copydex because that's what we used to do. We re-upholstered sofas and chairs, we used the same furniture, we just covered it with different fabric. I can still do that.'

Re-upholstery was something that Julian Fellowes developed into an art form! 'My first job was at Frinton Rep, where I immediately achieved fame for being able to cover the only sofa they had in about seventeen minutes. That sofa was covered and re-covered for every thriller and comedy they did.' If food was eaten by the actors on stage, which it frequently was, the responsibility for providing this rested with the poor benighted ASM. Alison Steadman still remembers a recipe for ice cream learnt during her days in stage management. 'The play *Roots* is a props nightmare. It starts off with a meal. There are no curtains on the stage so this meal had to be on set from the half. I had to cook this meal and leave it ready. One of the characters makes a cake, they have another meal, they have a tea party. I was so frightened of forgetting something I had a list in my pocket, a list in my dressing-room, it was terrible. At one point they had to eat some ice cream! I went to the props master and said, "How do you make Neapolitan ice cream that has to be on the set from seven o'clock?" It was a revelation! You use Cadbury's Smash potato and you colour it in three colours, then cut it into sections and make it into a block.' Being in charge of the prop food had its advantages, according to Vilma Hollingbery. 'We never had enough to eat, I used to eat the prop food, I used to have quite a lot of custard I remember, because we used custard to look liked fried eggs and I used to eat what was left.'

Drawing-room comedies tended to be a staple of many reps and at the top of the props' list for these was usually a drinks' tray. Lynn Farleigh recalls one terrible mistake she made, 'As an ASM in Salisbury I once poured a bottle of real whisky down the sink, thinking it was a prop substitute in need of washing up.'

Things that couldn't be faked were borrowed. Janet Whiteside says, 'I adored ASMing. I loved going to people's houses and saying, "Can I borrow this and may I borrow that?" There was one wealthy family in Kilmarnock who must have dreaded me coming, I borrowed their sofa once, a beautiful sofa, they did without it for a whole week, and I borrowed all their silver. They took great pleasure in coming to see the play and seeing all their furniture.'

Things of all shapes and sizes were removed from the houses of many a willing victim. To assist in this work, Alec McCowen had a hand cart in which to ferry chattels to and from the theatre, some of them possibly as bizarre as the prop Michael Kilgarriff recalls being sent to find. 'There was a time when I had to get a mole trap and I thought, "Where do you get a mole trap in Jersey?" So I went along to the local ironmonger's and said, "Have you got a mole trap? I'm from the theatre and I want to borrow one," expecting him to snigger at me, but without moving a muscle he said, "Large or small?" Thinking theatrical, I said, "Large," and he slammed this thing down on the counter, teeth and all.'

Barbara Leslie rose to another difficult challenge, only to find that her efforts were wasted. 'Patrick Cargill and I were doing a play where the summerhouse is blown up, this was when I was stage manager, and he had to come out of the summerhouse after the bomb had gone off, with the remains of a piano keyboard all round his neck. I saw on the prop list I'd got to get a piano keyboard and it never occurred to me to say I can't get this. You were so dedicated and naïve. So I combed the old second-hand and antique shops of Buxton and I found a man who'd got a broken old piano and he let me have the keyboard from it and I lugged it all the way back to the theatre and Patrick Cargill said it was too heavy to go round his neck and could I make one?' Liz

Crowther found herself embarking upon some obscure trails. 'When I was looking for props, I once had to find a glass eye for an actor. I also had to get some coffin-wood samples from a funeral director. We used to borrow tennis trophies from David and John Lloyd's family to dress the set with.'

Requirements frequently went beyond the odd glass eye or tennis trophy. In one show at the Penguin Players, Michael Cochrane really had his work cut out for him. 'My first production was a thriller. It had four sets: a bathroom, a lounge, a kitchen and a bedroom. On the opening night I hadn't yet got the bath in which the murdered person was found, I hadn't got the cooker into which somebody else had their head shoved, I hadn't got the sofa under which they had to hide the murderer and I hadn't got the dagger or revolver, so I was fired. There wasn't much point in firing me because they opened in two and a half hours, so I was reinstated. I had two and a half hours to go round Bexhill-on-Sea and find a bath, a cooker, a sofa, a dagger and a revolver. I went rushing back to my digs, which were owned by a postman. He said, "I'll tell you what I'll do, I was a plumber in my time ...". To cut a long story short, he got his bath out of his bathroom, his cooker out of his kitchen, put the cooker on the bath and put them both in the back of his van and took them to the stage door of the De La Warr Pavilion.'

Bernard Cribbins was also tested. 'I remember you used to get your prop list on a Tuesday morning, I used to have to get strange things like a goat. There was a farm up on the moors about Oldham and I borrowed a goat and I used to have to bring it to the theatre on a bus. The driver used to make me go upstairs. I'd ask for one and a goat to Rose Bank, which was near the theatre.'

As well as private individuals and even local farmers helping the theatres, many shops and businesses were happy to lend a hand in exchange for a mention in the programme and the spin-off benefits derived from the general public seeing their goods displayed on stage in what amounted to an early form of product placement. As small shopkeepers are forced out of the high streets by large chain stores, Liz Crowther believes that this will happen less. 'Propping would be different now because the shops aren't local, they are branches of national chains,' a pity, since the rep theatres have always been dependent for their survival on the commitment of the local community and the borrowing and lending of props was one way in which links could be forged.

Just as the jobs themselves were often idiosyncratic, so the people who carried them out were usually colourful characters. Brian Cox remembers, 'We had this wonderful drunken stage manager, who doubled as the priest in *Hamlet* and one night he was drunk and he fell into the grave of Ophelia and we had to crawl under the stage to rescue him.' Bernard Hepton says, 'At York there was one stage director who nobody quite liked, he was a bit of a bully, he used to lose his composure quite easily. There was one wonderful night when he actually went up with the curtain. He was hanging on to the curtain shouting at people and I was on the stage waiting to open the play and I watched him go up about six inches into the air.' Evidently, stage-managing could be hazardous. Brian Cox again: 'One day the stage manager was giving me gun drill. He was holding the gun by the barrel and he said, "You never, never point the barrel at anyone, you always hold the barrel away from you and you make sure the chamber is open, then you close the chamber." He handed me the gun and I pulled the trigger and the gun went off and he got a very black nose. I'd burnt his nose.'

Given the enormous amount of work that an acting ASM was expected to do, it is not surprising that the length of their hours compares with those of junior hospital doctors today. Derek Nimmo says, 'As a stage manager one worked Sundays as well, that was when one struck the old set and erected the new one ready for the supposed dress rehearsal on the Monday, which one hardly ever got through because there was so much going wrong with the props. It was a period of extraordinarily hard work.' Bernard Cribbins stresses how meagre the financial rewards for all this labour could be. 'When I was a stage manager and we had to do the get-out and the get-in on a Sunday to be ready for the dress rehearsal on a Monday morning, I had three brothers, the Joneses, and they were all cotton-mill operatives, they were my stage crew and I used to pay them something like five shillings an hour, it was double time on a Sunday, and I used to get ten shillings for the whole day.'

Tom Conti was none too pleased by the ratio of effort to reward either. 'A changeover weekend was when you finished the play on a Saturday night after two shows, having had a run through of the next play in the morning. Then you took the set down on a Saturday night, gathered all the props together for the next play, the set went up on the Sunday, you stayed pretty well the whole of Saturday and Sunday night in the theatre, slept in the green room for a couple of hours, dress rehearsed on a Monday morning and opened on the Monday evening. It was a killing routine for the princely sum of eight pounds a week.'

In spite of all these hardships, it could be a thrilling way of life, as Clive Francis admits. 'They were wonderful days, I cherish every moment of them and I learnt so much. When I left Bexhill I knew everything there was to know about the theatre. I could light a show, I knew how to put a production on, it was invaluable, not the sort of thing you get taught any more.'

Stephanie Cole shares his sense of indebtedness. 'I had a very broad experience of ASMing, which I loved actually, I'm very practically minded. In those days I had a lot of energy and an enormous amount of enthusiasm and commitment, so I really enjoyed that. It does give you an understanding of what it's like when you're on the other side of the curtain trying to make the set work, get the props right, cue things on time.' Although the financial rewards were necessarily small, the work when it was done well was not without recognition, in Peggy Mount's experience. 'Marie Fontaine came to me once and said, "You have pleased me, you have been a very good stage manager," and she gave me a little parcel and inside it was a diamond clip.' In his own way, Alec McCowen received acclaim as well. 'I shifted scenery and at lunchtime often worked in the box office. It was a wonderful start in life. I played a variety of strange parts. The first one was an elderly manservant called Mickey in a play called *Paddy the Next Best Thing*. I got a notice in the paper, not for my performance but for how good the scene changes were.'

Scene changes could not be relied on to run smoothly, however. Stephen Moore remembers a performance of *Arms and the Man* in Colchester when the first act took twenty minutes and the first scene change forty-five because the set was too big for the stage.

People tend to become nostalgic about their early days as ASMs, but Bernard Cribbins gives a warning about over-romanticizing what it was like. 'I don't know what it was about the good old days, because they weren't good old days when you think about it, it was bloody hard work,' and Martin Duncan says, 'I remember seeing dawn come up over Lincoln Cathedral many times and thinking, "This is agony."'

Perhaps the lot of the acting ASM is best summed up by Patricia Brake, who says, 'I was a lodger in Salisbury in the house of a brigadier and his wife. I remember the brigadier's wife saying over breakfast one morning that she thought I would have a much easier time in the army. I think she was right!'

3

Theatre Buildings

'*Not the Inigo Jones!*'

Tom Osborne Robinson

OVER MANY CENTURIES Britain has developed a rich theatrical tradition, which has found its physical expression in a legacy of buildings quite breathtaking in their beauty. Sir Christopher Wren rebuilt Drury Lane in 1674, Sir John Vanbrugh constructed the Haymarket Theatre in 1705 and architects of their stature set high standards for others to follow. In terms of regional theatres, notable disciples have been John Paty, who in 1766 built the exquisite Theatre Royal in Bristol from plans which were modified by a carpenter called Saunders, who had worked at Drury Lane. Nearly a hundred years later C.J. Phipps designed enchanting theatres in Brighton in 1866 and Northampton in 1887. A prolific theatre architect of the later Victorian period was Frank Matcham, who was responsible for the Palladium and the Coliseum in London, His Majesty's in Aberdeen and the Everyman in Cheltenham, among many others. Men like these helped to create what the actress Josephine Tewson, talking about Matcham's Royalty Theatre in Morecambe, describes as 'the most blissful theatre, a proper little gilt opera house'. These beautiful buildings were an expression of civic pride and were usually located centrally in their towns and cities. Their interiors were frequently lavish, with ornate plaster work, sumptuous gilding and plush seats which were intended to create a sense of occasion for the audience, although it must be said that the people in the cheapest seats had sparser accommodation in the gallery or 'gods' and were not allowed to come in through the resplendent foyers, but used a separate and unadorned entrance.

The Royal Theatre in Northampton, which C.J. Phipps constructed, was lucky enough to have the services of the talented scenic designer Tom Osborne Robinson during the middle decades of this century. One evening a chandelier broke from its hanging and came crashing down. Osborne Robinson's first reaction was 'Not the Inigo Jones!' – a splendid chandelier reputed to have been made by Jones hung in the auditorium, and his initial concern was for this rather than for the safety of anyone who might have been underneath it. Happily the Inigo Jones remained intact, it was an inferior chandelier backstage which had fallen, but this anecdote indicates the powerful attachment that the fabric of these old buildings evoked in those who worked in them and came to love them.

Dennis Ramsden's description encapsulates people's image of the ceremony and excitement associated with these old-fashioned buildings. 'His Majesty's Theatre in Aberdeen is the second largest in the country after Drury Lane and was run by the Donald family. Staff were lined up every evening on the aisle, they wore white gloves and their gloves were inspected. Dust sheets were put over the stalls after the performance every night, the ashtrays were sparkling, they were cleaned and polished every day. It was a magnificent theatre.' Dorothy Tutin still remembers the atmosphere generated by one of the best examples of these theatres: 'The Bristol Old Vic is a theatre that has magic attached to it. It is extremely old, it has a lot of history, the proportions of it are so intimate that it draws out whatever you have in you. It's not intimidating, it's encompassing and wonderful.' Though members of the audience are aware that the structure of an auditorium can influence their comfort as well as their ability to see and hear a play properly, they may be unaware of the effect it has on the way in which an actor performs. Robin Bailey believes that the design of the celebrated old repertory theatre in Birmingham facilitated performances of greater intimacy. 'Because of the Birmingham Rep's seating arrangements, to go on to the stage of a night was like walking into a wall of faces, they were so accessible, the rake was so steep. It was a great pleasure, playing in it, even though it was tiny.'

One of the most appealing factors about the repertory tradition is the enormous variety of theatres that it embraces, ranging all the way

from the splendour of His Majesty's in Aberdeen to something altogether more makeshift and humble, such as the little theatre in
Frinton-on-Sea. Nickolas Grace describes it. 'Frinton Rep is in the
Women's Institute Hall, the seats aren't raked and the stage is fifteen
foot by ten foot.' Josephine Tewson tells of a similar encounter with the
less lavish types of regional theatre. 'I went to Darlington and it was
twice-nightly weekly rep in the Mechanics Hall with wooden tip-up
seats and a platform up one end. If you went off-stage on one side that
was it, three feet and you hit a wall. There was one huge dressing-room
with a string across and blankets thrown over it, with girls on one side
and chaps on the other.' Buildings such as these and the Regent
Theatre in Hayes offered facilities that could only be described as
minimal, as Shaun Sutton recalls. 'It was a tiny theatre. One dressing-
room for girls and one for boys, and the stage was tiny. I remember
arriving and saying, "Oh the lighting's not in yet, is it?" and they said,
"That is the lighting." '

Another small-scale enterprise was to be found at the old Castle
Theatre in Farnham. Tenniel Evans says that when he worked there, 'if
it rained the audience tended to put their umbrellas up because the
roof leaked'. The old theatre in Salisbury was reasonably watertight,
although Roger Leach remembers, 'If a storm was particularly noisy
the corrugated-iron roof made a hell of a row.'

There were varying degrees of comfort on offer front of house in
most repertory theatres, but conditions backstage were grim. To
understand some of the problems faced by actors and stage crew, a
brief description of the geography behind the scenes may be helpful.
From a position standing on stage and looking out front, the left side
of the stage is known as prompt side because it houses the prompt
corner, where the person on the book sits to control the performance;
the right hand is called 'OP', or Opposite Prompt. The stage is
flanked on both sides by the wings. A wing is a canvas-covered flat
placed at the edge of the stage and facing the auditorium to mask the
side of the set, or scenery. In the space behind the wings the cast wait
to make their entrances and the expression 'Winging it' derives from
the actor's need to rush off into the wings to check what his next
line is.

Above the stage are the flies, the domain of the fly man. This is
where all the backcloths, which are attached to planks of wood or bars,

are hoisted up and tied off to a rail on the fly floor or gallery, where they are stored when they are not being used in a scene and from where they can be lowered into position as required. Above the flies, right at the top of the fly tower, is the lighting grid. Here the electrician sites all the lamps and lanterns needed to light a show. They are plugged into sockets on a metal grid and hung from bars that can be moved to meet each show's individual needs.

Most stages are hollow to allow for the use of trapdoors or hydraulics and have an area beneath them that can be utilized variously for dressing-rooms, storage or workshops. Access to the orchestra pit is usually from under the stage. The paint shop is sometimes above and to the side of the performing area, where the scenery for each production is made. In the paint shop is the paint frame, a contraption to which the canvas flats are attached before they are painted. Once they are finished, the paint frame is lowered through a gap between the paint-shop wall and the floor, to stage level, where the flats can be carried into position and fixed. As well as these technical areas there are dressing-rooms, props rooms, a wardrobe and a green room, so called because in the old days it was painted green or possibly because a green baize door led to it, where actors meet to chat, make tea or have a meal.

In most theatres there is access from one side of the stage, round the back or underneath, to the other. This was not the case at the Arts Theatre in Ipswich, as Doreen Andrew recounts. 'The Arts Theatre Ipswich was a converted hall of some kind with partitioned dressing-rooms. It was a great barn of a place and if you had to make an entrance on the other side of the stage you had to go upstairs, round the back outside the theatre and in the other door, in all weathers. Ian McKellen was playing Henry V and I was doubling Mistress Quickly with the Queen of France. I had this costume with enormous sleeves, ermine up to my armpits. Having changed into that from Mistress Quickly, I had to go outside, jump into two feet of snow and trudge round to go and stand on the podium and be the Queen of France. It was ridiculous!' Actors in Ipswich were out in all weathers and some even had adventures between exiting stage right and entering stage left. One of these was Stephen Hancock. 'I was playing a policeman, wearing the full rig. To get round to the other side of the stage you had to go out into the street and back through the stage door, and there was a bloke hanging around with his car and he said, "Oh, oh, is it all right if I park here?" and I said, "Of course it is, of course it is."'

Alec McCowen remembers vividly the crude conditions backstage in Macclesfield. 'There were no dressing-rooms, we dressed under the stage with a curtain between the men and the women and there was no running water and I had to go to the pub next door with two buckets and get a bucket of water for the men and one for the women, for the show.' At least the theatre at Colchester had dressing-rooms, but, as Philip Voss recalls, 'They were like horse boxes and there was a terrible lavatory.' Peter Bowles did a stint in Nottingham, where the state of the facilities left him with a long-term concern about his health. 'At Nottingham Rep, which was putting out the most wonderful work, there were only two dressing-rooms, one for men and one for women, under the stage. They were partitioned with the sort of partitions you'd make chicken sheds out of, some sort of asbestos, which has always worried me ever since. There was a boiler somewhere to heat the theatre. The fumes were unbelievable – some of us were taken to hospital. We used to have to have glasses of water secreted about the stage because the fumes coming up from underneath the floorboards were so awful.'

Roger Leach is equally disparaging about the area behind the scenes at the old Arts Theatre in Salisbury. 'Backstage at the old Salisbury Rep was dreadful, it was like the wartime spirit. People made the best of it. Coal was kept in the corridor on the left-hand side of the stage, we had to be careful of our costumes when we went to make an entrance.' He also remembers, 'We used to have to get in and out of the wardrobe through a window. The wardrobe store was always full of pigeon shit as the roof needed fixing.'

During the 1940s in Scarborough Doreen Andrew worked in conditions which nowadays would cause Public Health Inspectors to close the building down. 'We were in the old opera house, which was still boarded up from the war and completely rat-infested. You had to be very careful to put away your make-up otherwise you'd find these little teeth marks in your sticks of Leichner.'

Several rep companies used to be housed at the ends of piers, where conditions were understandably primitive. John Warner discovered this when he worked in Bognor Regis. 'The theatre was at the near end of the pier. I remember the previous week we'd had performing dogs in the dressing-room, and I mean performing! The leading lady was called Beulah Garrick, no relation. I remember going into her dressing-room, daring the girls' dressing-room, and she was sitting on a chair over the sink, peeing.'

Actors were not always driven to these lengths, although the marine setting of the pier theatres could add an extra dimension to some of the plays that were produced. William Franklyn recounts, 'I went to meet Barrie O'Brien, who had repertory companies on the Isle of Wight, at Southsea on the pier and at the Palace, Bournemouth. I got a job as a try-out in *Arsenic and Old Lace* on the pier at Southsea, playing two parts. What I remember about it is that the theatre is actually on the pier and between the floorboards you could see the water underneath and in the play itself there's talk about one of the characters, Teddy Roosevelt, going down to the Panama Canal, so there was in fact a reality on stage, you could look down and see little rowing boats and small launches going underneath the stage while you were acting.'

Peter McEnery started his career on the pier in Brighton, where all the fun of the fair was to be had, as he relates. 'The Palace Pier at Brighton had a weekly rep company that did north country comedies and West End successes. They were usually pretty tacky, but it was my first job and I was only sixteen. I was taken on as ASM and I was paid thirty shillings a week. I loved it, I thought it was fantastic. I can tell you that the Palace Pier is a third of a mile long because I walked up and down it so many times a day getting props. It was at the far end of the pier. It was a proper little theatre with front-of-house bars on two levels. It had a dress circle and the stage door looked out on to the bumper cars. During the plays you'd get the noise of all the screaming from the bumper cars, the vibrations, the thump of the sea below. Because I was the ASM, during the interval the other actors would send me out to fetch them refreshments. I would delight in this because I would go out to the stall in full make-up and I thought that people would recognize me. And of course they'd look at me in horror because of my brick red make-up!'

Jean Anderson recalls factors which compensated for the spartan conditions in pier theatres between the wars. 'In summer in rep you played on the piers. I did straight plays on both Brighton piers. We used to dive off the pier into the sea between the matinée and the evening show.'

Although they could not boast of bathing facilities, many land-locked theatres had their own particular attractions. There is a long tradition of ghosts haunting British theatres and the regions are not excluded from this. Simon Williams says, 'The theatre in Bath is supposed to be haunted. When I was there, I once saw a figure in the stalls. I thought that someone was kidding around pretending to be a ghost, but nobody was and when I went out front to have a look I found that one seat in the row was down.'

Patricia Marmont is more sceptical about the visitations that were supposed to occur in York. 'The theatre at York was lovely, it was an old theatre, it was haunted. It had been a nunnery and a nun had been walled up or suffered some grisly demise and the wardrobe mistress, Mrs Lowther, had second sight and she was the only person to have seen the ghost. It used to go along the back wall. Everybody fantasized that they had seen it but I don't know if anybody did. One did believe that Mrs Lowther had seen it.'

Liza Goddard says, 'The Castle Theatre in Farnham was a very old building and it was also haunted in the costume department by a very old gentleman in top hat and tails who suddenly appears in a place where there is nowhere to get in,' an account verified by Sheila Reid: 'The Castle Theatre in Farnham was riddled with ghosts. I was sitting in rehearsal and a man in Puritan clothes was suddenly having a very nice time enjoying the show next to me.' Alison Steadman is equally convinced that such things can happen. 'Lincoln did have a ghost. When we were doing the fit-ups or the strikes we'd have a tea break in the green room and there was a big iron pass door just outside the green room and we often used to hear that bang although we were all there having our tea. That was the ghost of the theatre.'

The most graphic account of a supernatural encounter comes from April Walker, who began her career working in Chesterfield. 'When I was an ASM it was my job to bring the iron in. I had to go across to the far side of the stage, up an iron ladder to the fly gallery and wind in the iron. It was a huge great winch and, once you got started on it, it did not want to stop halfway. I was just about to start cranking this winch, when I looked along the fly gallery and saw a man sitting on the rail. He was a shadowy figure of a man, wearing a dark coat or cloak and what looked like a stovepipe hat. I said, "Oh, I didn't realize there was anybody in. Do come on down because I want to get the iron in." The hairs on the back of my neck started to stand up, and I thought, "I don't think I like this very much. I think I'm just going to go back down." I knew that underneath the stage there was the carpenter, so I went down to him and I said, "I feel absolutely petrified, I think I've just seen something, or someone, up on the fly floor." "Oh," he said, "you've seen George." "Who's George?" I asked. "George Stephenson, who built the Rocket." Apparently, before that theatre was built, he had offices in a building that were at about that level.'

These wonderful old structures, with or without their resident ghosts, have a patina, an ambience that their more modern counterparts have had insufficient time to acquire, a feeling corroborated by Alison Steadman. 'When you're working in a modern space it creates a different atmosphere for a group of actors from these lovely old Victorian theatres.' That is not to say that many of the modern buildings do not have a convenience and a staging potential with which the older ones find it hard to compete. After the Second World War there was a wave of new building lasting through the 1950s, 1960s and 1970s. Jennie Lee, who was Minister for the Arts from 1967 to 1970, injected money into the repertory movement via the Arts Council. The Belgrade Theatre in Coventry was the first civic theatre ever built, as part of the city's reconstruction after it had been blitzed by the Luftwaffe. The Belgrade was a people's theatre, which had and still has the backing of the local council. Named in honour of the Yugoslavian government, which provided the timber with which the auditorium is clad, the success of its construction led the Arts Council to authorize the building of theatres like the Crucible in Sheffield, the Octagon in Bolton, the New Repertory Theatre in Birmingham and many others.

Oliver Ford Davies has a point to make about the conception of the theatre in Birmingham, believing that in many cases, where two auditoria exist, the main house has been over-extended at the expense of the studio space. 'The Birmingham Rep had to move to a better theatre, but the move from four hundred and fifty seats (rarely full) and a small stage to the new Rep – nine hundred seats and a vast stage – brought many problems. The desire of civic authorities to have large theatres and tiny box-like studios has proved a disaster in many places. Instead of nine hundred and two hundred seaters, we should have built six hundred and three hundred and fifty seaters. The West Yorkshire Playhouse has at last got it right.' Built in the 1980s, the West Yorkshire

Playhouse in Leeds is a testament to the success of more modern buildings to entice the community inside them, but many actors retain a fondness for the older, shabbier edifices in which they started out. However, in spite of their atmosphere, in spite of their considerable beauty, several of these have failed to survive. The advent of the cinema scythed away many, which were converted into picture houses; the arrival of the television in its turn put paid to many cinemas and some remaining theatres, which were redesignated bingo halls; the development of video and computerized entertainments has done further damage to the surviving number of regional houses. The loss of these old theatres can have a profound effect on those who once worked in them. Lionel Jeffries says, 'I worked in a weekly rep, Lichfield in Staffordshire, the David Garrick theatre and it actually was David Garrick's theatre. Samuel Johnson put the money up for it, I believe, but the Lichfield people will put me right on this, although I don't think any of them are interested, there is no interest at all, it's sickening the lack of interest. That lovely theatre is now a storeroom. The stage, all the original boards that Garrick actually played on, were ripped up and burnt. My wife and I went back there recently and I cried.'

4

Repertory Theatre Managements

'What do you want to go to New York for? You're in Liverpool!'

Attributed to Maud Carpenter by Richard Briers

JUST AS THE repertory theatres themselves were an eclectic range of buildings, so the people who ran them were a wonderful collection of colourful, dedicated, but sometimes eccentric, personalities. None more so than the legendary Maud Carpenter, who started work in the box office of what was then called the Liverpool Repertory Theatre when it first opened in November 1911. The theatre, which stands in Williamson Square, was renamed the Liverpool Playhouse and in 1923 Maud Carpenter became its general manager, a position which she held until the mid-1950s. Under her extremely firm hand, the Liverpool Playhouse maintained its position at the forefront of the repertory movement. Many actors remember her with a mixture of awe and affection and the stories about her are legion. Richard Briers says of her, 'She started front of house selling tickets and she became a legendary figure who controlled everything. She was a galleon-type of lady with an ample bosom; she went round like a very large ship. She wore a long black dress and pearls. The Playhouse to her was Covent Garden.' This impression is echoed by Moray Watson. 'Maud Carpenter was a legendary figure . . . She didn't know anything about the stage itself, but she ran the front of house beautifully, but beyond the curtain she knew nothing at all. There's a story once that she went through the pass door on a Saturday night, which she very rarely did, and heard the stage director saying, "All right boys, strike," (meaning take the scenery down) and she said, "What's the matter, do I not pay them enough?" She managed to get things wrong, a little bit like Mrs Malaprop. There's a wonderful, legendary, naughty story about her and Mr Carpenter going to bed together for the first time and she said, "Well, you can put that away for a start." Another story about her – she threw a party one Sunday in the summer and she said, "All right, that's enough drinking inside now, we're all going outside now for the cold copulation."'

Caroline Blakiston remembers, 'She came back from a holiday in Venice declaring, "We drove down the Grand Canal in a Lagonda,"' and Richard Briers reiterates her confusion about the appropriateness of certain words. 'She would do malapropisms – instead of saying, "It was a mere bagatelle", she would say, "It was a mere bag of shells."' John Warner remembers her as 'a sort of Lilian Baylis. She once bumped into Gerald Cross, who was the director, and said, "Why do you keep doing all these bird plays?" and he said, "What do you mean?" and she said, "Well you've just done *The Wild Duck* and you've done *The Seagull*, why can't you do something nice like *George and Phyllis*?" She was a great character. She was more the business side, management, she knew really nothing about the theatre. But it was her theatre. The directors were very much under her thumb, I think. The directors chose the plays but she'd object if she didn't like them.'

The directors were not alone in being under her thumb. Jean Boht recalls, 'It was Maud Carpenter's policy that her artistes must always be dressed formally outside the theatre – the men were not allowed to wear sports jackets, for instance, and later I learnt that many of the company would hire a taxi from just around the corner to fulfil her "Stars" arriving at the stage door requirement.' Brigid Panet remembers similar regulations. 'At Liverpool actresses were not allowed to go out wearing trousers.'

Richard Briers says that her strictness extended into the economic as well as the sartorial aspects of theatre management. 'Maud Carpenter was very much a down-to-earth businesswoman. I was paid eight pounds a week there and I was playing all these large parts, so I went to see her and I asked for ten pounds a week, which was a lot of money in those days. She said, "Now look here, love. You're getting good parts, aren't you?" And I said, "Yes, Miss Carpenter." And she said, "Then don't fuss about the money. Eight pounds a week is very good money these days."' To her, the notion of anybody looking beyond Merseyside for artistic or financial fulfilment was incredible, as Richard Briers once again relates. 'Pauline Yates was there and she was in an Elmer Rice play. Someone came over from American to see the production, a friend of Elmer Rice, and they told her she had a chance of going to America, to New York. Maud Carpenter would on no account release her. She said, "What do you want to go to New York for? You're in Liverpool." She couldn't understand that people had a life outside the repertory theatre, where the top salary was about fifteen pounds.'

In spite of her severity, Miss Carpenter was not without a sense of humour, as the following anecdote by John Warner illustrates. 'The Playhouse was doing *The Diary of Anne Frank* and Dr Cohen was the chairman of the board, a Jewish doctor and he later became Lord Cohen and he used to come every first night. Maud rang him up on the first night of *The Diary of Anne Frank* and said, "I hope you're coming tonight to the play," and he said, "I'm terribly sorry, Maud, but I can't because I've got a Jewish function on tonight," and she said, "So have we."'

The Playhouse must have inspired loyalty in all those connected with its running, as Moray Watson tells a story concerning the same Lord Cohen. 'I made a great mistake at a party one day. A gentleman called Sir Henry Cohen said, "Are you enjoying yourself here, Watson?", and I said, "Yes, very good, wonderful. Marvellous sort of means to an end." I don't know what made me say it. He said, "What do you mean? Means to an end?" I said, "Well, I'll be leaving at the end of the season, going to London." He said, "Liverpool *is* an end in itself, Watson, we have a very high standard here and it is not a means to anywhere." He was very angry.'

Judy Campbell did her time in Liverpool and comments, 'Later on in one's career, theatre programmes always used to say, "Started in rep at Liverpool Playhouse." But you didn't, you finished in rep at Liverpool Playhouse.' Her sentiment, that the Playhouse represented a pinnacle of the repertory movement and was the ultimate goal of anyone working in it, is widely acknowledged to be true and Maud Carpenter undoubtedly contributed to its lofty status.

Another figure of pre-eminence in regional theatre and a contemporary of Miss Carpenter's was Barry Jackson. Born in 1879, he first became involved in amateur theatre with a group called the Pilgrim Players, who met at his father's house in Birmingham. This company assumed professional status when Jackson built a theatre for them in

Station Road in 1913 and the famous Birmingham Rep was born. He also inaugurated the Malvern Festival as a showcase for Bernard Shaw's plays and was knighted for his services to the theatre in 1925. As patron of the Birmingham Rep, ultimate power over the theatre's running was vested in him, but he preferred to adopt a low profile and delegate much of the day-to-day running of the company to a succession of directors whom he employed. As well as staging performances by Lord Olivier and Sir Ralph Richardson, the Birmingham Rep launched the careers of many illustrious actors, including Sir Derek Jacobi, Albert Finney, Michael Gambon and Ian Richardson.

The fullest account of what it was like to work with Jackson comes from Bernard Hepton, who was initially taken on in Birmingham as an actor, but, in a move characteristic of Sir Barry, became the last director to be employed by him. He believed in giving people the opportunity to explore their potential. Bernard Hepton says of him, 'Barry Jackson was in charge. He was a sort of shadowy figure. He didn't actually come in every day, he lived in Malvern. When he came into the coffee break during rehearsal, he didn't often do it but when he did he would stand there and have polite conversation. He would never, or very rarely, give an opinion about the current play to an actor, which I thought was absolutely right. He would give his opinion to the director. The first note I got from him was in a Linklater play, *Abraham Lincoln* and I was playing the Southern Gentleman, and the note came via the director Douglas Seale saying, "Tell that young man his trousers are too short." That's the first note I ever had from Sir Barry.'

Paul Daneman remembers, 'Sir Barry Jackson was the great, famous figure, the *eminence grise*, he would arrive, tall and stately, with a cigarette in a long tortoiseshell holder. He only had to say one word, "That one's quite good," and you were in. His word was absolute law, quite right, it was his theatre.' Bernard Hepton also says, 'He was a great influence in my life. It was not until I was directing that I came much more into contact with him. He invited me to his house and we had talks about what plays to put on. I got to know him fairly well. I considered him to be a very cultured, cultivated man. I don't know how clever he was. That's a different thing altogether. His genius was actually allowing people to fail. Giving people the opportunities to succeed, in other words, and encouraging people by giving them those opportunities.'

It is worth mentioning here that in discussing the contribution working in rep made to their careers, actor after actor comments that it provided them with the opportunity to fail. If one production was less than successful, then the ground could always be made up the following week, fortnight or month. This enabled them to take risks that they would not have done otherwise. Sir Barry Jackson was significantly responsible for creating this climate within the repertory movement, which was why his theatre became such a crucible for talent.

Bernard Hepton includes in this tribute to Sir Barry mention of his instinctive vision for staging Shakespeare. 'He was a great editor of Shakespeare. He said, "As far as editing Shakespeare is concerned, there are certain plays that need it, because if the audience doesn't understand it or doesn't know what is going on then they're going to be bored and you're going to fail." He was always thinking of the audience. For instance, the three parts of *Henry VI* were done. He edited them brilliantly and they worked like a charm. When they transferred to the Old Vic the eminent scholar John Dover Wilson was seen at the end of *Part Three* sitting in the auditorium on his own and the manager went over to him and said, "I hope you've enjoyed these three plays, Professor?" and Dover Wilson replied, "Yes, I realize now that I spent ten years editing them and I realize it's ten years wasted."'

'Sir Barry's credo was "If you come across something and you don't really understand it, read it again. If you still don't understand it give it to somebody else to read and if they don't understand it, cut it! Because the audience only have one opportunity and if they don't understand it you're lost."'

Charles Simon embarked on a career in theatre production as a result of the frustration he felt as both an actor and a director with the policies of existing managements. He maintains, 'When I was running a company, it was very difficult to convince theatre proprietors that they were just as likely to make money in their theatres from classical stuff as from fur coat and no knickers, so in the end I decided that the only thing to do was not just to own the company but to own the theatre as well. So I very recklessly took a lease on a theatre in Darlington, which was the only one I could find, a beautiful old Theatre Royal, a Royal Charter Theatre, one of the few in the provinces.

'When I took the Theatre Royal Darlington it had been playing third-rate revue for years. It was on its last legs, so I thought, "Right, the only thing is to show them boldly what I'm going to do and if they don't want it, well bugger them." I went even further than was necessary. In my first year there I did *Hamlet*, for instance. I had a wonderful company of people who really knew what they were doing. In a complete week in the large Theatre Royal we played to the glorious sum of thirty pounds. The public hated it, they couldn't understand what I was doing. I did *Hamlet* every year. I got to the stage when I could announce my year's programme and the sixth year we did *Hamlet* by the end of January we had sold out for the production, which was to be in November. I was secretly very proud of that. When you're young you do things you wouldn't dare do when you are older and I had made up my mind that I was in a better position to know what a good play was than any member of my audience. The idea of running ballots – Which play would you like to see? Please tick them off – to me was nonsense. Managements all over the country used to do that. I said to myself, "The only ones they're going to tick off are the ones they've already seen because they like them and they wouldn't be coming again, anyway." I proceeded on the assumption that I should know or I shouldn't be in my job.'

In spite of this self-assurance, which characterized Charles Simon's early work at the Theatre Royal in Darlington, his initial efforts were stymied. 'I struggled for a year to convert the audience from a review audience to a play audience and then the theatre was sold over my head and knocked down and they built a cinema instead.'

Undeterred and with the conviction of firmly held beliefs, Simon continued with his mission. 'I was so furious that I heard on the grapevine that the Temperance Society, for which the town was famous, had a beautiful hall but were in financial difficulties. I was able to get a lease on that and I converted it with the help of the public. I only had two weeks. I enlisted the help of the public through the local press and they all came in and screwed down seats and put up drapes.'

Having involved the community in this project of building a theatre for themselves, Simon continued to produce plays with increasing success throughout the late 1930s, until his efforts received another setback with the outbreak of war in 1939. He joined the Royal Air Force and delegated the running of the theatre in his absence. The Theatre Royal continued to flourish to the degree that Lord Haw Haw singled it out for a mention in one of his infamous broadcasts. 'We know what you're up to in Darlington and we're going to drop fire bombs on your lovely repertory theatre!' The theatre survived that particular German attack, but was hit by a bomb later in the war. Charles Simon remembers hearing the news. 'I was out inspecting RAF stations and I walked in to sign the adjutant's book on one station and the sergeant in charge looked at my signature and said, "Have you got a theatre in Darlington?" And I said, "Yes I have, why?" And he said, "Well, I'm afraid you haven't, it was bombed last night. It was on the eight o'clock news. Headquarters Bomber Command has been sending out a message to all stations because they don't know where you are, to let you know." When I got there all that was left were two gable ends, with an announcement on one gable end, "Next week: Aristophanes' *The Birds*". Everything went – tons and tons of scenery, thousands of playbills, costumes, everything. Then, with the assistance of the local council, I bought the cinema, knocked it down and built a theatre and got my own back.'

Simon was a prolific as well as a determined manager. His main company was based in Darlington, but during the summer months he took them to do seasons of the most popular plays from their repertoire in Aberystwyth, Eastbourne and Bournemouth. The damaging effect of the war was not limited to his Theatre Royal enterprise, these other ventures had to fight for their survival as well. He says, 'The day war broke out I had my senior company at Aberystwyth. Immediately, the government banned all public entertainment and the theatres were shut. I went to see the Chief Constable of Cardiganshire and persuaded him that the government had given him special powers, whether he thought this was true or not. I said, "We're in Aberystwyth, Gerry's not going to waste his bombs on us." So he let me open, but I might just as well have been shut because everyone was glued to the wireless waiting for news of the war. The following day, outside the Garrick Theatre in Charing Cross Road there was a huge long poster saying, "This theatre closed by order of the government, nearest theatre open – the Charles Simon company at the King's Theatre, Aberystwyth, two hundred and sixty one miles away." '

The boldness and tenacity which Simon showed had its own reward: in spite of being bombed out, his company continued to perform and flourish right up to 1951. He describes its eventual decline.

'In 1951 I found that the theatre I had built was too big for the town. During the war the Prudential Assurance had been sent to Darlington, so you had a hand-picked audience of people accustomed to going to the theatre, away from their own homes, with nothing to do but go to the theatre. The moment the war was over and those people went back to their homes, I found that the theatre, which held twelve hundred people, was too big. The mayor started a fund immediately to try to force me to stay and raised thirty thousand pounds, but I had to go to him and say, "You give me twenty thousand pounds and everybody's happy, but in two to three months I come to you and say, sorry old man but I've spent all that, can I have another twenty thousand?" This was well before the days of subsidy, you see. We had to close down and I took my company on tour with a mixed Shakespeare and Shaw rep.'

Charles Simon was more directly involved in his companies than Sir Barry Jackson, but both of them had a driving vision of what the theatre could be. However, the repertory tradition was not dominated by lone figures: married couples and sometimes whole families were involved in establishing and running companies. Most famous among these is the Salberg family. Derek and Reggie Salberg, together with their cousin Basil Thomas, were movers and shakers in regional theatre. Their father Leon ran the Alexandra Theatre in Birmingham, which Derek took over from him, while Reggie operated theatres across the land from the Preston Hippodrome to the Penge Empire, before finally devoting himself to the creation of a company in Salisbury. Basil Thomas was in charge at Wolverhampton. Peggy Mount differentiates between them in this way. 'Basil Thomas, who ran Wolverhampton was one of the Salbergs, he was a cousin. There was Reggie, who knew the plays, who could always choose good plays; there was Derek, who ran the Alex and knew all about the theatre and there was Basil, who was the money man. He wrote a lot of plays that went on into the West End. It would be wonderful to have them now. Some of the performances that I saw at the Alex would have stood up in the West End at any time. People like Billie Whitelaw and Peter Vaughan and Margaret Leighton, who are very successful now, started with Derek at the Alex. If you got to the Alex Birmingham you really were somewhere.' Joss Ackland remembers his love of cricket. 'I worked with Derek Salberg and I got into the company because when I went for the interview he asked me if I was a bowler or a batsman and

I said, "Bowler", and he said, "That's fortunate," and I was enrolled. They needed a bowler that week.'

Tenniel Evans recalls hearing a story about him, which perhaps explains his popularity within the business. In the days before the National Health Service, the wife of a company member was in dire need of an operation, the cost of which was estimated at a hundred pounds. In trepidation the actor approached Derek Salberg and asked if he would consider lending him the sum. When Salberg enquired how his employee would repay him, the actor suggested that an amount might be deducted from his wages on a weekly basis, a proposal that Derek agreed to. Imagine the actor's surprise upon opening his pay packet to find that his salary was exactly the same as it had always been and that the expected deficit had been swallowed up in a pay rise.

Reggie Salberg obviously shared his brother's generous inclinations, as Roger Leach remembers: 'Once at the end of the tax year, he had some spare cash left over in the budget and he gave everyone in the company a bonus.' The brothers were both awarded the OBE for their services to the theatre. Reggie describes the beginning of his career thus: 'I was asked to start a company at the New Theatre, Hull, which lasted six years and did rather well. That was weekly rep. We had a very good director, John Barron, a very good director turned actor. That sort of rep was so much more commercial in those days. You occasionally did something like *She Stoops to Conquer*, but on the whole it was commercial.' He puts the secret of his undoubted success down to having 'A good standard, a good company – Frederick Jaeger, he was the toast of the town, a comedian; Cherry Morris, who then worked with the RSC; It was a good company.' Cherry Morris is happy to return the compliment. 'Reggie Salberg had such a love of the theatre. He was always there, he was always available, he wasn't a remote figure. He was very good with the town people too, which is terribly important, and they adopted the theatre. He would try and go to places that hadn't got a theatre near them, so that the catchment area was such that it would bring people in.'

Salisbury was one such area and the company that Reggie ran there was among the first to receive assistance from the Arts Council when it was set up (he served on its drama panel for many years). He gives an exhausting description of his time in Salisbury. 'My job was a peculiar one because I worked in those days just with a secretary and Alan Corkhill, who was the theatre manager, the occasional trainee manager, including Sir Robert Scott, and that was it. My job with that small staff was to plan the season, choose the company, go to student shows as well as doing the finance of the company. That was done with the help of three people, nowadays I reckon there are at least four people doing my job alone. I wrote all the programme notes and that sort of thing. When I started there was more blurring of jobs – I would go and clean up the theatre between houses and things like that. We all did whatever came our way. I'm making myself sound like a bit of a saint, but I did work a six-day week and certainly most Sundays.' This belief that the administrative arm of theatres suffers from over-manning is echoed by Stephen Hancock. 'Each rep used to be run by about half a dozen people, not twenty thousand like they are now. A manager, a secretary, someone in the box office, a money person who came in once a week to sort the books out, and that was it. I worked at Leicester recently and you would pass people in the corridor and not know who they were. In the old days you would know everybody from the cleaner to the manager to the usherettes.'

Like Sir Barry Jackson, Reggie Salberg never directed plays himself, as Jonathan Cecil says, 'What Reggie used to do, he was very clever, he never directed himself, he always said he wouldn't know how to do it, but he always cast his plays, with some consultation with his director.' Casting was clearly something which interested Salberg and he used to trawl the drama schools looking for new talent. His instinct was usually sound, although there is always the exception that proves the rule. Lynn Farleigh recounts that he wrote 'No' next to Albert Finney's name in a RADA programme when he went to see him in a play.

In the tradition of families running theatres are Richard Burnett and Peggy Paige, who managed the Penguin Players, which were based in the De La Warr Pavilion at Bexhill-on-Sea. Peggy Paige was a person for whom the expression 'old trooper' might have been coined, as Vilma Hollingbery recalls, 'she was still playing the cat in pantomime at the age of eighty-six'.

Liverpool and Birmingham staged a different play every three or four weeks and theatres like Salisbury, although they may have started as weekly reps, eventually devised a schedule which allowed productions a fortnightly run. Companies at the popular end of the spectrum of repertory theatres, not dissimilar to the Penguin Players, not only produced a different show every week but did two performances every night.

The undisputed king of twice-nightly weekly rep was Harry Hanson. His company, the Court Players, performed in venues up and down the country. He bought the Court Players from an actress called Marie Fontaine, who stayed on as his leading lady. Donald Pickering says, 'Dora Bryan always tells the story about how she was working for Harry Hanson doing twice-nightly and she said to him that she wanted to leave because she'd been offered a job in a play by Emlyn Williams; this was her first big break, and Harry Hanson said to her, "Stay with me and I'll make another Marie Fontaine out of you." I mean, everybody knows who Marie Fontaine was, don't they? Dora would have ended up as the star of the Leas Pavilion in Folkestone!'

The loyalty which Harry Hanson demonstrated towards Marie Fontaine extended towards many members of the profession, as Peggy Mount, one of his protegées, remembers. 'He was wonderful because he had at least ten companies and in each of those companies he had at least ten people, so he had all those people that he employed. He was terribly loyal to his people and he had such wit.' Vilma Hollingbery, who worked in many of his companies for several years, agrees. Here she talks about her audition for him. 'Harry Hanson was a marvellous man, he actually cared enormously. He had a waspish sense of humour, but he cared tremendously about the standard of work. I auditioned for him in a hotel in Belgravia. They'd taken a room, his company manager was there, as well as the great man himself, who looked like the Wizard of Oz. I had to do eight speeches, an improvisation, show him my legs, and let him see how far I could project vocally. He was wonderful. In between jobs he'd write to me at home and say, "Look, you've got to do something about your voice," or something like that. He took such an interest. There was a sense of family. You were very proud to be a Harry Hanson Court Player.'

Hanson could be considerate towards those whom he thought to be tested and true, but he had a fearful temper. Paul Daneman says that he 'was a bit of an ogre and he had a stranglehold on rep', while Beryl Cooke reports that he would sack people if they were not DLP (Dead Letter Perfect means being 100 per cent accurate in knowing your lines). Those who knew him well were always on the look out for tell-tale signs that he was cross. Peggy Mount knew the warning signals. 'He was a little, short, fat man and he had three wigs. One wig was blond and if he was wearing that you kept out of his way because he was in a bad mood; a grey wig and he was all right; he had another one and if he wore that you knew that everybody was happy and nobody would get sacked.'

Peter McEnery, who worked for the Court Players in Peterborough, pays tribute to the scale of production that the company attempted. 'Harry Hanson's company at Peterborough did quite ambitious plays like *Paddy the Next Best Thing*, which has five acts with about four scenes in each, with sets including a country house and a railway station, and we did this twice nightly.' This was no mean achievement, a fact which Carmen Silvera recognizes when she says, 'Harry Hanson was the crème de la crème of twice-nightly weekly rep.'

Producers were drawn into rep theatre for a variety of reasons. Judy Campbell recalls working for a man who had a passion for theatre buildings. 'J. Baxter Somerville, known as JB, had theatres all over the south of England. He had a passion for theatres and as theatres had to have actors in them, he put up with actors. He used to travel all over the country by train, he was rumoured to live in a disused railway carriage. I got a job with him in Brighton because my father, who owned a scenery workshop in his theatre at Peterborough and made sets and props for plays, swapped me for some palm trees that JB needed for a production of a play called *Alomo*, which was set on a desert island.'

J. Arthur Rank formed an association with the theatres at Worthing and Bromley, not because he cared passionately about rep, but because he recognized the excellent training it could provide for actors, as Robin Bailey observes. 'The Connaught Theatre, Worthing, and the New Theatre, Bromley, which was in fact the old theatre Bromley too, were run by J. Arthur Rank, because during those days he had what was known as the Charm School, where starlets went to become stars. Very few ever did, but that was the idea. They were groomed for stardom. To give them a little acting experience – the least important aspect of their careers – they were sent down to Worthing to be in a play. Us run-of-the-mill actors had to carry them through it.'

Even though J. Arthur Rank might seem to have been using the repertory system for his own ends, there was a certain compensatory glamour in his association with the world of motion pictures. No such enhancement was attached to Charles Denville. He ran theatres like the one in Barnsley, where the routine made Harry Hanson's schedule look like a rest cure. Denville's company did twice-nightly like Hanson, but he also did two different shows a week. Barbara Lott braved a six-month season for him: 'When I arrived at Barnsley Rep Charlie Denville met me and said, "Now we've got two rules in this theatre; we have no dress rehearsal and we have no prompter."' This must have been a terrifying prospect.

In a similar mould was Harold G. Roberts, whose companies also performed two shows a week twice-nightly. An insight into how these companies functioned is offered by Philip Locke, who never worked for Roberts, but was in Oldham in a different company at the same time. 'Round the corner in Oldham was a company called the Harold G. Roberts Players, who did twice-nightly twice-weekly. The way they cast their season was to ring up an actress and say, "Do you play the Mother in *Heaven and Charing Cross Road*? Do you play the Grandmother in *Ma's Bit of Brass*?" and if the actress said, "Yes, those are some of my parts," she would be taken on to play those roles, because she had already played them. There was a snob element in not being in that kind of company. It must have been a pretty deadly sort of life to go round playing these parts.' Doreen Andrew worked briefly for Harold G. Roberts in Scarborough and recalls his cost-cutting ways. 'We moved from Scarborough to Keighley. Harold G. was a tight-fisted old so-and-so because he sacked me in Scarborough and re-employed me in Keighley so he wouldn't have to pay my train fare from one place to the other.'

Managements at the tattier end of the repertory scale seem to have been prone to these cheapskate habits. Michael Simpkin says, 'A friend of mine did a pantomime in some seaside resort. It was *Snow White and the Seven Dwarfs* and the management could only afford to employ three dwarfs, the other four were made of cardboard. The actors had to keep adding lines like, "Us three will go on ahead, you four stay here."' In spite of what those anecdotes might suggest, managements in some weekly reps insisted on a high standard of work. Jennie Goossens appeared at the Devonshire Park Theatre in Eastbourne. 'Michael Dover was a fair old snob, but in saying that, he strove for very high standards as well as being rather ruthless with some young ASMs who might not have a dinner jacket. The standards were high, so I was always taught well and the grounding was good. You always called the leading man by his surname, everything was much more formal.' At Colchester Philip Voss recalls a protocol similar to Maud Carpenter's in Liverpool. 'There was a strict code of conduct at Colchester Rep. Bob Digby insisted that we behave well. We weren't allowed to hold hands in the street.' Another martinet in Maud Carpenter's mould was Annie Peacock, who had the foresight to give Brian Rix his first job in the theatre. He says, 'Annie Peacock ran the White Rose players in Harrogate, she wore full evening dress to welcome in the audience on Fridays. Mrs Peacock went round in white gloves checking the surfaces to make sure the cleaners had done their job.'

Anthony Hawtrey, son of the actor-manager Sir Charles Hawtrey (1858–1923), followed his father into the theatre as a producer. Although working in weekly rep, his companies at Buxton, Croydon and the Embassy in Swiss Cottage produced work of an extremely high standard. Tony Hawtrey launched the careers of people such as Nigel Hawthorne and Joss Ackland. The latter remembers, 'Tony Hawtrey would go along to the box office before the Wednesday matinée and take all the box office takings to the racecourse and put it all on the horses. His wife Marjorie was in the company and her boyfriend worked in the kitchen and used to throw all these pots and pans at her. It was a fairly colourful time, a mad period, but thank God it was wonderful. One learnt an awful lot from it.'

Gambling was a passion that Arthur Lane, who produced plays at Wimbledon Rep, shared. Belinda Carroll says, 'He was a real rogue, but a very lovable rogue. He once put the entire earnings from the theatre for a week on a horse. (If he wasn't in the theatre he was at the bookmaker's.) Luckily on that occasion the horse came in. He was an actor-manager for many, many years, although he was always in trouble financially.'

Only a few managers and producers come into the category of rogue. Most were dedicated workaholics, risking their own money to keep actors employed and the public entertained. One such, a woman who holds an almost unique position in contemporary theatre as she still produces summer seasons of weekly rep, is Jill Freud. She says that she started the repertory company at Southwold ignorant of what was involved. For instance, during the first year of operations she didn't have a wardrobe or a wardrobe mistress and admits that an early weakness of the company was insufficient stage management. She works without a salary. Her total motivation is to provide work for actors, something she has been successful at, since she employed twenty-one of them in 1995. While many might be tempted to disparage the opportunities offered by weekly rep in the 1990s, when the expectations of the performers and public alike have become more sophisticated than they were in its heyday, Lady Freud remains committed to thinking small. 'If you get too ambitious then costs start to outweigh what the theatre can earn. The co-operative nature of the company is what makes it successful. I take a long time casting, it's very important. I try to squeeze as much rehearsal time as possible. By re-using the same actors I hope to create an ensemble feeling.' Her formula works. The theatre in Southwold is flourishing, while larger-scale reps such as Windsor and Leatherhead, which produce plays on a three-weekly basis, have narrowly escaped closure.

Whatever the degree of altruism or roguishness that producers and managements display, it is in the nature of employees to find something to gripe about, be it the conditions of work or the rate of pay. Jean Byam was given some sound advice by her father, a Harley Street doctor who had given financial backing to Roy Dotrice to run a repertory company in Guernsey. When Jean complained to him that the wage she was receiving as an ASM in Oxford was too low, he said, 'Never complain, offer to buy them out but never complain!'

5

Rep Companies

'*Surviving the siege at Lucknow.*'

Julian Fellowes

THE MANAGEMENT OF a theatre were responsible for assembling a company and the success with which they achieved this was reflected in what amounted to an unofficial league table among the repertory theatres. At one moment Bristol would be in ascendancy, at another it would be Nottingham or the West Yorkshire Playhouse. Jonathan Cecil describes the ratings when he began his career. 'There were two ways of starting in the business really, which were either to carry a spear in one of the big companies or to join one of the repertory companies. There were the chief ones which everybody sought after – Birmingham, the Bristol Old Vic and Liverpool, I think those were the three, possibly Glasgow Citizens and Sheffield, but they were on a sort of different level. Those ones were three weeks or four weeks. Then there were the weekly reps, and the fortnightly ones, which were the sort of middle-of-the-road ones, which is what I did.'

Within each company there was a similar hierarchy. This was certainly true in the 1940s, when Alec McCowen first entered the profession. 'There was a distinct hierarchy within the company: the leading man and the leading lady were the tops. People kept in their place, there was a sort of deference paid. If you were doing a scene with them it was quite over-aweing for a young actor.'

Lynn Farleigh agrees. 'Any hierarchy of rep was considerable and as an ASM you were very, very low. You knew your place and you were expected to keep your place. I think older actors deserve to be treated

59

with respect because it not an easy profession to survive in. If you've been going for thirty or forty years then you deserve a bit of something for having the stamina and the guts to keep at it.' Harking back to the 1920s when he began his career in Hull, Maurice Denham disagrees with Lynn Farleigh's definition of status within a particular theatre, 'There was no sense of hierarchy, the parts were evenly distributed,' and Jenny Seagrove appears to have been equally unaware of distinctions of rank within a group, although she served her time as an acting ASM in one company, but later returned to another rep as leading lady. 'There is a different perspective because you are treated differently. Suddenly you are having to rush around when you are a leading lady, doing all the publicity. But you know, to be honest, it doesn't feel that much different because to rehearse and to perform in the theatre depend on the people involved. And it is not so much the time that has passed since then, it depends on who you are working with. I look at acting ASMs now and they are treated pretty much like I was treated. It is a family, a happy family, or hopefully it is a happy family.'

Whether people pull rank or not, there are always individuals who stand out. From his early days with the Lawrence Williamson Players in Bolton, Derek Nimmo remembers an actor called Herbert Evelyn because he 'used to attend rehearsals in a morning coat with a silver nob cane'. Other actors who worked in rep were defined not by their rehearsal clothes but by the blazing quality of their talent, even if that was not always immediately apparent to the harassed observer, as this tale told by Oliver Ford Davies indicates. 'David Buxton, who was production manager at Birmingham, told me he was doing a get-in (putting the scenery up) in the mid-Sixties, when at about one o'clock in the morning two well-dressed figures walked on to the stage reminiscing. David angrily and wearily said, "Look, I know you're famous but I'm so tired I can't think who you are and will you please get off my stage!" Laurence Olivier and Ralph Richardson, who had come to remember their youth, left – not best pleased.'

Olivier and Richardson were once the young turks of the Birmingham Rep, and many of the generation of great actors who followed them also started their careers in Sir Barry Jackson's theatre. During his time as director there, Bernard Hepton admits, 'I suppose I was responsible for quite a few famous people. Albert Finney came when I was directing *Julius Caesar*. It was just when Douglas Seale was leaving and he said, "Well, you're going to take over, we'd better audition this bloke together." Albert is a lovely man, a great fellow, but he gets terribly flustered and when he was very young and he got flustered he went very pasty white and his hair was all over the place. We auditioned him. We'd had a marvellous report from RADA. The audition was just to give him some practice really, he was going to come anyway. He had an end-of-term show and it was agreed that he would come a week late. He was playing Decius Brutus, which was a very small part. When the cast list went up on the board at the theatre everybody rushed and had a look at it and they saw this strange name – Albert Finney. Who the heck is Albert Finney? Finney? He's going to have to change his name. He's a footballer – thinking of Tom Finney. Then we had the read-through and I had to explain that Mr Finney was going to be a week late and that he was coming straight from RADA, everybody went, "Oh God, oh dear, oh God, one of those!" He came. He was not just the week late, he was half-an-hour late as well, because at Birmingham you took the train, got off at New Street and nobody knew where the theatre was. It was astonishing. One of the most famous theatres in the country and the people of Birmingham didn't know where it was. It was just over the road in Station Street. Albert got lost! He was wandering about trying to find the theatre. He was very white and he had his old duffle coat on and his Temple edition of Shakespeare. We spent the morning rehearsing and at lunchtime we all went for a drink over to the Black Lion, as we normally did. Albert wasn't there, he'd sloped off somewhere with his script. And, to a man, everybody said, "He doesn't have to change his name – he's a star!" I've never come across that either before or since. He was nervous, he hardly looked out of his book, but you just couldn't look at anyone else on the stage. He stayed with us for two years, he did *Macbeth* when he was twenty-one, an astonishing performance. That was his peak.' Finney was not the only discovery to whom Bernard Hepton can lay claim. 'I went round to quite a few theatre schools. Somebody invited me up to Glasgow, to the end-of-term show. Ian Richardson stood out a mile. I asked whether he would like to come to Birmingham Rep and he said, "Of course!" and that was his first job as well. Ian did a remarkable Hamlet for us and many other interesting, marvellous performances. An extraordinary performance as Whitaker in *The Long, the Short and the Tall*. He's an extraordinary actor. He's very mercurial.'

Another graduate of the Birmingham company, although before Bernard Hepton's time, was Barbara Lott. She was given the opportunity to appear in *Man and Superman*, which was directed by Peter Brook and starred Paul Scofield. She describes her first meeting with him. 'He came in, this very tall man, he hasn't changed at all except his hair is white. My mother was terribly worried about him because he was lined at twenty-three. He came in and it was like neon lights switching on. It was just magic acting with him.'

Although so many illustrious people made early appearances in Birmingham, other regional theatres were also doing their best to foster talent. Liverpool can claim Anthony Hopkins among its protegés and Marjorie Yates gives us a glimpse of him in his formative years. She remembers him as 'a totally uncontrollable man who used to climb up drainpipes. He used to come and play the piano in my digs. My mother was a pub pianist, a real busker, she used to encourage me when I was starting out and if my mother was staying she used to sit and listen, he was a wonderful pianist.'

Elizabeth Counsell encountered the neon-light effect when she went to Billingham in 1968. 'I played opposite Michael Gambon in *Macbeth*. I'll never forget the read-through. Gambon was on a low chair, rocking with fright, almost inaudible, he had long hair and I could only see the tip of his nose, but watching him I thought, this man is going to be a star.'

Many of the great and the good went on to become stars because they received such an excellent grounding in the craft of acting from working in rep, a fact acknowledged by Sir Peter Hall. 'Of all the great actors I've worked with, and I've worked with nearly all of them, the most consummate technician was Paul Eddington and that was because he'd worked for twenty-five years in rep.'

The nurturing and exploring of a great talent could prove extremely irritating for fellow actors, as Hilary Mason comments about her time at Aylesbury. 'We were also joined by a young gentleman called Peter Ustinov. He was lovely, but he did insist on playing everything in a different accent every night. In a play called *White Cargo* he played the first night terribly Noël Coward, the second night he was French, the third night he was German, the fourth night he was Polish, the fifth night he was Russian and I can't remember what he did on the Saturday. Bertie, who was our leading man and manager, remonstrated with him and Ustinov replied (and I'll never forget this), "If I can't experiment in weekly rep where can I experiment?" We forgave him because he was a wonderful man anyway.'

Among the other luminaries connected with various reps, Jean Anderson recalls doing a play by W.B. Yeats at the Gate Theatre in Dublin before the war. 'He used to come into the theatre, a wonderful figure with all his capes and hat.' The memory has stayed with her for sixty years. Jean Byam was also subjected to the legendary Irish charm when she worked as an ASM and actress at the Oxford Playhouse during the war. Cyril Cusack, who was in the company, used to tease her by telling he'd been in the IRA and had put bombs in post boxes.

Although it is inevitable that certain personalities should stand out, one of the repertory system's strengths is that it provides actors with the opportunity to work in an ensemble situation, where the team takes precedence over the individual. Indeed, Sir Alan Ayckbourn believes that it is possible for the team to achieve its own celebrity. 'I'm a great believer in the company ethic, a group of talented actors can in a sense produce their own stardom by being identified as a group.' Paul Bradley says, 'At the time when I was starting in the Seventies there was a feeling that ensemble theatre was a good idea. You got to know people's strengths and people took risks. There was an ideal of an ensemble company, it was not just a group of actors brought together for one play, nor was it the case that a star would come in and take the lead role. There was a feeling that you had progression. You may start holding a spear, but by the end of the year you'll get to throw it, with a line attached. The only way you learn is by being given the responsibility of big roles, and that's what happened in rep. I started playing smaller parts and ended up playing leads.' What Fiona Shaw values about working with the same people over a period of time is the sense of shared courage. 'Collective bravery about a perceived unknown creates tremendous bonds. Moving towards failure is important. The dividing line between that and success is very slight.' In order to take the risk of what she calls 'moving towards failure', actors need to feel equal to and valued by their colleagues. Christopher Honer, the director, notes that, 'In ensemble companies the barriers go. The kind of barriers that exist when people first meet each other always take a bit of time to break through. There's no doubt that people familiarizing themselves with each other does benefit the work.'

Sir Peter Hall holds so strongly to this opinion that he has recently established his own company at the Old Vic Theatre in London, which he is running largely according to the repertory tradition. He maintains, 'Theatre work is essentially collaborative, there's no question that a group of people who have worked with each other a lot and know each other well and know how they dislike each other as much as how they like each other, are going to get a great deal more work done in a more creative atmosphere than a group of strangers.' From an actor's point of view the benefits are clear, as Richard McCabe points out, 'In an ensemble company not only do you get to know the other people, you get to know their work as well, which is also an advantage. You can cut corners, it's not always, "Will I offend someone if I try this?" It's a great advantage and I think it shows from an audience's point of view. You feel like a family.'

Sir Alan Ayckbourn claims that his early days in rep at Worthing, Leatherhead and Oxford, before he set up his own company in Scarborough, have helped to shape the way he writes for the theatre. 'Working in rep has given me a loyalty to the company system. I still work on the assumption that actors will support each other. It has certainly profoundly influenced my writing style. I think I am probably as fair handed as most writers in making sure that the sexes are treated equally in terms of numbers of roles. The number of female and male roles that I have written is virtually identical. If I do write a small part, I tend as a rule to double it up with something else so that the actor is never left with feeling he's a small-part player.'

His belief that actors should share equal status has led him to explore the potential of staging plays in the round, with the audience on all sides rather than divided from the play by a proscenium arch. He explains, 'Theatre in the round is a great equalizer. Any actor worth his salt coming on to the stage will realize he cannot dominate the scene without the help of his fellow artistes. Everybody in a sense is upstaging each other, or equal to each other; the listener is as important as the speaker. You get a forced inter-reliance. Working in the round explains why a lot of my plays don't carry the conventional leading role. My stuff is about six people, all of whom have equal responsibility, which is born out of working in a company theatre, where you have a lot of explaining to do if you kill someone off on the second page.' Sir Derek Jacobi is also enthusiastic about the opportunities presented by working in a tightly knit unit. 'That feeling of being a company, of being an ensemble, is hugely enjoyable. A great trust is built up and you can get much further much quicker. You know and you trust and you can move quicker and go much further.'

Although he had an eye for talent, Bernard Hepton remained a stalwart supporter of the company system while he was directing in Birmingham. 'During my four years we had more or less the same company. I had an ideal at that time, and I still think it's a wonderful ideal, to have a permanent company. It doesn't seem to work in this country at all. Other things like film and television are pulling at actors. One had been brought up with the Moscow Arts and the Berliner Ensemble. But even they didn't last for all that long. They needed a personality and once the personality was away it dissolved a bit. I tried to keep the company together as much as possible, but people did come and go.'

The problem of enticing actors to commit themselves to the same company over a period of time is one that Sir Peter Hall has also had to grapple with. 'I think that what's worth renewing in the repertory idea is the stable company, I don't quite use the word permanent because if you put an actor in a permanent situation he'll try to break out of it, but if you tell them they can go away then they'll stay. The best times in my life have been spent working in stable companies.'

Actors who stayed together over a long period through thick and thin could develop a sense of their own power, as John Warner relates. 'In Dundee I worked from cue scripts, you got the last four words of the previous speech and that was it. You had no idea what the plot was. We were sent a new play which we refused to do, we all went on strike because we thought it was so awful. So the director said we'd have to choose our own play and we luckily found *The Shining Hour*, which had the same cast and was a much better play to have done.'

Rupert Frazer worked at the Glasgow Citizens Theatre early on during Giles Havergal's tenure there as director. Havergal revolutionized the kind of work that the Citz did and his radicalism infected the whole company. Frazer says, 'The feeling at the Citz was, "That's how it used to be, we're going to show you how it is today."'

That theatre could be more militant still was discovered by Mark

Lambert, who was at Bristol when it became clear that the Little Theatre, which operated under the aegis of the Old Vic, was facing the threat of closure. 'Under Peter Postlethwaite's leadership we resigned from the company and set up the Little Theatre Company in order to save the theatre from destruction. We put on a season of three plays: *The Ghost Train, One Flew Over the Cuckoo's Nest* and *Waiting for Godot.* We all had allotted jobs in the morning – I was in charge of publicity – and in the afternoon and evening we rehearsed. We finished on a Saturday and opened on the following Monday. It was a hugely exciting and satisfying time and we made a profit of four thousand pounds at the end of it and secured the theatre's future for five more years.'

The advantages of being part of a close company are innumerable. Wendy Craig says, 'The benefit of a good company feeling was that everybody was there to help each other. Nobody wanted to hog the limelight or do each other down. It was truly supportive, you always felt secure on stage.' Amanda Redman felt the same: 'There was an atmosphere of family and actors stood up for each other and it was very much a company feeling, not in the sense of trying to outdo each other, not in the sense of stars, it was a company'; while Maurice Denham found that the sense of togetherness helped him to overcome stage fright: 'We hadn't got time for nerves. Company feeling helped.' In William Franklyn's opinion, 'That feeling of camaraderie is unique to repertory and it actually helps you work because you talk to each other – "I say, why don't you try such and such . . ." – nobody was ever too grand not to help somebody out.'

Actors can have a reputation for cattiness, a charge which Francesca Ryan defends the profession against, 'It's surprising how well actors get on with everyone. People have a kind of family attitude, by and large. Every one is kith and kin, you take people on board, you're connected for that time. People say that actors are more neurotic, or more egotistical or more selfish as part of their temperament and that may be true, but I've always found that they are often more open and more generous because they have to put themselves in situations where they're so vulnerable.'

The dynamics of any group of people, never mind those with the volatile temperaments of actors, can throw up difficulties, as Peggy Mount acknowledges when she comments diplomatically, 'The success of an ensemble depends entirely on who you're working with.' Tom Conti also tempers his praise of company life, 'Inevitably there were envies in the companies – why did he or she get that part? On the whole it was pretty friendly, we got on pretty well. It was play as cast, we never had a clue what we would be doing next.' Perhaps the note of caution in his remark stems from an encounter he had during his time in Dundee, 'There was a girl in the company that everybody was trying to lay, but she was kind of a professional virgin, it would appear, but we had a kiss in this play and we sort of pretended this kiss all the way through rehearsals because I was too embarrassed, I didn't know what to do. Then finally on the dress rehearsal, one had to actually do the proper kiss and this girl went completely wild, tongue and everything, and I was terribly off put, I found it deeply unpleasant, like an assault. It was not a comfortable experience.' This kind of unwanted intimacy also happened to Francesca Ryan. 'I went to the Library Theatre. I did *Fashion* by Doug Lucy, then I did a double bill which had been on at the Royal Court, *Our Country's Good* and *The Recruiting Officer*. That was notable for the fact that the guy who I was playing opposite in both plays, who was the love interest, we didn't get on. Relations were very strained by the second play. There was a big kiss at the end, which was quite loathsome to me and I'm sure to him, and when he was feeling very angry with me he'd stick his tongue in my mouth. That's the only time I've never really got on with anyone, mostly you can contain it.'

Hostilities when they do occur can develop into extreme feelings, as Faith Brook confirms. She was doing a season at the Bristol Old Vic: 'There was an actress who was brought in to play Arkadina in *The Seagull* and we thought she was rather starry and we were all together and there were no stars. We were all one big happy family and we didn't like this grand behaviour, so we made an effigy and stuck pins in it! It was a dreadful thing to do. A few days later she got terribly ill! It was a terrible thing to do, but we hated her.'

Anna Calder-Marshall discovered to her cost what it felt like to be excluded by a clique of people when, as a very young actress, she secured her first job in the theatre at the Birmingham Rep. 'It was terribly exciting to be going there, to be given the chance of making mistakes and of learning. I really found out how tough it is. I felt quite lonely at times, not feeling very liked and one of the other actresses said, "You can't expect to play a main part and be liked as well." That seemed incredibly hard to me.'

Rep gave many novices their first taste of human and, in particular, sexual relationships. Richard Pasco admits, 'I was a virgin till I was twenty-three, everyone was brought up strictly. You didn't do it. I got ditched, my heart was broken', a theme which Brian Rix takes up, 'I was very young and sexually aware, very fond of one or two of the ladies in the company.' Peter Bowles puts it more succinctly, 'Once that initial excitement of having got the job was over, the real power force, the real excitement, was the thought of the sexual life you'd have when you got there. This was a tremendous driving force with all the actors I've talked to. You just don't get that now because you do an episode of *The Bill* and then you all go home. One of the great memories of Oxford, Nottingham, Leatherhead, Coventry, is growing up through falling in love. I wanted to mention it because it's a very important thing in the development of actors and actresses – being thrown together, having to fend for oneself and create a theatre, work desperately hard, I mean really really hard and yet manage to have a really good and exciting emotional life.' As Gemma Jones says, 'That unit of people in a repertory company become enormously close. It was very incestuous, of course, lots of love affairs, dramas, squabbles, a very particular way of life.'

Other actors tell a different story. Richard Bebb explains, 'It wasn't that we were a particularly virtuous group of people. Very few people were living together, one or two. It was just very hard working, there was no time for socializing,' a thought amplified by Donald Pickering: 'You lived much more in each other's pockets in those days than you do now. I don't know if that was a good thing. I don't think people were particularly promiscuous, we were all too busy learning lines and trying to get someone to hear them.' This is vividly borne out by Vilma Hollingbery, who recalls that the night she and her husband Michael Napier Brown were married, which was a Sunday, they sat up in bed learning their lines for the Penguin Players' production which was to open the following day!

Because of the proximity in which people worked, relationships did develop and many actors married partners whom they met in rep. In Scotland this became endemic, as Anthony Tuckey relates. 'Though not in the top rank of repertory theatres, Perth enjoyed a reputation for high standards and extreme eccentricity. Everybody who went there, I was warned, got married. (Well, perhaps not everybody but to be honest there wasn't a lot else to do.) So bad had this marital madness become that on one occasion when Marjorie Dence, the manager, was told about another pending marriage she turned to the artistic director and said, "David, sack Jo and Tony immediately: it'll be babies next and then we'll never get rid of them."'

Barbara Leslie describes her wedding to Shaun Sutton when she was an actress and he was both directing and acting at Buxton. 'Shaun said, "We can get married on Wednesday afternoon because we're not rehearsing." So we got married and it was awful, we were rehearsing *Jane Eyre* in which I was playing Adèle, aged eight, and Shaun was playing eighty. We had a party after the show which went on all night, we didn't go to bed till half-past five. Joan Sanderson got married two weeks after us, during *You Can't Take It with You* and they very unwisely had a party in the middle of the day. She and her husband were going off together because they weren't in the next week's show, they were having a week off. There was no food left and people got drunk. Half the cast was drunk and all the guests were in front that night. One of the cast, a great friend, lovely girl, couldn't say her lines at all so I had to shake a lot of talcum powder over Penny Williams, who was the acting ASM and she went on and read the part. She was about seventeen.'

Brian Cox's wedding was an equally drunken affair. 'I got married in Birmingham Rep. Michael Gambon and I played Othello and Iago. I was the only one who was sober, we had the reception in the morning, *Othello* in the afternoon and *Romeo and Juliet* in the evening. After the reception we got back to the theatre and I was sharing a dressing-room with Mike. For costumes we all had uniforms and he embarked on this extraordinary comic business trying to get his braces on. It took him about ten minutes. They kept pinging all over the place. He finally got all his clothes on and we were ready and "Beginners" was called, then I looked at Mike and I realized he didn't have any make-up on. And he was playing Othello! I said, "Mike you haven't got any make-up on," and he looked at his sticks of make-up and said, "That's all right," and he gathered up the make-up and held the sticks under the lightbulb until they went soft and then rubbed them all over his face.'

Barbara Lott and her husband Harry's was another rep wedding. 'The blitz was just starting because Harry and I met in Brighton in September and we married in December and I know that we were married during an air raid. I can remember that because the congregation were on their knees, not in prayer but in fear and the vicar's hand shook so much he dropped the ring twice.'

A close company did not only provide a climate in which relationships could thrive, it acted as a conduit for the relaying of certain traditions within acting, which is essentially a living skill. Although the plays are printed and the basic moves are written down in the prompt copy, many bits of business would be lost if they weren't passed on verbally from generation to generation. Richenda Carey says that when her husband Nigel Stock was rehearsing *She Stoops to Conquer* at the Bristol Old Vic, 'one of the actors asked if he wanted to know the Tony Lumpkin business [the tricks of timing and gesture that the actor playing the part of Lumpkin might use]. This was passed on orally from production to production.' Other great comic roles benefited from the same kind of advice, which was inherited with them, as Sir Peter Hall testifies. 'I remember Ralph Richardson telling me that after working at this funny little theatre in Brighton, he toured with Ben Greet's Shakespeare Company and did all the Shakespeare parts. An old actor in the company taught Ralph Bottom, taught him the business, and Ralph played Bottom about three times in his career, once at the Old Vic, and it was based on that handing on.'

Elizabeth Counsell can verify this, as she worked in a company with an elderly actor, who told her that as a boy he had been in a production of *A Midsummer Night's Dream* playing one of the Mechanicals. During rehearsals an elderly actor in that company had given him the business associated with his character, which had been handed down over hundreds of years from Will Kempe, the actor who played the comic roles in Shakespeare's own company.

Sir Alan Ayckbourn recalls being a beneficiary of this oral tradition, although he is rather more sceptical about its value. 'When you were in the dressing-room there were several old actors ready to give advice, often it was quite ill-founded really, which was probably why they were playing small parts in weekly rep, but none the less it was so well meant that there was a great feeling of team.' For Jan Francis, who started her career as a ballet dancer and had no formal theatrical training, it was a positive help. 'The wonderful thing about rep is that it really was like a family, the other actors helped me so much. They said, "Look, there's a problem here, we'll teach you about voice production and breathing and so on." They were so kind to me, they helped me with exercises and gave me classes. That was a sort of special spirit that you got in rep, it was wonderful.'

However, company life within the repertory system was no bed of roses. Conditions could be harsh and would often test actors to their limits. Tom Conti paints a grim picture, 'It was a miserable existence in many ways, it was terribly cold and the theatre was always freezing. They didn't put the heat on during the day because it didn't matter if the actors died of bronchial pneumonia. They heated it a bit for the audience. Not a lot, they'd take it to just above freezing for the audience. It was terribly harsh. There were people who lived all their lives in rep, they just went from one company to another and they lived in digs for decades. I suppose they look back on it fondly in some ways, the ones who are still alive, but it could be a miserable and lonely existence. Everybody would hope when they went into a company that there would be somebody warm to go to bed with for a few months.'

Almost by definition actors in repertory theatres are badly paid, as Rachel Kempson knew when in 1957 she went to Frinton to see her daughter Vanessa Redgrave in her first job. Vanessa earned four pounds a week and had to make her own costumes. The Redgraves took a hamper of food down to feed the whole company with as they were all so underfed and poor.

Although the youngest members of the company were the worst paid, it was often the elder members who suffered the most, as Eileen Atkins points out. 'Up to the age of about thirty-five, being in rep is huge fun, but if you think of old people in rep, that is when it must get awful. To have been in weekly rep in your sixties must have been ghastly, it must have been awfully harsh.' Peter Copley agrees, 'Middle-aged couples, actor and actress, often found themselves in a sad situation. They'd never really made it and spent their lives going from rep to rep. They were useful because they had built up a good wardrobe, but they were sad because they'd been engaged on a joint salary of, say, seventeen pounds a week between them instead of ten pounds each. It was a convenience for the management because they were getting an experienced middle-aged actor and actress cheaply. It was a dead-end situation for the actors, they never ever made enough money. They were expert menders and repairers of their clothes, they were always making and remaking costumes.' That rep could be a dead end for the older members of the profession also occurred to Derek Nimmo. 'Rep could be a very lonely life and there was no escape from it. Looking back, a lot of people couldn't really have had much ambition. They liked acting, but it was more of a trade than a profession because they just got stuck in it, there was no escape from it.'

Jenny Seagrove concedes that there is a down side to company life: 'It can be terribly lonely if you are in a company where you don't really get on with people and you are in digs that are cold and damp and miserable and you can't afford to change them.' The stresses of this way of living can wreak havoc in an actor's private life. Oliver Ford Davies remembers that when he was in a company in Cambridge, 'It was all-consuming. One had no other life. Outside relationships were very difficult to maintain. Only two people were married and both had broken up by the end of the season.'

Although a long stay in one company can cause personal difficulties, Fiona Shaw warns against it for creative reasons. 'Ensemble playing facilitates a shorthand, but people flog themselves out, groups don't last for ever. You have to watch for that moment. It created trust but I'm nervous about taking a sentimentalized view. It's easy to become institutionalized within a group.'

Voices like this tend to be in the minority. For many people rep was a stimulating time during which they formed friendships which lasted a lifetime. Shaun Sutton says, 'A happy rep is a community that goes on for ever. All the people I worked with, a lot of them came into television with me and they all remained friends. We retained our friends from those days in rep.'

The bonds created in rep often go deep, as Peter Bowles knows. 'A few years ago now I did an episode of *Rising Damp* and everyone warned me to be careful with Leonard Rossiter. I'd worked with him for a year in rep and we got on very well. He was the star of the show and on the first day that I arrived I made a suggestion as to how we might do the scene. People literally dived for cover. Of course, Leonard was wonderful – "Let's try it out" – and they were amazed. There is this bonding that takes place in rep.'

Julian Fellowes describes the bonding as 'that lifeboat feel that I can't honestly say you get anywhere else and because of that I still have friends from rep. Because those early days were forged in such fire, you have the feeling of having all survived the siege at Lucknow,' or as Nickolas Grace comments, 'When you've only got a week you've got to start to love each other pretty quickly.'

6

Fit-up Theatre

*'Doing fit-up you just touch with your fingertips the continuous line
going back to Burbage.'*

Barry Foster

THERE USED TO be a niche in the world of repertory theatre which was
occupied by a particular kind of company, the fit-up. These companies
were a synthesis of two major branches in British theatrical tradition –
the emerging form of repertory and the great custom of touring.
Charles Simon records, in parenthesis, 'The great touring system was
unique to England – number one tours, number two tours, number
three tours. It was possible to tour a play for five years, fifty-two weeks
of the year and never go to the same theatre twice.' Borrowing from
this tradition and capitalizing on the popularity of permanent companies performing a variety of works, a group of actors was assembled,
often by an actor-manager, and a repertoire of as many as six or eight
plays was prepared and taken on tour around a circuit established by
the company. Sometimes the fit-up theatre would stay a week in one
place, doing a different play every night, sometimes only a couple of
days. Rep companies operated a slight variation on this system;
although based in a permanent theatre, they had a touring arm, which
would do the same play for a week, but in a different venue each night.
The following week or fortnight they repeated the same circuit, but
with a new production.

The concept of a company touring a repertoire of plays was by
definition regional and flourished primarily in Ireland, but also in
Scotland and Wales. Charles Simon recalls, 'Ireland then was full of

fit-ups run by very famous actors indeed. The famous companies were Anew MacMaster, Michael McLiammoir and the Dobells, who even travelled their own orchestra to play the overture every night.' Simon worked with none of these, but describes his own company, 'The fit-up company was run by a lady called Dorothy Grafton, whose father had been the first Irish actor to go to America and make silent films, but she was still running the rep. As far as I can remember, in my company there were five men and three or four women. The moment you set about melodramas like *The Silver King* you need a hell of a lot of people.'

Carmen Silvera worked on the mainland with the Peter Allen Repertory Players. 'There was a young man and his parents. His mother when I met her hadn't got her teeth in, and his father had a cast in one eye. There was also a chap with a child of ten, who was on the run from his wife. The little boy was an atrocious little chap who followed us all about. There was an old lady who I don't remember much about and another young man and this was the Peter Allen Repertory Company.'

Barry Foster had the good fortune to work with one of the greats – Anew MacMaster, known as Mac. He says of him, 'Mac was a very famous and tremendous Othello,' and goes on, 'unlike other actor-managers of his day who might have been frightened to have around them young people who might be rather good, he wanted you to be as good as you could be because it reflected well on him. He wanted fast strong players sending the ball low over the net, so that he could hit it back. The whole thing was most exhilarating, a lesson.' Secure in the knowledge of his own considerable talent, Mac's reputation spread and at one point he was seduced by an offer to appear in the West End. Charles Simon describes the consequence, 'Anew MacMaster was one of the finest Hamlets I've seen in my life. He went over to London to work with Gladys Cooper and became an overnight matinée idol success, but at the very end of the week he went to see Gladys Cooper and said, "I'm sorry, dear, but I'm leaving," and she said, "What do you mean, you're leaving? You've just made your name in London!" He said, "I can't be doing with this business of saying the same lines every night. I'm going back to my fit-up."'

The lure of the fit-up evidently could be strong, but for a young actor starting out in one of these companies initial impressions could be disconcerting, as Ray Cooney discovered. 'I joined what I thought was a weekly repertory company in south Wales and I turned up on Christmas Day with all the things that you had to have in those days – they made you have your own riding breeches and dinner jacket and tails and two suits – and I couldn't see the theatre in this place and it was a very small village and I thought, "I hope I've come to the right place," and I asked at the pub. I said, "I've come to join the theatrical company here," and they said, "The electrical company?" and I said, "No, the theatrical company." And they said, "No theatrical company here, boy, but there's a village hall down there." So I went down to the village hall and I saw a poster on the top of which was Midland Productions, and that was the company which I'd joined, and I thought, "That's funny, they've put six weeks' plays up on this bill," and there was *Wuthering Heights, Jane Eyre, See How They Run, Deep are the Roots, Smiling Through* and I thought, "This is most strange," and I looked closer and I saw Monday, Tuesday, Wednesday, Thursday, Friday, Saturday. And I'd joined the last of the touring fit-up companies, where they do a different play every night. They broke you in gently at first by giving you only two parts to learn in the first week.'

Charles Simon sympathizes with Cooney's plight. 'I was totally innocent, an innocent abroad, I couldn't believe it when they handed me six scripts when I arrived – having to do that and cope if you hadn't learnt it well enough, once you'd done that no audience in the world could frighten you.' Barry Foster also found himself thrown in at the deep end. 'I got straight in from drama school. I went across to Ireland and plunged into rehearsals straight away, it was a repertoire of about seven or eight plays. The company already knew mostly what they were doing, so it was a question of getting me into the shows. I played Lorenzo in *The Merchant of Venice*, three small parts in *Hamlet*, the leader of the chorus in *Oedipus Rex*. I was a senator and a few walking-on parts in *Othello*.' The selection of plays described here gives an idea of the high standard of Mac's company, as does the fact that the other juvenile actor was the young Harold Pinter.

Carmen Silvera was not so lucky. She remembers, 'I wrote for a job in *The Stage* which was advertised, "Juvenile character actress required for the Peter Allen Repertory Company. Please send photograph and details." I got a telegram back, "Can offer you contract, Commonwealth Terms." I thought that was a different sort of contract to Equity. Happily I packed my cabin trunk. The train arrived at half-past four in the afternoon and a very attractive young man met me, he recognized me from my photograph. He arranged for my trunk to go to the theatre and said, "I've fixed up digs for you, full board for thirty-five shillings a week." He took me to my digs, saying "They're in the same road as the theatre, so that's all right, and you're not playing tonight[!]" I said, "What time is the rehearsal tomorrow?" And he answered, "Oh just till about eleven."' His words sounded ominous and filled Miss Silvera with justified foreboding. She describes the next morning. 'It was my first rehearsal and I said, "Have you got a script?" And they looked at each other – script? Nobody had asked for a script for years! They got this exercise book and in it was a précis for the play we were doing that night, turn it upside down and there was a précis for the play we were doing the next night! When we rehearsed, using the exercise book for a script, they said, "You come on and you've got to get these three points over. Dad will ask you some questions and you just answer them, but you've got to get these three points over. Dad will ask you so and so and you must tell him that, on your second entrance you've got to come in with some gossip." In performance they just made up the dialogue, Dad would chat away and you'd keep the conversation going for about five minutes and then he would give you the nod to go off. That's how they did their plays. They weren't plays that they'd made up, they were real old melodramas like *Face at the Window*, *Maria Martin*, *East Lynne* and so on.'

Once the rehearsals were over it was time to get on the road. The travel from venue to venue took many forms. In the 1920s Charles Simon remembers, 'We had a horse and cart and in the summer the actors all travelled on top of the scenery in the horse and cart.' Thirty years later, with the West of England Touring Company, Phyllida Law had a comparatively luxurious experience. 'We got on this bus in Exmoor, where we were stationed, and went to Plymouth, Exeter, all round Devon, with extraordinary luminaries like Joan Plowright, who used to make rugs on the bus.' Ray Cooney did not fare quite so well, 'We used to travel in whatever cattle truck was available, with all our scenery and everything,' while Barry Foster's mode of transport was in keeping with Mac's elevated status. 'Harold and I and a couple of other actors usually travelled with Mac in his huge old limousine and the others went with the sets in the lorry.'

On arrival in a town digs had to be found for the night or alternative arrangements had to be made. Charles Simon recollects, 'Frequently in the summer if you were a bit hard up, which you inevitably were, you would sleep under the cart,' and Ray Cooney became used to accommodation which was equally rough and ready. 'Sometimes if there were no houses around you might have to sleep in the village hall. In one hall I remember, there was a huge snooker table, it doubled as the snooker hall, the fellas slept on the snooker table and the girls slept in the dressing-rooms.'

The first priority when the fit-up company arrived in a village or town was to prepare for the show in the evening. The tasks were numerous and divided amongst everybody. Phyllida Law describes what was entailed. 'In the fit-up company the men did the set, they did the nailing, which was very difficult in places like Dorchester because the town hall had a teak floor and the nails kept bouncing out and people always had wounded thumbs. The boys used to put up the set with French braces and we would nail them in position at the bottom. Because it was a fit-up company and the stages were all of different dimensions, sometimes we had to leave bits of the set off. The timing of it was astounding. We could put the set up in very little time. We did the ironing, us girls, the costumes came with us on rails in the back of the bus and we got them ready. We were very quick getting on to the bus at the end and of course we got home quite late. Sometimes we had to extend the stage with card tables. I think Joan Plowright once went through one. In between acts leading actors in their dressing gowns would help to change the sets.'

Ray Cooney recalls that his job was to assemble the props required. 'You'd turn up in the morning at ten-thirty and you'd have a quick run-through of the play you were doing that night, then you'd go round to whatever houses there were to borrow the props for the play that night while the other members of the company erected the set. We carried about six basic sets and some backdrops.' Transporting these sets, which had to be loaded and unloaded on a daily basis, could be an onerous business, particularly if they were heavy. Bernard Horsfall remembers desperate measures sometimes had to be taken: 'In one of the theatres we toured to with the Dundee Touring Repertory Company, the footlights were made of biscuit tins. In another place they built the stage of trestle tables. In *Random Harvest* we had a very heavy iron gate, which was meant to be part of the railway scenery.

After a very short time of touring with it, we stopped the van one night and threw it off.'

In common wtih the repertory movement as a whole, actors were expected to provide their own costumes, which travelled with the set on the van. Charles Simon: 'We had to provide our own costume. In those days all contracts relating to actors said, "Must dress well on stage and off." In other words you must not let the company down. Props were found for you, but you had to provide everything else – make-up, wigs, in those days you travelled with your entire belongings in a theatrical basket. When an actor arrived to join a new company, the company wouldn't look at anything except his theatrical basket, to see whether he was a successful actor, that was the measure of the man. There's a story, I don't know whether it's apocryphal or not, about the actor who didn't have a wardrobe, he'd had to flog it all when he was unemployed, but, determined to make the right impression, he filled his basket with building bricks.' In wardrobe as everything else, Mac's company set a different standard from the others, as Barry Foster relates. 'The costumes were made for us. Mac's wife Marjorie was tremendously gifted, she was Michael McLiammoir's sister and she had some of his talents for design. She used to design and make the costumes and also maintain the wardrobe.'

The venues were many and various. Speaking of Peter Allen's company, Carmen Silvera says, 'They used to play what was known as the Smalls – little villages and towns in and around Wales and Ireland and Scotland. They travelled round and you stayed in one place for about a week or a fortnight, depending on how big it was and how long they could put up with you.' Barry Foster describes the wide range of theatres and halls that he appeared in. 'You're struggling all week to get a play on and just about the time you've got it right, it's time to say goodbye to it. In Mac's company, always you knew you were going to come back to a performance, albeit in totally different conditions. One week you might be in a perfect Georgian horseshoe theatre like the Opera House in Cork, or the Theatre Royal, Waterford – a wooden horseshoe where Edmund Kean and Sarah Siddons played – or you might be on the front apron of a cinema, as you were in Galway, or we would erect trestle tables in a post office in a little village called Hospital in the county of West Cork. Very often we were in schools or halls where we had to put rostra up and with a few sets of drapes and a few spotlights you could do almost any play.'

The portable nature of fit-up is emphasized by Charles Simon. 'The idea of fit-up was that you carried the kind of equipment that enabled you to play in a field or in an inn yard, which we frequently did, or in a hall or in a theatre. The equipment was so constructed that it could all be folded up and put in the cart.' Carmen Silvera gives a description of the kind of venue she faced in South Wales. 'The auditorium was in a church hall. It was all on a level, but they had chairs with arms, then chairs without arms and then benches. The prices were four shillings, three shillings, two shillings – this was in a mining village and it was packed every night.' From church halls to hotels, the choice of venue was nothing if not eclectic. Tony O'Callaghan records a one-night stand he did during a period with the Century Theatre, which bears all the improvisatory characteristics associated with fit-up. 'When I was at the Century Theatre, Keswick, the director suggested doing a Sunday night show based on Wordsworth, his sister Dorothy and Coleridge. He offered me fifteen quid for the night or a meal at a fancy restaurant. The first night was at a hotel and the set was this beautiful bay window that they had overlooking Lake Derwent, this was our backdrop. We rehearsed this forty-five minute show in the director's living-room. It was made up of poems, letters and songs. The hotel gave us the linen store to get changed in, it was a cupboard. I remember sitting in the cupboard thinking, "Oh my God, has it come to this? I'm in a cupboard and I'm dying with nerves. I don't believe it! What happened to Hollywood?"'

Conditions were often basic, as Phyllida Law remembers. 'With the West of England Touring Company at some venues when you exited from one side of the stage you had to go outside to get to the other. Also you could never get to a loo, so people used to pee in paint cans behind the cyclorama, then someone would kick the paint can over, a stream of liquid would cross the stage, hit the floats [footlights] and explode.' As well as being rudimentary, the venues were often very cramped. John Warner says, 'At St Andrews I remember the stage was so small, we were doing *Twelfth Night* and literally the stage ended as you got off the set, so you had to jump on to a theatrical skip.' However, nobody can have appeared in anywhere as intimate as Malcolm Farquhar, 'I went to the Arts Theatre Salisbury, which was a monthly rep. We did three weeks of one-night stands then a week at the theatre. We travelled extensively from Southampton to Dorset. It was part of the Arts Council contract that we were taking theatre to the small places. We went to a very small village and we played *Present Laughter* in somebody's sitting-room. It was a very large sitting-room and had a sort of minstrels' gallery. We played to about fifty people sitting on chintz sofas and chairs.'

For a time the format of fit-up was considered sufficiently successful and popular to be worth exporting and, rather than playing in Wiltshire sitting-rooms, some actors found themselves touring plays to more exotic regions. Stephen Hancock was one of these. 'The RAF had an entertainments arm and it started up this Middle East Repertory Company based in Cairo, which I auditioned for and got into. I went straight from school into the army during the war. We went round all sorts of units in the Canal area. We had WAAFs and civilians playing parts. Nobody quite knew how to treat us, they didn't know whether to take us into the Officers' Mess or the Sergeants' Mess, or to split us up. We did plays like *The Wind and the Rain* which was about medical students. It was a beautiful, romantic, gentle comedy, the least likely thing to take round rough army units. We played in hangars, we played in NAAFIs, we had a highly adaptable set. We had all the stuff in a truck and as we went through these Egyptian villages, people used to clamber on to the back of the truck and pinch things. I used to sit in an armchair, which was part of the set, with a shotgun across my knee and the driver had an axe to bash people with.'

In mainstream fit-up theatres the repertoire the companies chose was every bit as varied as the places in which they performed. Charles Simon remembers that Dorothy Grafton's company did more than one show a night. 'You played three different sections on the bill. First off was variety and everyone in the cast had to do something, sing a song, do a bit of conjuring, recite a poem, something. Then you did the play itself; then in the old custom of the Theatres Royal at Drury Lane and Covent Garden years ago, you played a farce.' Carmen Silvera recalls that for Peter Allen's company, Friday night was the high spot of the week. 'Friday was All Star Variety Night. Each person had a talent for doing something: the man with the child used the little boy as a ventriloquist's dummy, one of the young men was a good tap dancer and he played the ukulele, the father played the guitar, he and his son did a stand-up comedy routine, they got the local ballet school in to do a turn and there were also some sketches which I had to do. "Do you sing?" they said and I said, "No, not very well." "What about dance?" "Oh yes, I can dance, I was trained as a dancer." "How many evening dresses have you got?" I said two. "Right, two five-minute spots, one in each half. Tell the pianist what to play, he can play anything, then give him the nod when it's time to go off." '

Working in Ireland meant that the normal copyright rules did not apply. Charles Simon explains, 'It was then (in 1926 and 1927) the Irish Free State, not the Republic of Ireland. There was no copyright agreement then, so it enabled Irish companies to send shorthand writers over to London to take down the latest popular success and play it in Ireland without having to pay royalties. Quite frequently you were playing a slightly garbled version of something that was still playing in London. We did Irish plays, melodramas like *Under Two Flags*. It was quite remarkable what they could do, these very skilled fit-up people and I've never been sorry I had that experience.'

Part of the benefit of working in this way was the fact that an actor was given the chance to play a wide range of roles, something for which Ray Cooney remains grateful. 'I owe a hell of a lot to the two years I spent with the fit-up company, it really gave me the feeling of an audience and one got to play such wonderful diverse roles. One night I'd be playing the German officer who shoots Nurse Edith Cavell. They did such wonderful plays as *Maria Martin* and *The Sign of the Cross*. I loved it all. Wonderful feeling of teamwork.' For Jean Anderson the opportunity to play a string of leading parts was a bonus. 'I did three tours in Ireland doing, if you can believe it, a different lead every night of the week. I had one night off, we played Sundays. I had to keep five leading parts in my head.' She goes on to describe the audiences who were the beneficiaries of all this hard work. 'In a lot of places they'd never even seen theatre except going back to the days of melodrama. The Shawlies [the groundlings who used to sit in the cheap seats] used to sit in the front, engrossed. The thing that really got them was Shakespeare. They could understand it almost more than a modern comedy. It makes you realize that there is something so basic about Shakespeare, they got the message. A sophisticated comedy they couldn't get.'

Charles Simon agrees, 'You would find that your audience could

recite the Shakespeare speeches with you. There was this great tradition of competent theatre even in the wildest parts.' Shakespeare was
deemed to be suitable fare, but a form of censorship did exist, as Simon
reveals. 'You'd arrive at a town and the first thing the manager would
do would be to go to the local priest and present him with the plays you
were proposing to do. The priest would put a notice up, stating the
plays which the audience may see.' Simon points out that working in
rural communities meant that special adjustments sometimes had to
be made to suit the requirements of an audience of farming folk. 'I
well remember that we went to a little village on the banks of Lough
Ree. You always planned to go up at seven-thirty, but you never did,
you waited until they'd finished work. The harvest workers would have
to stop because the dusk was coming up and you saw the lanterns
coming down the hill, the place would be full and you'd hear a voice
saying, "All right, you can start now!" Sometimes you wouldn't ring up
the curtain until eleven o'clock at night and you would knock off at
about two in the morning and then the audience would expect you to
go out and sit with them, so they could tell you how much better so and
so was last year. Then they would take you off and command the local
bar to open and you would learn how to drink Guinness and be joined
by the local priest and a couple of civic guards.'

Conventional repertory companies were prone to making the occasional mistake, but the likelihood of this happening was far greater in
fit-up, where there were so many variables to contend with. Being in a
different theatre every night or so could be confusing to the actor and
lead to incidents like the one described by John Nettles. 'I worked with
Tony Church at the Northcott Theatre in Exeter. In the company were
David Suchet and Robert Lindsay. There were three companies
including the Theatre in Education company and we toured throughout the south-west. On one occasion we visited the Minack Theatre in
Cornwall. We lost an actor during a performance. He had to make an
entrance stage right and to do that in those days you had to go down a
cliff path. He got completely lost and all we could hear was, "Help,
help."'

Some of the theatres and halls were dilapidated, ramshackle places
whose fabric was in such poor condition that accidents were bound to
occur. Jean Anderson remembers two incidents, 'In Tralee we played
in what had been a beautiful old theatre in the main street. In *The Moon*

and the Yellow River there's an enormous explosion. That was set off under the stage and the first time it happened everything fell down from the flies – dead birds, everything. How we kept straight faces at this very serious moment I'll never know. There was another splendid time in that theatre. I had to make a very snooty exit as an English lady in this Irish tragedy we were doing by Maria Edgeworth. I made my snooty remark and marched off and my down-stage foot went completely through a floorboard up to the knee. There was a gasp from the audience and somehow I had to pull my leg up and get off.' Even the great Mac's company was not safe from the odd mistake, and on one occasion Barry Foster recollects that Harold Pinter was the culprit. 'Harold was playing Bassanio and Mac was Shylock and in the trial scene Bassanio says to Shylock, "Take this six thousand ducats," which is twice what he's asking for, and for some extraordinary reason Harold said, "Take this six thousand buckets." His entire face froze. Mac stared at him, then converted the whole of his next speech – "If every bucket were in six parts and every part a bucket . . . I would have my bond."'

Even before conventional rep came under threat, the writing was on the wall for the fit-up companies, which could not withstand the competition first from cinema and then television. The actors involved in fit-up remember it with great affection. Carmen Silvera confesses, 'It was wonderful really, when I look back on it, that I had that experience. I wouldn't have missed it for anything because I learnt a lot of what not do do.' Ray Cooney says, 'In the fit-up company you just lived and breathed everything together. When I started there were about five or six of them, mainly in Ireland and Wales and a couple in Scotland and there was one I think in England. I saw the end of them really.' Perhaps the potency of the spell they cast on those who worked in them is best summed up by Barry Foster, 'It was a tremendously joyful time altogether. Doing fit-up you just touch with your fingertips the continuous line going back to Burbage, of the actor-manager with his company barnstorming round the country.'

7

Directing in Rep

'Always give an answer, even if you don't know what the answer is.'

Attributed to Peter Dews by John Warner

IN THE EARLY days of the repertory movement, theatre companies in the regions tended to be hierarchical, although as the century progressed the idea that actors should work together in an ensemble became increasingly popular. As Peter Hall observes, 'Theatre work is essentially collaborative, although it requires a chairman or a leader – it may be the leading actor or the director or the writer. It finally requires an editor and an inspirer.' In exceptional cases the person at the head of the company may be an actor or a writer, but it is more common for the position of editor and inspirer to be held by the director.

Bernard Hepton was the last person appointed to this post at the Birmingham Rep by Sir Barry Jackson and describes the work that it entailed. 'In those days directors did everything. They directed the play, they chose the cast, they went up and down to London to interview actors, they talked to writers. I don't know how one did it but one did, one had to. Now it's unheard of: people have assistants or invite people in.'

The advent of assistants has become necessary as more and more of the director's remit concerns administration. Christopher Honer is the artistic director at the Library Theatre in Manchester and he estimates that he only spends fifteen weeks of the year in rehearsal with actors and 60 per cent of his time is absorbed by administration. He cites an example of the kind of problem which preoccupies him: 'Manchester City Council banned Norwegian wood because of the Norwegian whaling policy, which meant that no one in council employ could use wood from Norway at all. I had to ensure that the theatre workshops didn't use it. This is the kind of bureaucracy that takes up my time.'

Robin Herford, who worked as director in Sir Alan Ayckbourn's company at Scarborough, believes that increasingly pressure from higher up the chain of command can compromise a director's artistic vision. He says, 'Running a theatre is becoming less and less of an attractive job, a sort of siege mentality afflicts anyone who takes on the job of artistic director. Now it's possible for the charitable trusts who oversee the theatre board and the theatre director to be held personally and financially liable for deficits. There was a test case recently – if you are knowingly trading in deficit and pushing yourself further into deficit, then people on the board can actually be held financially liable. These are voluntary posts, people do it out of the goodness of their hearts. If they are going to be held liable for debts that we incur, then quite understandably they are going to say, "You can't do this and you can't do that." '

As well as being overburdened by bureaucracy or accountable to defensive governors fearing their own financial liability, directors can also, as Bernard Hepton noted, come into contact with writers, an experience which gave the director Charles Simon enormous satisfaction. When he was directing in his own theatre in Darlington before the war he included many plays by George Bernard Shaw in the programme. 'Shaw came to see several of our productions. He was the most wonderful gentleman, I adored him. I remember once going to see him in Hertfordshire to discuss what I was doing with his plays. I ventured to apologize to him for the very small royalties accruing to him from my productions. He looked at me and he said, "I wrote them to be performed, my boy." When I was preparing a production of *Back to Methuselah*, I wanted to make certain cuts – the temerity of youth – I remember writing to Shaw and saying that certain parts of it were unShavian, too long, and could I send him my proposed cuts? How daring you can be when you are young! Straight away he sent me a telegram: "Cut what you like but for God's sake don't show me!" '

Simon recalls another encounter with the great man, when he staged a production of *St Joan*. 'There's a big tent scene between Warwick and Fauchon, a long discussion that's usually played as a drama. I always thought it was a comedy scene and I played it that way.

Shaw came to see it and I thought, "Oh dear, now what's he going to say?" Afterwards he said, "Very interesting, very interesting, you think I write comedy do you?" And I said, "I'm sure you do, Sir." "You're thinking of the tent scene . . . well done." He always insisted that he wrote comedies, high comedies and that any attempt to make his plays over-dramatic was a great mistake.'

Although obliged to wrestle with bureaucracy and sometimes take on whole committees, in spite of the occasional gratification of input from the likes of Bernard Shaw, a director's chief area of concern is his actors and how to coax the best performances out of them, both in rehearsal and when the show is running.

Like Robin Herford, John Warner has worked both as an actor and as a director. He believes, 'The best directors are actors because they know the problems. Directors who haven't been actors tend to be umpires – they tell you what not to do, not what to do. If you've been an actor you can help somebody with their performance.' After years of experience as a performer in theatres up and down the country, the Glasgow Citizens Theatre invited him to direct a production of *Waiting for Godot* for them. Self-deprecatingly, he says, 'I kept one lesson ahead of the class. Martin Esslin's book *The Theatre of the Absurd* was a great help.' He goes on to admit, 'You learnt Director's Bluff. Peter Dews defined it – always give an answer even if you don't know what the answer is.'

Directors need to prepare themselves thoroughly before rehearsals begin. Sir Peter Hall says, 'I spent six months at the Oxford Playhouse as director. I did some rep, but I didn't do as much as I should have done.' This was possibly because 'Doing a play in a week was horrible, horrible and I resolved never to do it again.' His experience at Oxford taught him that 'The disciplines of rep very much affected how a direc-tor behaved. A director's virility was measured by the scale of his preparation. You really were compelled to work out the staging and the moves beforehand and give them to the actors. You did it by having a model of the set and cardboard figures.' This process is called plotting the moves or blocking the play and in weekly rep there was rarely time for any other approach to the work. Shaun Sutton, who started his career directing for Anthony Hawtrey before working for BBC Drama with great distinction, reiterates that comprehensive preparation before rehearsals is a vital prerequisite of the job. 'I used to make a point about homework, the absolute necessity of a director in weekly rep coming with everything worked out. Until the actors knew their moves and what they were going to do they weren't happy, so I used to work on the scripts very hard. I worked out all the moves and then set the whole play in one day, which wasn't difficult, that got all the moves out of the way.'

A mainstay of repertory companies, particularly for those involved in weekly rep, was French's Acting Editions of the plays being performed. Published by Samuel French, these were usually transcripts of the prompt copy of West End productions and contained both set designs and details of the actors' moves. For directors and actors under pressure they could be life-saving. Sir Peter Hall found, 'You couldn't survive in rep unless your director gave you the moves, having done the homework. That's why the reps loved French's Acting Editions.' Shaun Sutton learnt how to work under the pressure of inadequate rehearsal time. 'There wasn't an awful lot of time for motivations and things. You know what somebody once said – "Why do I move and look out of the window?" – "Because it says so in the French's Acting Edition." I didn't always adhere to French's, I worked out my own moves.' Wendy Craig worked with the director Val May in rep, who 'took no notice of French's Acting Edition, he made each play his own. He directed them as though they were being done for the first time.'

Although they could provide valuable assistance when time was short, Dennis Ramsden, who used French's Acting Editions when he was directing in Aberdeen, sounds a note of caution about them. 'As a director you had to work out the moves. French's scripts had too many moves usually. You have to beware of French's scripts because every move that anyone has ever thought of is in them; even though the director may have subsequently taken them out, they are left in the prompt copy.' French's Editions provided a safety net for some hard-pressed directors, but others found that the pressure could be stimulating, as Jonathan Church, currently artistic director at the Playhouse in Salisbury reveals. 'Practical pressures can create extraordinary improvisation and I rather enjoy that.'

The constraints of weekly rep were considerable, but with the extra rehearsal time afforded by two- and three-weekly rep, directors could afford to take a more fluid and exploratory approach to the work. Martin Duncan, now in charge at the Nottingham Playhouse, remembers the formative period he spent working in two-weekly rep in Lincoln. 'With Philip Hedley we often didn't reach the text until quite late. He'd be very strong on character and movement and the whole Laban theory of effort – a pushing effort, a kicking effort and a jabbing effort to build character. He'd divide the text into units and you'd rehearse saying, "I come on and I berate you," and the person you were working with would say, "I argue with you, I block you." It wasn't so much what you said, it was all to do with feelings and actions. Then maybe he'd get you to read a scene through, then put the book down and improvise. The last thing that happened was actually learning the words. You'd done the whole background to your character, what your feelings were, what your thoughts were, what you'd come on to do. That was very important, what your intention was. Not just, "I'm saying this," but, "I'm saying this in order to do that." That did take a lot of rehearsal time, but there didn't seem to be a panic about learning lines. Philip Hedley wouldn't allow French's Acting Editions. His methods have stayed with me all my life. I don't block shows, I leave it up to the actor to decide. In rehearsal if an actor asks me where he should go, I say, "I don't know, you're the actor, you're up there, you're playing the character." '

Not all directors are as flexible as this (and indeed some actors are unnerved by those who are!). Malcolm Farquhar is one who espouses the opposite point of view. "I have always preferred it and I think sixty per cent of artists prefer it, that you have the blocking structure ready. It can always be altered, but the actors feel safer. They can't bear directors who say, "Where would you like to come on from? Which chair would you like to sit in?" Actors curl up straight away. It's give and take with direction, but the director must be in charge.' While acknowledging the authority of the director, Farquhar believes that the fruits of leadership must not be misused. 'As the director you have power, but you mustn't abuse that power. What I've always tried to do is to find a compromise in one's personality in the way you hold the discipline of the theatre together without being an absolute bastard. I found the only way to do it was to say, "My office door is always open if you have problems." '

Although directors may strive to be accessible to their companies, actors, who feel that their future employment may be at stake, often remain wary of them. Peter Bowles gives a succinct description of the awe which directors can inspire. 'Some directors are good and some directors are bloody awful. The people who run the reps, they are gods, you are in their thrall. You don't worship them necessarily, but there is a power play going on. One of the things which is a terrible hold back for young actors is that when you start on a play what you really try to do is please the director. You're hoping that he likes you, you're hoping that he likes what you are doing and you are hoping that he will employ you again. It may be subconscious, but that is what is going on and you are not one-on-one with the character you are playing or with your talent. It's a killer, of course, and it can hold you back for years. Any experimentation, any release of your own talent is gone. You start to use what is known as technique and craft simply to produce this thing that is liked by the director and it has nothing whatsoever to do with your own creative talent, so you never develop.'

Bowles's opinion that an actor's desire to please the director can sometimes result in the inhibition of his potential arises when directors bully their casts. Bowles suffered humiliation at the hands of one director, which he has never forgotten. 'At Oxford I was rehearsing with Frank Hauser and I asked him how I should say a line and he replied, "I'm paying you ten pounds a week to know how to say that line." It wasn't the abruptness of the way he spoke to me, it was the fact that he mentioned my salary. I come from a working-class background where money was never spoken about and to have my wages mentioned was a sexual insult as well, it was extraordinary, I've never forgotten the hurt of that.'

Anna Carteret remembers the man who was in charge of the Butlin's Rep in Skegness. She describes him as, 'sort of short and stocky with red eyes and a bull neck, he sacked me several times and forgot about it the next day. He used to drink a lot. He slashed his wrists halfway through the season and went into a mental home in Lincoln. I thought this was typical of theatre. He used to shut his eyes when directing us and sort of conduct us as if we were an orchestra or choir, and give us our inflections through his conducting.'

Peter Penry Jones remembers equally colourful scenes from his early days in the business. 'The director at York would have tantrums, the kind of tantrums where he would lie on his back with his legs in the air,' while Donald Pickering recalls one who 'used to kick us in rehearsals, "Give me more, give me more!"'

Not all directors' behaviour was so extreme, although Derek Nimmo describes his director in Bolton as, 'a pretty sadistic man, he bullied me, the only thing he taught me, which is something that has always puzzled me, he said, "Whatever you do, always use Roger and Gallet soap and when you've got down to the last little bit, keep it in the breast pocket of your jacket."'

Dulcie Gray also suffered at the hands of the head of the company. 'The director at Harrogate had a lot of affairs, he had an affair with Sonia Dresdel, who had been there before me and I think he wished to continue with someone, it didn't matter who. He pinched my bottom every time I went past him. I did not like being pinched every time and one terrible day when he did it I said, "I wonder if you could change the monotony and not pinch me every time I go past you?" My days were numbered after that.' She was not alone in being pursued by her director. Paul Daneman appeared in many productions at Sir Barry Jackson's Birmingham Rep and describes one of the directors there as, 'a brilliant man, but the trouble was that he was a bit of a martyr to his genitalia, he couldn't leave the girls alone and got into all sorts of scrapes.' However, it was not only young women who found that physical advances were made to them. Richard Bebb tells of a gay director at Richmond, who loved pulling the hairs out of young actors' legs!

Another actress who, as a fledgling, had an unhappy experience with a director was Jenny Seagrove. 'I do remember as a young actor at Newcastle, fresh out of drama school, full of ideas and things and there was a big notes session after rehearsals one day and I remember the director giving us notes and I put up my hand and I made a suggestion and there was this kind of silence. The director said, "Jenny, I think you can go home now." I was so hurt because I was enthusiastic and I felt really rejected, but I didn't realize that in those days young actors didn't make suggestions in note sessions. You just took your notes and said, "Thank you very much", and if you wanted to say anything, you sort of quietly did it in rehearsals and preferably not at all.'

Actors are bound to complain about their directors, with varying degrees of justification. William Franklyn voices the kind of opinion which is often heard. 'Directors varied from being utterly incompetent, to being bullies, to being very talented and it was the luck of the draw which one you got. Some of them were good administrators but no good as directors and that was where the team spirit would take over because the actors would save the day. Actors have many many times saved directors, but I don't remember many occasions when directors have saved actors.'

An actor's view of a director is subjective and often influenced by the personal chemistry between the two of them. Therefore one performer may be full of praise for a director, of whom another is critical. A case in question is Willard Stoker, who was born in 1905 and worked initially in Perth rep, before going on to the Oxford Playhouse and theatres in Worthing, Birmingham, the 'Q' in London and then a long stint at the Liverpool Playhouse. Moray Watson worked with him in Liverpool and formed the impression that, 'Willard Stoker was good, but he was no good if you were very young and inexperienced. I was very lucky that I'd been at Whitley Bay and Leatherhead because one or two actors joined us straight from drama school and they floundered. He liked to have a strong cast and rather let you get on with it. He cast well, each play, and of course he gave notes and directed the play. Some directors are awfully good, they manage to teach at the same time as directing, but he couldn't do that.'

Richard Briers, another graduate of the Liverpool Playhouse, remembers him too. 'Willard Stoker used to pace himself, he was doing a different play every three weeks; he had a light touch on the wheel. He wasn't a megalomaniac, he wasn't selfish like some of them are.'

Malcolm Farquhar, who was employed by Stoker at the Birmingham Rep, was also comfortable with his methods. 'Willard Stoker at Birmingham hadn't really plotted it, but it looked as though he had. He'd say, "You sit there and you sit there, and mmm, we'll sort that out in a minute, dear," and eventually we'd get to the end of the morning's work and he'd throw the book in the air and say, "I don't want to see that again!" and then he'd start, like a piece of music, mar-vellous.'

Directors inspired different responses in the actors they worked with; some were unanimously liked or loathed. Many were judged by the degree and the type of help that they offered. Performers like Rachel Kempson, who worked with William Armstrong at the Liverpool Playhouse in 1935, were content with what Richard Briers called 'a light touch on the wheel'. She recalls, 'Willie Armstrong used to say at rehearsals, "Oh my clever company, I just follow them."' While some may appreciate being allowed a liberal rein in this fashion, others may experience this artistic freedom as being given no help. Derek Nimmo understands the director's plight. 'The director was usually in the play too so he hadn't got much time. There wasn't much finesse about it, you had to be reasonably confident and get on with it. I don't remember receiving many notes.' Leslie Lawton recalls a similar lack of advice, but comments that, even when it was given, there often wasn't enough time to make use of it. 'You didn't have directors, you had glorified stage managers, really, because the moves were all in the book. You just had to make sure you did the moves and remembered the lines, or an approximation of the lines! I don't remember being directed in weekly rep. In twenty weeks the only note I had was, "Try and make it a bit smoother." Occasionally some young blood would come along and start giving you notes and of course you simply couldn't take them in.'

When Rosemary Harris started work at the Roof Garden Theatre in Bognor Regis at the tender age of eighteen, she admits, 'I didn't know what being directed was, I had nothing to compare it with. If you were on board, if you were part of the team, you were expected to know what you were doing and you were trusted to do it. One was taught by one's elders and betters, that's who you learnt from, I don't remember being taught by the director.'

Many of those who persisted in asking for help from the director rather than from other company members were frequently disappointed in the response they received. Brigid Panet found herself puzzling over some textual interpretation. 'I was playing a witch in *Macbeth* at Chesterfield. I asked the director, "Are we male or female, real or imaginary?" And all he said was, "Yes".' Rupert Frazer was baffled by Philip Prowse in Glasgow. Prowse began as a designer and, although he is now an acclaimed director, when Frazer encountered him he was still feeling his way. 'To begin with Philip Prowse wasn't a director he was a designer, so when he started to direct it could sometimes be exasperating. He'd say, "Oh do it like Bette Davis at the end of *Dark Victory*," which isn't much help if you haven't seen *Dark Victory*!' Keith Drinkel recalls being nonplussed during his time at the Birmingham Rep. 'If you asked Peter Dews what your subtext was, he'd say, "Your salary at the end of the week, love,"' while Fiona Shaw was frustrated when she worked at Bolton by a director whose input consisted of lines such as, 'You have an eating scene. We in the theatre always eat marshmallows.' Tom Conti received what he thought was unhelpful advice during his time at Dundee, when he remembers the director putting his head in his hands and saying, 'Oh Boy, for God's sake, *act*.' Conti's response was, 'This wasn't the most encouraging thing a director could say to a young actor. I wanted to say, "I rather thought that was what you were supposed to avoid." However, they wanted acting – people still do, unfortunately.'

Directors can be reticent or unhelpful during rehearsals and that creates problems for the cast, but a director who is intrusive and imposes his own views too stridently can be equally bothersome. It is a fine line to tread, as Jill Gascoine points out. 'The best directors are good at doing what you can't do, which is seeing the play as a whole. All the bad ones impose their ideas on things.' Paul Williamson shares this opinion. 'Nowadays you find directors don't know what's important in a scene because they've intellectualized it so much, or they and the designer together have wanted to make a statement that has nothing to do with the play.'

The wish to intellectualize during rehearsals is a great drain on time, but is very much part of the Russian theatrical tradition, as Christopher Honer discovered when he invited a member of the Mali Company in St Petersburg to direct a play in Manchester. He takes up the story. 'In 1994 Manchester was designated City of Drama. There were friendship links between Manchester and St Petersburg, so I invited Grigory Dityatkovsky, who was the associate director of the Mali Theatre in St Petersburg, to come here and direct a play. I managed to squeeze eight weeks' rehearsal for him, and he complained at the shortness of the time available. "How can I do it, how can I do it?"' Francesca Ryan, who worked at the Library, fleshes out the detail. 'Christopher Honer had a Russian director over from the Mali Theatre in St Petersburg. They're used to rehearsing for months and months, maybe even two years, minimum six months. Chris was doing an exchange because Manchester is twinned with St Petersburg. He managed to eke out the budget to give him eight weeks' rehearsal, which for a rep theatre in England is pretty big cheese, and this guy came over and was distraught – "But please, what I can do in eight weeks?" He was astonished by the attitude of English actors, being English actors we like our tea breaks and lunch breaks, but in Russia you started work at nine and you finished when you finished.'

Not only do English actors like their tea breaks, they also like to have a certain amount of confidence in the director's ability to cast a play. Many met their match in Donald Sartain, who was director at York for a number of years. John Newman reports, 'He was an inspired director and a martinet, but rather over-enthusiastic when it came to casting. Sometimes several actors turned up for the same part.' This often did not become clear until the read-through, when a number of actors all opened their mouths to speak at the same time.

The follies and foibles of directors are legion. Mark Buffery recalls one, 'who was narcissism incarnate. He wore army-style clothes, had a crew-cut and would take a break every hour. In that break he would have a pint of milk and crack six eggs into it, mix it together and then drink it. Then he would sit down and breathe for a bit. He was a fitness fanatic and was constantly prinking and preening. He paid more attention to his own body than he did to any of the bodies on stage.'

As a breed, directors can be prone to all sorts of whims, as Jocelyne Page discovered during a spell at the Nottingham Playhouse in the 1950s. 'At Nottingham a Czech director called Kosta Spaic came to do *Yerma*. During the rehearsal for a storm scene someone pulled an ancient loo chain above the stage, the reverberation from the flush went on for one full minute. "Excellent, magnificent, keep that noise in," called Kosta, so every performance someone had to pull the chain.' The Czech was eager to give notes to his cast, who sometimes found them rather perplexing, as Jocelyne Page continues. 'Kosta was electric and so different in approach to what we had known, it was very exciting and unpredictable and he was very funny, loving the expressive "Oh Boggarty" – "Bugger it!" – and talking in several languages at once. He kept saying, "Brighter, brighter", which seemed odd in a tragedy, but he was using the German word for "broader".'

The orders which came down from on high sometimes proved very challenging, particularly to those working in stage management, as Juliette Mander describes. 'Michael Bogdanov was quite difficult to work for because he expected rabbits out of hats for no money. I did a show about boxing where all the actors had to go off for six weeks to train to be boxers. Michael's first words to me were, "Find me a Lonsdale belt," and I did. In about two days I found him a Lonsdale belt. It had to be insured for enormous amounts of money and put in the safe each night.'

Not all directors are martinets and the perception of how good or bad they are may well be influenced by the change in nomenclature. As late as the 1950s and even into the 1960s directors were known as producers and Stephen Hancock believes that this is an accurate reflection of the working style at that time. When the producer became more engaged in the rehearsal process his title changed and what is now referred to as Director's Theatre was born. 'There is a difference between the word "Producer" and the word "Director". In our day we had a producer who sat there, saw what was on offer and produced something from you, which is very different from someone standing out front saying, "You go here, you go there." That's very simplistic but it does make a point.'

Carmen Silvera worked in rep during the era of the producer and gives a clear description of the working relationship. 'You had to pick up the director's messages pretty quickly. He would have plotted the play and would have got in his mind how he wanted it played. You would then offer your performance to him and if you were not on the right track he would very quickly guide you until you were.' Patricia Marmont recalls a scene which must have been repeated in reps up and down the country, and reflects the amount of direction that actors were frequently given. 'I remember in one particular play the director, Alexander Scott, wanted me to cross from stage left to stage right, but he never gave me a motive for doing it. So as I went I decided to pick up a piece of paper from a desk and crumple it up. I said, "Could I have a wastepaper basket?" And he said, "What do you want a wastepaper basket for?" "So that I can cross over and throw the paper in it." "What for?" "So that I have some motivation." "Oh, these Americans and their motivation!" The standard thing was if you were told to move up, down, left, right, you didn't have to have a reason to do it. A good enough reason was because the director told you to do it.'

In spite of the testimony describing wilful or obstructive directors, many actors give accounts of others who were prepared to give not only guidance, but positive and practical help. Alec McCowen was lucky in this respect, 'You did as you were told, there wasn't time for argument or, "I don't believe this." You didn't say, "Why am I making this move?" – "Because I told you to!" The director at York, Geoffrey Staines, I remember as being a very good and sensitive director. Philip King and Falkland Carey wrote a play called *Murder at the Ministry*, in which I played an ordinary little man in some post at the ministry and he turned out to be a German spy and I was shot in the arm at the end and had a rather grand exit, and the audience seemed very impressed but quiet and I remember Geoffrey Staines saying to me, "Would you like to get an exit round?" and I said, "Ooh, yes, how do I do it?" and he said, "You just pat your arm where you've been shot as you go out of the door and you'll get a round." I didn't believe it, but I did it that night and I did get a round and I did for the rest of that week. He knew things like that.'

One director who receives almost universal praise but whose help was rather less specific is Oliver Gordon, who worked at Salisbury among many other places. Among those who benefited from working with him was Jonathan Cecil. 'We had a splendid old chap directing at Salisbury, from whom I learnt a lot, called Oliver Gordon.' Robin Ellis, another graduate from Salisbury, says, 'Oliver Gordon didn't go in for long discussions in terms of motivation or theory. His direction was more – "Piss off there, cock." Maybe some modern directors could take a leaf out of his book, as rather surprisingly it seemed to work.' This point of view is amplified by another of Gordon's hirings, Chris Harris. 'Oliver Gordon was great, he could block a show in a day. You had the afternoons off to go and learn your words. What you learned from that man! He was totally professional – in terms of theatre craft and theatre knowledge, timing laughs, opening doors, when to put a cup down – he was wonderful. He had age on his side, he was a much older man. He was a dream to work with. If you said, "Why am I moving here?" he'd say, "You'll know by Wednesday." There was never time to give you the motivation. It was always, "Piss off down left, cock." That was his phrase – "Cock." It was always, "Cock this, cock that". He used to come in for the run-through, which he didn't really like, and he'd ask for the house lights to go down and before long you'd hear him snoring and he would sleep through the whole of the run-through. On one particular occasion we stopped and said, "Oliver's asleep." So we called out, "We've finished, Oliver," and he woke up abruptly and said, "Right, come on stage and I'll give you notes." So we all trooped on to the stage and he said, "Now, the timing – good God!" His face was a picture – we'd only been going about ten minutes. But everything stopped for cricket – at your audition he'd say, "Do you bat? Do you bowl? Are you a fast bowler? Are you right handed, left handed? By the way, you're playing Hamlet."'

Another who, like Gordon, inspired affection and admiration in equal measure, was A. R. Whatmore, known as Whattie, who began his career by founding a repertory company in Hull in 1923. He went on to work in many theatres, including Dundee and Ipswich, and wherever he went seems to have provided insight and inspiration to his casts. That he set many extremely successful actors on their way in the theatre is a telling indication of his talent. The roll of honour is impressive, as Joss Ackland points out. 'I worked at Salisbury during the end of A.R. Whatmore's time. He was a wonderful character. He ran an incredible repertory company before the war at the Embassy Theatre in Swiss Cottage. Robert Donat, Donald Wolfit, Edith Evans and Eric Portman were all juveniles for him there.' Among others who worked for him was Nancy Mansfield. 'A.R. Whatmore was outstanding. He was happy in Dundee in his little domain. He was God and it suited him very well. What made Whatmore a brilliant director – what makes anyone a good director – is that he had an infallible instinct for what is right. His stagecraft was impeccable. He was one of those directors who lets you have a very free rein unless it was wrong and then he was down on you like a dose of salts. He had a very brusque manner. He'd do all the moves and leave you to do the character. He told you if it was wrong, but he never inflicted his ideas upon you. Usually you were happy with them because his instinct was so unfailing.'

Stephen Hancock adds to the eulogy. 'My first rep was with A.R. Whatmore at Ipswich. He was absolutely marvellous, he was a big man in all senses. We always rehearsed on stage and he used to sit out front and say practically nothing and every hour or so he would make a remark which would just click everything into place. If it was comedy (and he was terribly good at comedy) he would just stroke his moustache and say, "Hrrrmph, make it funny." And you did. It made you think, "Oh well, if that's what you want . . ." and he'd say, "No, you've gone too far now." His comedies were always glorious. If you had a spark of comedy in you it would come out.' Hilary Mason agrees that Whatmore's particular gift was for comedy. 'A.R. Whatmore was one of the best comedy directors I've known in my life. He didn't give much direction, but what he did give was marvellous. He was a splendid comedy director, he knew it inside out.'

Another tribute to Whatmore comes from the distinguished actress

Barbara Jefford. "In the summer of 1949 I knew that I was going to go to Stratford to play Isabella opposite John Gielgud in *Measure for Measure* in 1950. My then agent thought, "Ah, this girl needs experience," and he managed to get me into Dundee Rep and I went there in the autumn of 1949. A.R. Whatmore was very eccentric, I suppose you could call it. He always called me Shakespeare, because he knew I was going to Stratford in 1950. "Come on Shakespeare," he'd say, he used to tease me quite a lot. He was very bluff I remember, and very practical – there was no nonsense. When you are running a repertory theatre you have to be not strict exactly, but you have to get on with things. He was a splendid man, I remember him with great affection and he taught me a great deal. He was a good director because he organized his time very well. I don't remember standing about, he organized himself so that he called you only when necessary. He was brisk, but then he had to be brisk.' If conclusive evidence were needed of Whatmore's stature in the repertory movement, then let it come from Dulcie Gray. 'Everything that A.R. Whatmore touched turned to gold – his sets were always ready on time, everything was perfect, we all knew our lines and were raring to go. I just thought he was a kind of God.'

Not all directors had the good fortune or merit to achieve this god-like pre-eminence, but there are many whose work deserves recognition. Among them is Stephen Joseph, whose contribution to repertory theatre is summed up by Robin Herford. 'Stephen Joseph was a director, an academic, a man of enormous vision. He'd seen theatre in the round in America and brought it back to England and started it off in Scarborough. Starting in Scarborough was a brave thing to do, you can't do it overnight. It comes from a tradition which Stephen Joseph started of encouraging new writers to write. He encouraged Alan Ayckbourn to write. Alan apparently was acting ASM and the story goes that one day he was complaining about the size of the part he'd been asked to play and Stephen said, "Well you write something better and bigger and you can play it." So he set out with the aim of writing lead parts for himself, then he discovered other people could play those lead parts better and concentrated on writing and directing.' Arguably Stephen Joseph's comparative lack of recognition in the history of the repertory movement is because latterly he has been overshadowed by the fame of his protégé, who further explored not only his interest in theatre in the round, but also his belief that actors need to be eclectic in their skills.

Robin Herford says of Ayckbourn, 'Alan was very good at getting people to broaden their skills base. If you were a designer you might find yourself doing something else, if you were an actor you might find yourself directing. He had this belief that "men of the theatre" are more use if they really are that, if they really have a knowledge of more than one skill, otherwise you tend to get pigeon-holed.' Russell Dixon was another company member on whom Ayckbourn made a lasting impression. 'I worked at Scarborough with Alan Ayckbourn. He had a total concept of every play he did, the actors and technicians took several weeks to catch up with him.'

Among other directors who have garnered praise during their careers is Douglas Seale, who worked for Sir Barry Jackson in Birmingham. Richard Pasco remembers that his preparation for rehearsal, with all the moves plotted out, was as meticulous as 'an architect's drawing', and Paul Daneman speaks of him as, 'a marvellous man, I loved him dearly. A very good director, much better than he's ever been given the credit for.' He goes on to say that Seal may have provided Sir Peter Hall with some of his inspiration for his acclaimed production of *The Wars of the Roses*. 'Barry Jackson wanted to do *Henry VI*. He said, "The trouble is it hasn't been performed for ninety years, it's unactable. *Part One* is totally unactable, *Part Three* doesn't make sense unless you've seen *Parts One* and *Two*, but we could perhaps do *Part Two* on its own.' We did that, and it was a huge success largely because Dougie Seal invented a way of doing it, a way which all the directors who have done it since heavily imitated.'

Liza Goddard has fond memories of a director with whom she worked at the outset of her career. 'Joan Knight was an extraordinary woman, a big woman with a big personality. She smoked cheroots and she was extraordinarily good at directing young people, she gave us a great sense of confidence. She called everyone darling and she laughed a lot, she had a lovely laugh.' Another Joan who wins plaudits, this time from Doreen Andrew, is Joan Kemp Welsh, 'She was amazing. She was a difficult taskmaster but she was marvellous, exhilarating to work for,' although Doreen Andrew found Sir Lewis Casson, Sybil Thorndyke's husband, less exhilarating. She was directed by him in the Travelling Repertory Company, which was run by Basil C. Langton. She gives the following account of rehearsals. 'One did learn an awful lot by watching and listening. You didn't say, "I don't think the line should be said like that," you were given the inflection and told how to say it. I can remember Lewis Casson saying to someone after a good deal of rehearsal, "Well, you're still as dull as mud, go on to the next bit."'

Charles Simon, of Theatre Royal, Darlington fame, attracts a good deal of praise from those who remember happy days in his company, among them Barbara Leigh Hunt, who declares that, 'Charles was the most wonderful director, he was urbane, he was witty, he had the most beautiful voice and he was a very good teacher.'

Love them or hate them, as Peter Bowles observed earlier, directors have an enormous amount of power over the repertory actor. An incident which demonstrates the extent of this is related by David Horovitch. 'I suppose because you become very bored and very tired during pantomime it does become diverting to try and make each other laugh. We were doing *Aladdin* and the director Ian Mullins was playing Abanazer. Towards the end of the play he has this scene where he comes on saying, "New lamps for old, new lamps for old." He was carrying this tray of lamps, all of which were stuck down except for the one he was to give to Aladdin's girlfriend. One matinée she pointed to one of the lamps that was stuck down and said, "I don't want that one, I want this one." After a struggle he pulled it off the tray and you could see all the glue stuck to it still and he gave it to her saying, "Here you are, a new lamp to light you on your way to a new job."'

Without doubt actors show ambivalent feelings to those who are in charge of their work, but the directors are not without compassion for the performer's plight and may even feel a sense of helplessness at their own ability to overcome what can be mountainous challenges. Sir Peter Hall must certainly speak for many of his colleagues when he says, 'In weekly rep all you can do is sympathize with the actors and make sure they don't bump into each other.'

8

Digs

'I once had digs in a place called Ham Row, which seemed very appropriate.'

Chris Harris

THE MANAGEMENT'S RESPONSIBILITY was to appoint a director and his brief was to assemble a company. For the actors, who arrived in some unknown town ready to start work in the local rep, their first task even before rehearsals began was to find accommodation.

Digs and the landladies who preside over them have become a powerful part of theatrical legend, in the repertory movement as much as anywhere. Every theatre had a digs list and many actors compiled their own, based on word of mouth or personal experience as they moved from job to job. To secure a room with one of the renowned landladies, like Dorothy Kelly in Liverpool, was a prize, but much of the time it was a question of taking pot luck.

In the first half of the century the service offered by the best landladies was considerable, as Robin Bailey records. 'Mrs Spratt of Station Road in Worthing prepared three meals a day for us, always ready on time. We were not, and often came back late at night to find her patiently waiting to serve supper. Every Thursday morning, when I was free from rehearsal, she turned on the geyser and ran a bath for me as I finished breakfast in bed. And all for two pounds a week.'

Derek Nimmo was equally well looked after. 'In digs we used to have what were called single combined rooms, which meant you had a single bed and a moth-eaten old armchair and a table and chair. First thing that happened in the morning was your landlady came in and lit the fire and when there was a nice cheery fire you got up and she'd bring your breakfast in too.'

In Stockton-on-Tees Michael Kilgarriff secured accommodation with the local lamplighter. 'He used to go out with his bike and his ladder and his pole every night and light the gas lights at dusk.' Kilgarriff has the following advice to give. 'Given a choice, the best things to go for were digs where they had grown-up sons – like me – young lads, so the landlady would feed you and mother you and cry on you when you left.' Alec McCowen took this counsel when he went to Macclesfield for his first job, 'In Macclesfield I paid thirty-seven and sixpence a week and the landlady was so fond of me she used to give me two and sixpence as pocket money. I saved a pound a week on a three pounds a week salary. One became very fond of some of the landladies. The old digs were homes from homes, they were wonderful. Of course, it would depend on the character of the land-lady, but many of them were theatrical landladies because they loved the theatre and they loved actors. They realized actors' tempera-ments and would forgive you if you were a little late home for supper, or if you didn't leap out of bed at seven in the morning. I remember the coalfires in one's bedsit, particularly at York. I remember Mrs Lythe coming in with the porridge. You'd come home for lunch after rehearsal and she'd have a Yorkshire pudding waiting as a starter and then the roast beef. Huge teas with ham and lettuce, and supper! Four meals they would provide. I left York after eighteen months with Mrs Lythe and for some reason she wasn't at home when I came to collect my case on the last Saturday night and I met her in the street and I can remember now hugging her and weeping, sobbing in the street. She only died this year and we've kept in touch.' Barbara Lott describes the lodgings she had in Barnsley before the war. 'The land-lady had digs for about eleven shillings a week and I used to buy my food in the market, which the landlady used to cook, and I can remember now waking up and seeing her coming in with a shovel of hot coals to put on the fire to get the fire lit. Of course, no central heating. The water had coal dust in it.'

There are no qualifications in Vilma Hollingbery's account of her experience in digs, which she says, 'were wonderful. There were theatrical landladies and it was their job and they loved their actors. You could get a hot supper if you could afford it when you got back from the theatre at midnight. The landladies were proud to be theatrical landladies. They didn't leave you to it, they looked after you, there'd be a bottle in your bed and your washing done. They knew what you liked and what you didn't like, it was bliss really.'

Janet Whiteside entered the profession when she was very young and rather timid. 'I was terrified of my landlady. I didn't like liver. I was only there for three weeks, but we had liver once a week and I used to wrap it up in newspaper and hide it in my suitcase and when my father came to take me back to Birmingham, I said, "Do you mind if I open my suitcase in a field . . . ?" and I got rid of the liver like that.'

She might have done better to use the local greasy spoon, as Jocelyne Page used to do. 'We all used to fall into a café in Hornchurch which saved us from cold and starvation every day – wonderful smog on all the windows. Eggs, bacon, mushrooms, sausage and beans and over-cooked cabbage. I think it was run by Maisie, who one day called out, "You'll have to wait, I'm cutting my toenails in the back."' Perhaps it was more advisable to emulate Jean Anderson and stick to landladies whose hospitality and cuisine could be guaranteed. 'I remember my landlady used to light the fire in my bedroom while I was still in bed, she provided three good meals a day. She was a wonderful landlady, she used to invite me into her kitchen after supper to watch television when it first came in. She used to interrupt all the programmes – "I've 'ad 'im, I've 'ad 'er too."'

One actor who shared Alec McCowen's luck in finding accommodation with women who proved to be treasures was Hilary Mason. 'We were doing *Ghosts* in Aylesbury the week before the war broke out and I was playing Mrs Alving. The management said, "We can't afford to give you a costume, Hilary," so I went home to my landlady and she said, "You will go to the market and buy me five yards of hard linen at two and sixpence a yard." She ran me up the most beautiful Edwardian costume that I had ever seen.' Kindness such as this inevitably endeared landladies to their lodgers. Michael Kilgarriff recalls a company determined to show their appreciation of one who was held in general esteem. 'One of the boys in the company had a landlady called Mrs FitzGibbon, who was a sweet old duck, and she used to come and see the show Friday first house, and the joke was that we would always get her name mentioned in the play. You'd walk on stage playing a character called Jones and someone would say to you,

'Good morning, Mr FitzGibbon', or if there was a pub mentioned it would suddenly become the FitzGibbon Arms.'

In their turn landladies often took a proprietorial pride in 'their' actors. Carmen Silvera says, 'When I was in Warrington there was a junior ASM at the theatre who was very green, he wasn't very good at all but he actually had to go on in one of the plays and say, "My Lord, your carriage awaits." He was so excited about it and he did it and they even mentioned him in the bottom of the crit in the local paper. It said, "John so and so was adequate." Now his landlady didn't know the meaning of this long word and she thought it was very good and she kept saying to him, "Oh, you're adequate, it says you're adequate," as if this were the best possible praise. It became a kind of catch phrase in the company – "Oooh, you were really adequate in that!"'

Sometimes the landlady's friendliness could become a little onerous, as Ian Hogg remembers, 'Mrs Tomms in Nottingham ran an actors' digs. She had dropsy, unfortunately, and she was very fat. She had great big trousers on and a heavy sweater and a cloth cap. She had the pay-phone outside her bedroom and it was the only communication with home. I came down to breakfast one day and she said, "Having trouble at home are you, Mr Hogg? I heard you on the phone last night and I thought, there's trouble there." Then she asked, "Do you dine out after the show or would you like to dine here? I can provide you with nour-ishment." I said, "Oh, all right, yes." I thought if I got back quickly I'd be able to watch *Newsnight*. So I got back, reached forward to put the telly on and she came in with a tray of something and I said, "Thank you." I started watching *Newsnight* and I felt this hand on the back of the chair. She was standing behind me and she said, "I'm against capital punishment, what's your opinion about that?" There was a different topic every night and on the last night she said, "I suffer from dropsy, Mr Hogg, what's your opinion about miracles?"'

Some digs were segregated, as the landladies made nice distinctions between their eminent guests and those who were more humble, or between straight actors and variety artistes. Richard Pasco reports, 'The first lot of digs I had in Birmingham were in the Bristol Road, my landlady was Mrs Faulkner and I remember that Emlyn Williams came to stay. Mrs Faulkner used to put me in a room with a tray while he had the grand dining-room. She was a terrible snob, there was terr-ible class distinction.' The social divisions which some landladies underlined could have had awful consequences. Dulcie Gray was horrified to discover, in one place where she stayed during the war, that the household cats took precedence over the servants. 'I had digs next to the Lyceum Theatre in Edinburgh and during the first air raid the landlady shooed her guests to a passage in the house that had no windows in it and told us to lie on the floor and put cotton wool in our ears; she took all her cats with her but she wouldn't let the maids come with us, they had to stay in the kitchen.'

The most well known of all the landladies was probably Dorothy Kelly, who let rooms to Moray Watson. 'In Liverpool I was very lucky because I had some kind of an introduction. She didn't normally take people from the rep, she preferred people week by week. Miss Kelly was a legendary lady who lived up behind the cathedral, a good twenty minutes from the theatres. She lived in what looked almost like a slum, very unprepossessing houses, she had two awful yappy dogs called Peggy and Trixie, but she did cook divinely.' The status of Miss Kelly was reflected in the calibre of the guests she attracted, although some-times their qualities were not immediately apparent. Watson contin-ues, 'While I was there all sorts of people came through – Flora Robson, Coral Browne and Vincent Price. One particular memory I have is of *South Pacific* coming. I had a separate dining-room to them. Miss Kelly came in to me one day and said, "Oh Mr Watson, the gentleman in the front, if you can call him a gentleman, insists I try and introduce you and I don't want you to meet him, he doesn't wear his shoes, his socks smell, he puts his feet up and I'm quite happy for you not to meet him." Next day she said, "He's still saying he wants to meet you, would you go in, his name's Mr Sean Connery." I didn't know him, he was completely unknown, a chorus boy. I said, "Why does he want to meet me?" and she said, "Because he thinks you'll get him into the rep." So I went in on the Wednesday night. He'd been to see my matinée. He was indeed looking very scruffy and was rather offhand and surly and asked me to come and see his show the next day. I went to the matinée and without being wise after the event, he did look very good and stood out slightly. He said, "Right then, will you introduce me to Willard Stoker?" I said, "I don't think it's a good idea, he's not good with beginners and you're a beginner really. I don't think he'd be good for you and I don't think you'd get on particularly well. He'd probably fall in love with you and it won't help your career at all. But I will if you want!"' Alec McCowen chafed against his enforced separation from other guests. 'In a lot of places they used to have two separate lounges, one for the straight actors and one for the variety artistes and they didn't like us mixing. They didn't think it was right; they didn't think we would want to, although I longed to get in with the comedians and the jugglers and the singers and dancers.'

Although many actors were offered an impeccable service, in spite of the social engineering that occasionally accompanied it, others did not fare so well. When June Whitfield complained to her hostess that she had found bed bugs in her bed, the woman accused her of importing them! On another occasion, 'I had invited some of the cast back for a sherry and had bought a bottle. When I returned after the show it was half-empty. I mentioned this to the landlady and she said, "Yes, I hope you don't mind, I had some friends in." There was no answer to that!'

For Philip Locke the drama in his lodgings was equal to that at the theatre. 'In Oldham I was living with a Yorkshire family who were always having fights and rows and things. Furniture would be thrown around and in the middle of one night a mattress was hurled down the stairs. It was like something out of a play.' What Clive Francis describes is like something out of a horror story. 'When my father was very young he was playing a rep up north and he got these terrible digs at very short notice. When he arrived he felt very uncomfortable about the place. It was dark and dingy and he was actually given a candle to take himself up to bed with. He went up to his room with his little suitcase and he got on to the bed, then he thought he'd put his suitcase under the bed, but there was something there. He put the candle down to see what it was and it was a coffin. He never slept, he just sat in a chair all night, waiting for the dawn to come up. He went down to breakfast next morning and the landlady was serving up the bacon and eggs. "Did you sleep well, Mr Francis?" "Well no, actually. What's that under the bed?" "Oh it's Dad, sorry did it get in your way? He should have gone yesterday, but don't worry, he'll be gone by this afternoon."'

From the macabre to the simply odd, landladies came in different hues. Maria Charles recalls her first job, which was in the north of England. 'By the time I got to Oldham I was quite tired and I had nowhere to stay, I hadn't got a clue about anything. I stood in the station and said, "Now what do I do, I can't go to an hotel," so I asked

the taxi man if he knew of any theatrical lodgings. And he said, "Aye."
It was all cobblestones and I was teetering on my high heels. He took
me to this lady. I was quite horrified because I'd never been anywhere.
There were all the factories and the windows with the lace curtains and
people were still in clogs. He took me to this house. It was tiny, it wasn't
dirty, but it wasn't like I was used to. I can't remember the lady's name,
but she had a daughter called Yvonne, who had an illegitimate baby by
one of the actors. And she had a husband who hadn't any legs and
made false teeth in the kitchen.' This might almost have been the
establishment tracked down by Robin Bailey, who, when he described
to his potential landlady the nature of his work and his working hours,
was told, 'That's perfectly all right, we're very bohemian here. We
often sit on the floor.'

Jocelyne Page found herself staying in a bizarre place when she was
working in Ipswich. 'I lived in these wonderful digs over a petrol
station, they were closed down later because they were totally illegal,
gas fires everywhere! The smell of the paraffin stove stays with me still.
They had a budgerigar called Joe, who used to be let out at breakfast
and he used to perch on your plate and pinch the bacon off it.'

Occasionally there was not even refuge to be had above the petrol
station. Harriet Walter recalls a fellow actor finding an ingenious solution to his homelessness. 'There was an older actor in the company and
he didn't really have any digs, so he asked the management if he could
be the caretaker of the building. So they paid him a fiver or something
and after the show he would go to his dressing-room and put up his
little camp bed. They saved money on a caretaker and he saved money
on digs.' A similar fate befell Richard Johnson in Perth. 'The time that
I was there was one of extreme austerity. It was weekly rep and I lived
in the gallery bar, with David Steuart, who ran the theatre. We had
hospital-style beds put up in the bar, because the gallery was closed and
we lived up there and we got fed by the usherettes and the theatre staff.'

For Juliette Mander, working as an ASM in Leicester in the 1970s,
the gallery bar would have seemed like a blessing. 'I stayed in a squat
right opposite the theatre. It had electricity because they bypassed the
meter, but it didn't have heating. It had a bed with a mattress, the
shower didn't work, but there was a basin with a little water heater
above it that worked. The place was freezing, absolutely freezing, and I
was all on my own, it was very frightening. There was no kitchen and I

had to use the loo at the theatre. One night, it was Hallowe'en and there was a party after the show. I came home very drunk and I had an old lemonade bottle which I decided to fill with water from the heater, to act as a kind of hot-water bottle. The water was boiling, with the result that the glass cracked and the bottom fell out of the bottle on to my foot, which started to bleed profusely and of course I was scalded by a litre of boiling water. There was I in this icy building, stark naked, with a foot that was quite literally pumping blood. I was in shock, so I didn't kind of feel it. I hobbled back to the theatre, screaming, and luckily the hospital was quite close and the stage manager took me to casualty, where I was stitched up unceremoniously without any anaesthetic because I was pissed.'

Sanitary arrangements were often a bone of contention. Tom Conti says, 'I got digs in Dundee with a nice elderly lady. There were all sorts of rules – about baths and things – you were only allowed two a week, the rest of the time it was a wipeover with a damp cloth.' Joanna McCallum recalls her chagrin when, 'I remember arriving at one lot of digs to be greeted by the landlady who said, "Hello dear, what bath night would you like? Saturday is free." You had to buy the plug in order to have a bath.' For Dulcie Gray in Scotland, having a bath was not an option at all. 'I had some digs in Glasgow where you couldn't have a bath because all the landlady's vegetables were in it.' Unfortunately, it was not only the bathing arrangements which could be primitive, as this story from Jocelyne Page demonstrates. 'Edgar Wreford arrives at new digs on a wet day and is ushered into the kitchen to have high tea with the landlady. He is dying to pee and after a few minutes says, "Er, could you please tell me where the loo is?" Landlady, very loudly: "Alf, pass the soft paper off the bread, Mr Wreford's going to the lavatory."'

The rules which Tom Conti mentions extended to the matter of overnight visitors and on this issue landladies proved to be implacably moral. In the 1930s, although he was legitimately married, Robin Bailey had difficulty finding rooms where both he and his wife could stay. 'On joining a weekly repertory company in Worthing, none of the recommended theatrical digs had a vacancy. I found a room at the Firs, or was it the Pines? When my wife came down unexpectedly for a night, I asked if it would be all right if she shared my bed and my breakfast. "Where are your lines?" asked the proprietress. Lines I thought were what I had to learn by Monday. The lines she was speaking of, however, were not related to Act Three, marriage lines were what she needed before she opened the door. Even then, long before the liberated Sixties, my wife and I had not thought it necessary to carry them around with us, and it was only very reluctantly, with no proof of the legality of our relationship, that the dragon lady allowed us in.'

Vilma Hollingbery and Michael Napier Brown managed to rent digs together in Bexhill before they were married, but only by dint of a certain amount of deception. 'When Michael and I got married we'd been living together in digs for a year and we hadn't told the landlady we weren't married. We got married on our only day off, which was a Sunday, and we saved up and went to stay the night in the White Hart Hotel in Rye, which we thought was frightfully posh, and on our wedding night we sat up in bed learning our lines for the next production, which was *Pride and Prejudice*. Our one fear was that we had to get back to our digs first thing on Monday morning before the landlady saw the paper, because there were photographs of the Penguin Players' marriage, with us on the front page in our wedding gear and the landlady would have known that we hadn't been married, we'd been living in her house in sin. We crept in, stole her paper, and ran off down the drive.'

When he worked at Northampton, Tony O'Callaghan was told a story about the Royal Theatre's most infamous old boy, Errol Flynn, who began his career there as acting ASM. 'He used to carry his girlfriend to his bedroom on his back so that the landlady would only hear one set of footsteps on the stairs.'

Most landladies were anxious to prevent any illicit relationships from soiling the character of their boarding houses. However, sometimes their suspicions were unfounded, as Derek Nimmo explains. 'I was even more pompous then, would you believe, and the leading actress was called Maureen Norman, she was an immensely glamorous figure to me, I was about twenty-one and she must have been all of thirty-five. She did seem very glamorous, she had green fingernails and red hair. I used to quite innocently sit at her feet in her bedroom while she regaled me with stories of the theatre after the show. Anyway, my landlady mentioned that she thought I was having an affair and I was outraged at the thought that I was besmirching Miss Norman's reputation, I was absolutely horrified and being so pompous I went off to a solicitor and a letter was sent to the landlady, which cost me a guinea, which was quite a lot, that unless these scurrilous stories ceased I would take action against the landlady.'

On rare occasions it was not the poor actor who was caught with his trousers down, but the landlady herself. Simon Williams says, 'An actor called Arthur Lane was in digs after the war and the landlady served up a huge amount of meat always, although there was still rationing. One morning he forgot his script and had to go back for it. He found the landlady on the kitchen table *in flagrante* with the butcher's boy and a huge tray of chops. They didn't interrupt the proceedings, but as he tiptoed past, the landlady looked up and said, "Oh Mr Lane, you must think I'm an awful flirt!"'

The Swinging Sixties saw a loosening of public morality and by the 1980s the dragon ladies of theatrical digs had all but disappeared and a more tolerant attitude prevailed, as is shown by this last, anonymous tale. The actress in question was in a play at the Theatre Royal, York, and after the first night the whole company got roaring drunk and she took an actor back to her digs with her. In the middle of the night he got up to go to the loo. Time passed, and he didn't come back, and he didn't come back . . . Eventually there was a tap on her door and her landlady's head appeared, 'Excuse me dear, but did you bring somebody back here with you tonight?' 'Yes, actually, I'm afraid I did.' 'Well, he's just got into bed with me.'

9

Rehearsals

'Dancing round each others' egos.'

David Tennant

REHEARSALS ARE A core activity in repertory theatre, more than in
other branches of the profession, where once the play is open actors
have their days to themselves. In rep, as soon as one play is on, the
company starts rehearsing the next, embarking on a schedule that
begins at ten or ten-thirty in the morning and finishes twelve hours
later, six days a week. Maria Charles describes her debut in Oldham
during the late 1940s. 'My first rehearsal was in a wooden hut up
wooden stairs, quite a nice little hut, but you know . . . it's a hut! I
dressed up for this first rehearsal – I wore a very full skirt with about
four petticoats underneath, fishnet stockings, ankle-strap shoes, an off-
the-shoulder blouse and I put my hair up in Edwardian style, earrings,
a choker and a little fur jacket and I teetered up the stairs and I opened
the door to be greeted by this sea of faces, which didn't faze me, I
thought, "Well, why aren't they dressed up? They've all got slacks on."
At the end of the first day Douglas Emery, the director, took me to one
side and he said, "Very good, you're on the right lines and everything,
but you don't need to dress up quite so much."'

Often the stage at the theatre is occupied by the set for the current
show, so the choice of a hut to rehearse in is fairly typical. Church halls
are a popular venue, but some actors find themselves working in more
unusual places. During his time at the Birmingham Rep, Sir Derek
Jacobi recalls, 'We rehearsed on stage if we could or in a room above a
pub – the Market Inn down the road.' Francesca Ryan describes some

stressful circumstances which led to the company rehearsing in a place that was considerably more outré than the Market Inn. 'I worked for Ian Forest at the Duke's Theatre, Lancaster. We did *The Country Wife*, which was remarkable for the fact that the lead actor had a nervous breakdown during the technical rehearsal. Both his parents had died the previous year and he hadn't estimated how worn out he was. He just flipped and dropped out of the tech and somebody went on for the performance carrying the script. And after we'd opened *The Country Wife* we started rehearsing *'Tis Pity She's a Whore* and as a treat the director arranged for us to have the read-through in a crypt by candlelight. A wonderful introduction to this Jacobean play and a treat because we'd worked so hard.'

In the 1930s Judy Campbell found that she was under pressure in rehearsals too, since she was working simultaneously in Cambridge and Brighton. 'I remember driving between the two theatres with Richard Wattis and we were rehearsing Portia and Bassanio as we went along. The car used to boil because I didn't know about putting oil and water in it and I can remember pulling over into a lay-by, continuing to rehearse while we waited for the car to cool down.' The director Anthony Tuckey recalls his early days rehearsing in Perth, 'Sometimes in a church hall with heaters mounted about ten feet high on the walls and pointed at the ceiling, sometimes in the Cathedral Chapter House, which had huge but luke-warm pipes, and occasionally at the Old Prison, which had no heating at all. (If you've ever seen the New Prison at Perth, you won't actually believe there could be an old one.)' No matter how varied the venue, the level of discipline required of a company was constant and demanding – time was always in short supply and the clock had to be carefully watched, as Malcolm Farquhar testifies. 'Rehearsals always started at nine-thirty in the morning and if you were half a minute late you had to apologize to the entire cast and give a reason why. It seemed a bit churlish until you got into it. It was regimented.'

Just how much activity companies managed to pack in to the time available is demonstrated by Derek Nimmo's description of a typical schedule in weekly rep. 'You had to block straight away, there wasn't time for a read-through. Monday was always the dress rehearsal [of the current play] and that was it. Whatever state it was in, you had to go ahead. On Tuesday you'd start the new one and you'd block the whole of the first act and on Wednesday you probably had a matinée and you'd rehearse the first act without a book. Then you'd rehearse Thursday, Friday and Saturday and that would be it. There was always that moment on Saturday night when you looked at the noticeboard to see what you'd be playing next week.'

In some weekly reps it was the custom to rehearse only in the morning so that the afternoon could be given over to the arduous task of learning lines. Leslie Lawton remembers that occasionally actors would crave extra time, 'We would only rehearse in the morning. We used to go to the cinema in the afternoon! Maurice Jones, the director, didn't think it was necessary to rehearse in the afternoon. We were doing a play called *Ladies in Retirement*, which was quite difficult and more dense than the stuff we normally did, so we offered to come in for an afternoon to rehearse and he banged about the theatre all afternoon doing jobs because he was very cross with us for rehearsing, he didn't want us to rehearse, he thought we'd get stale.'

Not only did the director Shaun Sutton rehearse his company in Buxton all day, to his astonishment they wanted to work on the play on a Sunday too. 'We were doing a play, *Miss Mabel's Story*, Gwen Watford was playing Miss Mabel. I said, "Look it's a simple enough play. Let's have Sunday off, let's all go to the Goyt valley," and my wife and I set off to go to the Goyt valley and we passed the theatre and we heard the murmur of voices and they'd come in by themselves to rehearse. So we went in. We didn't go to the Goyt valley.'

There were companies like the ones run by Charles Denville and Harold G. Roberts, where two plays were staged a week. Rehearsals were so negligible that most actors appear to have no recollection of what they were like. What they do remember is the odd occasion when the statutory amount of time in weekly rep was eaten away. Moray Watson describes a nightmarish situation which occurred when he was appearing in Whitley Bay. 'We were all gathered together one Tuesday morning to read a play by Somerset Maugham. On the Wednesday, before the matinée, the director, who was called William Rotheray, said, "We're breaking early to have a company discussion." We were all told to sit down and he said, "We're going to make a very dramatic decision. This play is not working. We're now going to have a discussion about what to do next week instead." This was already the Wednesday! He said, "Have any of you got a play that you know well and would like to do again?" It was my first job, so I kept quiet, and the leading man suddenly piped up and said, "Well if nobody's got any better ideas we'll do *Murder Without Crime*, there are only four characters, one is off almost immediately, there's a girl and two fellas. I'll play the older man and Moray, you play the other man." I didn't know anything about this *Murder Without Crime*. I had the play Wednesday night, off the train from London, and we started on Thursday and opened on Monday. I'll never ever forget it. It wasn't a play that you could wing, I knew that once I was on stage it was like being in prison. How I did it I don't know, but somehow I got through, the way one does in a heroic, mad, theatrical way.'

The following story, which was told to Richard Bebb, goes beyond even the heroic, mad and theatrical. It concerns Richard Wood, who was the father of the playwright, Charles Wood. He directed a play at Blackpool, and for some reason there was a delay in obtaining the scripts, which did not arrive from London until very late in the week – on the Saturday before the Monday on which the play was due to open. The actors learned the lines on Sunday and opened unrehearsed on Monday.

When television first became available in the early 1950s public expectations of acting were raised by the standards of naturalism inherent in the new medium. Repertory companies realized the necessity of finding longer rehearsal periods for their actors, even if this meant that shows had to run for two weeks instead of one. Timothy West declares that, for those schooled in a weekly tradition, this came as something of a shock. 'When Salisbury started doing fortnightly rep the actors were all saying, "What will we do with the extra week?"' The answer to this is supplied by John Moffatt, who discovered, 'You found that if you had two weeks' rehearsal, you sort of sat back during the first week, so consequently by the second week you weren't nearly so far ahead. Also, you'd started to investigate, you'd started to pick it to pieces, you'd started to think about it and you realized then that you needed two more weeks.' For Wendy Craig, who worked in Ipswich, 'There was time to work on characterization in fortnightly rep, there really was. Usually we got the script well in advance of each production, so that we could start preparing before rehearsals began,' although Patricia Hodge found that even with two weeks there was not enough time available to tackle ambitious or demanding plays. 'On a

Pinter text in repertory it's no use spending two weeks trying to measure the pauses because you have no time for the rest. It's not an ideal way to try and explore the great writers.'

It may be surprising that many actors see a danger in having too long in which to rehearse. Among them is Barbara Jefford, who remarks, 'You can become very self-indulgent if you have too long to rehearse – sometimes now we have eight weeks and you really long to move on, you get to the stage where you really need an audience.' This point is echoed by Dorothy Tutin, who says, 'It's a truism that you can go on rehearsing a play for ever and never be ready. What you can do and think of is endless, but on the other hand if you don't perform it you lose out because you learn so much from the audience. The audience teaches you and you need to have that experience quite quickly, I think.' Alan Ayckbourn comments, 'I do think sometimes rehearsals expand to suit the time available, you can fill it with useful things. There are a lot of plays that don't benefit from having months spent on them.'

While it is true that any company worth its salt can find things to fill rehearsals with, for actors brought up on a diet of blocking, learning and then performing a play, some of the exercises that now accompany this process can appear pointless. John Warner records, 'Now I often feel that when you've got six to eight weeks sometimes, I think directors don't really know what to do with that time. I can remember at Bristol in rehearsal having to mime pass the parcel and eventually it came to my turn and I mimed an actor waiting to start work!' Jill Gascoine shares his scepticism about the value of immensely long rehearsals when she says, 'Nowadays you have about ten weeks' rehearsal and deep down inside me I think that's far too long – everyone's sleeping together after the seventh week!'

The director Ian Mullins makes an interesting point when he says that technically actors used to be much quicker than they are now, presumably because they did not have the luxury of several weeks in which to work. 'Actors in those days had a mental and technical process that worked faster than actors these days. They had to learn faster, assimilate faster, rehearse faster, but within the confines of the length of time for rehearsal there was plenty of time to discuss and to study the play profoundly. There was a danger in weekly rep of skating over it rather superficially, but there was usually time to examine it, analyse it, dissect it as much as you wanted, though actors knew throughout that process that they were going to have to go through it in their own privacy, because there wasn't enough rehearsal time. I do think that the general standards achieved in repertory during the Sixties were remarkably high.'

The Glasgow Citizens Theatre earned a reputation for being avant-garde under the directorship of Giles Havergal, so although Rupert Frazer's story about rehearsing for a production of *Hamlet* there in 1970 is not necessarily typical, it does throw light on some of the elements which contribute to the process of preparing a play for performance. 'The stage was empty at the beginning of the season, Giles Havergal was standing on it with a great black space behind him and he said to his PA, "Darling, can I have the company list?" and he went through this cast list saying, "You can be Polonius, you can be Ophelia, you can be Hamlet," It was all entirely arbitrary. I thought it would just be for the first day, but that is how we stayed, that is how he cast. Gertrude and Ophelia were played by men, I was a twenty-four-year-old Polonius, the set was black, we were all dressed in black, we had to wear jock straps and, if we were old, blankets down to the ground, if we were young, they were down to mid-thigh. The theme of the work as far as the actors were concerned was physically based, that was what it was about – physicality, that was why we were all young. All of us were under thirty, half of us were straight from drama school, none of us had any experience. We all took to this, we thought it was fabulous, exciting, extraordinary. We blocked, but we never improvised. "Oh God, how embarrassing," [Havergal and his co-directors] would say if we suggested improvising. After a while we got them round to it a bit. Rehearsals were surprisingly conventional. They'd get hold of an idea, one idea in a play, and really blow it up. What it means is that other aspects of the play are ruthlessly got rid of, pushed to one side, ignored and no apologies made. I am one hundred per cent behind that approach, I think it's wonderful. The play will go on existing, this is one three-week production of it. After four weeks' rehearsal we opened, and that night six thousand school children had their tickets cancelled for them. We stayed on the front page of the *Glasgow Herald* in Scotland day after day after day. In the end it ended up being an extended run, you don't get publicity like that every day of the week.'

Richard Pasco admits, 'It wasn't till many years later that I got into the truly creative side of acting. In those days it was a question of learn the lines and don't bump into the furniture.' This was largely true of weekly rep, but within the confines of the time available actors were able to develop their own individual approach to the work. Amanda Redman highlights the necessity for working on your own as well as in rehearsal. 'Rehearsals were very, very concentrated and the days were long. You did the read-through and launched straight into blocking, you didn't have the luxury of sitting round a table for ages and discussing it. You had to be very concentrated, very focused and you had to do a lot of homework.' The introverted nature of much of the work is accentuated by Gemma Jones, 'Essentially my method remains the same. It's always been quite private, but when I was younger I would be very secretive in my way of work, which I think was quite difficult for people working with me. Then I used to work things out in my head and be quite slow to arrive at something. Now I'm braver at throwing myself at something.' In contrast to this, Jill Gascoine finds that the most fruitful part of her preparation does not take place alone but in the context of group work. 'I read it and read it and read it and read the play, so that I know what it's about and what I believe, I talk to the director about what the concept is, find out the importance of my particular character in the story, get to know who that person is, or who you think it is. I do work on my feet in rehearsals, I do much more work there, my work at home is mainly cementing the lines.'

Russell Dixon adopted an systematic approach to his work in Manchester. 'I worked at the Library Theatre when David Scase was in overall charge and Howard Lloyd Lewis and Clare Venables were directing. We used a unit system for rehearsals, scenes were broken up into segments, each of which had objectives.' This method borrows much from the teachings of Laban, whose most notable disciple within the repertory movement was Philip Hedley.

After training in the Laban Method at drama school, Alison Steadman worked with Hedley at the theatre in Stratford East. 'When I was at the East Fifteen Acting School we were very much taught to base everything on character work rather than just learning lines and plotting moves. It's all to do with where would your character go, where would your character move to, motivated as we are in life, and to try and relate that to what the character is feeling and expecting. Because of the training I'm still very much in that mode. Each play I'd break down into units and objectives, which is how we were taught at drama school. Plays are broken down into acts and scenes, those are the units you are given, then they are broken down into smaller units. The first unit might be that you sit down and have a cup of tea, "How nice to see you", the second unit is, "How's Geoffrey?" The next unit might be that someone else comes into the room. It helps to give you a secure structure to work with, it helps you narrow things down. What is your character's objective in that scene? What does she want? We tried very much to stick to those rules. Philip Hedley used to organize warm-ups in the morning before rehearsals, so we'd spend time doing phys-ical, vocal and mental work-outs. A lot of people would have said, "We've only got ten days, what are you spending an hour on that for?" but even a very elderly lady in the company came along, so no one was excluded. It wasn't compulsory, as far as I remember. It gave everyone a good feeling of company morale, it helped everyone work as a team.'

Many performers place emphasis on instinct before analysis in their work. Among them is Eileen Atkins. 'When you rehearse in rep you do the first thing which comes into your head and hope for the best. Oddly enough, when you're working on a part, your first thoughts about it are absolutely correct. Your first instinct is usually right, but what you often do, when you have a proper rehearsal time, is undo it all and find out the reason why.' She sounds a note of caution about per-formers who don't underpin their intuitive work with a knowledge of technique. 'A lot of people who don't learn the craft of acting do rather well because they get the attention all evening and the critics don't know the difference.' Vilma Hollingbery reiterates the dangers of having to jump in with both feet when rehearsal time is short. 'I had to unlearn a lot of bad habits, instant characterization. You have to sum up a character in your first morning, there isn't time. Although sub-sequently I have found that very often your first instincts are right. You'll go all round the world and find other dimensions, but very often you end up where you started.' Even when several weeks are available for rehearsal, the central process often remains the same, in that actors begin with an impulse and then explore what this has suggested in an amount of detail which depends on the time available. Stephanie Cole sums it up. 'What happens now when you have four, six, eight weeks' rehearsal, you do a read-through and it's rather good and then you have that incredibly painful process of why was that good and why did it work and you feel as if you can't walk or talk, then you go back to the instinctive, but behind it is the whole weight of the knowledge of why, which allows you to reproduce the feelings and so forth.'

Another champion of actors' intuition is Sir Alan Ayckbourn. 'I think rep gives you a trust that sometimes, not always but sometimes, a thing can happen right first time. In a read-through of a play an actor can hit it so right that you want to jump up and say, "You've got it!" Very often you say to people, "Trust that first instinct." There are other times when the weeks that follow the first read-through will uncover all sorts of treasures that you would never get at in an ordinary weekly rep situation. There are also things you discover in a weekly situation that you can discover pretty fast if you want to. There are things that, if they come together on day one, then you ought to leave them alone.'

As Richard Pasco observed earlier, rehearsal in weekly rep chiefly consisted of learning the lines and not bumping into the furniture. There was rarely time for the finer points of characterization. Patricia Marmont endorses this point of view, 'In terms of characterization, nothing was ever discussed. It was what you brought to it', as does Peter Jeffrey, 'There was not time to dig and delve into character, you had to learn the lines and get the play on.' A further reason for this, apart from the time factor, is that knowledge of psychology, certainly as expounded by Freud, is a relatively recent acquisition for most people, when set against thousands of years of acting traditions. Many chose to stick to more tried and tested text-based study.

Edward Jewesbury says that, 'Characterization was not very subtly done. Obviously you would discuss who your character was, but the psychological side of the work has developed much more over the years. Shaw was interested in the words, which were wonderful and that was his approach to it, that you get it all through the language.' Maurice Denham, who began his acting career in Hull in 1934, declares, 'Characterization never worried me, if you think and feel hard, you become the other person.' Gemma Jones takes a different tack: rather than translate herself into another person, she attempts to project herself into the situation that faces the character she is playing. 'If you try to pretend to be someone else it is never quite as true. When I was younger I think I tried to be somebody else, but I think I've become more confident about coming back to being a version of me, with all the technicalities that one acquires.' Hilary Mason explains that an actor's development of character is not something which occurs in isolation. 'Your character was often formed by the people you were working with, often you'd have an idea about a character and then during rehearsals you'd think, "Well I can't play it like that because so and so is doing something similar." Your level was set by what other people were doing too.'

Broadly speaking, an actor's approach to a role falls into one of two camps. One is the text-based strategy that Edward Jewesbury referred to when he was talking about the importance which Bernard Shaw placed on words. In this, Jewesbury finds himself in sympathy with Sir Derek Jacobi, who says, 'You couldn't, dare I say it, waste time with too much chat about characterization. It was a question of doing rather than talking about doing. It's very easy, it's very attractive, to talk a part, to spend a day talking about it and then you get up on your feet and it's very different. I always try to work from the inside out. I envy people who say, "Oh, if I've got the right shoes I've got the character." If only it were easy as that, I'm always a bit suspicious of that. I tried to always be true to what I thought the playwright was getting at. I thought and still think that the most important person in the process is the man who wrote the play, without whom directors couldn't direct, lighters couldn't light and I couldn't act. I think you need to be true to what was written and to explore, to explore the words, not to show off one's talent as an actor but to take that as read for oneself. I'm an actor, I can act. Now let me put that at the disposal, at the service of this particular play by this particular man. I'm very much into text rather than externals. I want to make it sound right, to sound real, as if it were spoken thought, that behind what was being said there was a person, not necessarily me, that was coming through me. I couldn't do very much to alter the way I looked although I tried, but that was somehow less important than making what they heard sound real.'

Jennie Goossens is another who gives the text supremacy. 'You get your character out of the script. You beetle through it looking for clues rather like a detective, then in your mind you put the person together.' Peter Copley agrees. 'You are bound by the script and what the script reveals.' He speaks in cautionary terms about the other main approach to creating a character, which is predominantly visual. 'In rep a visual approach, funny voices, accents, walks, served for the creation of character, but in fact obscured it.'

There are many who would qualify this statement, for whom the creation of a visual entity is crucial in discovering the emotional truth of the character they are playing. Nyree Dawn Porter says, 'I always work out what the character looks like first, but basically there's nothing like shovelling in the lines. In rep you had to make your strokes boldly, quickly, as fast as you could and as well as you could and then the audience taught you the rest. It's a very courageous way of working but it is also very wonderful.' Richard Bebb is more specific, 'One always tried to find the character's walk.' Daniel Massey describes how he came unstuck with one role during rehearsals and that it was the discovery of particular visual clues which put him back on track, although he is careful to stress that one must not rely upon externals alone. 'You took a pragmatic approach to characterization. There are times when you get into a bind in the theatre and you can't put your finger on it and this happened to me when I was playing Luke Finch in some comedy and I said to Michael Bryant, who was in the company with me, "I'm in a terrible confusion about this part," and he said, "Take a piece of paper and write down on it gesture, accent, where you come from, how you walk, what you wear," and that helped me start to put things together rationally and logically. I'm a terrific pragmatist, but if I haven't got the character inside then there's no point in me going outside. It may not work, but unless I've formed some kind of empathy or understanding with the character then it hasn't got much meaning for me and it won't have much meaning for the audience.'

Part of the pragmatism adopted by many actors, bred by the shortage of time, was the use of certain short cuts, as Estelle Kohler points out. 'Time means organic growth; when you are short of time you have to take short cuts. We managed and the standard was quite high.' Paul Daneman describes a tendency which he observed in himself and his fellow actors. 'We used short cuts to characterization, modelling ourselves on actors who'd played the parts in London, rather like painters copying Great Masters.' In Stephanie Cole's opinion, 'I think the danger in the old days of weekly rep was that if people did that sort of rep for too long they took very short cuts and easy routes to things, they lost the facility to go down deep into themselves, so sometimes the acting became rather shallow.' Dorothy Tutin started in rep when she was very young, with the following consequence, 'I didn't really use short cuts because I was too inexperienced to know what they were.

But you could pick up bad habits like indicating an emotion without thinking it through and doing the subtle thing with it. There isn't the time to do the subtleties at all, but the plays that they were choosing to do were not those sort of plays. *The Admirable Crichton* and *Julius Caesar* are very well-made plays and you're not going to have to search for ways to make them work. They chose good plays that were done straight.' Sir Peter Hall summarizes the situation: 'In rep the actor's first priority was to learn the lines, then he might think about acting, then he might think about relating to the other actors. Everybody learned to cut corners in everything you can think of, but on the other hand, rough and ready though it was, it was often ready, surprisingly.'

The taking of short cuts was not limited to the actors, managements often resorted to one particular economy, the mention of which can strike fear into a performer's heart. This was the use of part or cue scripts. In these, the actor received only his own lines and the three words of the line before his, which gave him his cue to speak or enter. The result could be baffling, as Alec McCowen explains. 'I worked with cue scripts, you didn't know what the plot of the play was or how long your waits were. It was a revelation when you actually heard the entire play. They were very grubby little oblong things, very raggedy with bits missing. Maybe it was something to do with economizing with paper because of the war, but I think it went back further than that.' Derek Nimmo believes that to some actors, who were reared on them, these scripts became indispensable. 'One of the things one used to get were part scripts. You never knew what the play was about. You'd just think, "Oh, I haven't got many words in this." You didn't know how it all fitted together. Some actors were so used to that. Later on I worked with Robertson Hare. He'd get a BBC television script and he'd turn it into a cue script. He used to write it out in immaculate copperplate writing because he couldn't work in any other way.'

It is possible that learning by this method could have a detrimental effect on the final performance, in Vilma Hollingbery's opinion. 'When I first started, in the early Fifties, we used cue scripts. They were banned in the mid-Fifties. You were given however many sheets of paper with your lines on stapled together. There were your lines and just the last line of the speech before. You had no idea what the play was about until you came to rehearsal on the first day. This is what caused people to learn like parrots. You were learning lines without being sure of the context of them.' She mentions that cue scripts were eventually banned, which was partly in response to disgruntled companies, who were fed up with using them. One who agitated on this issue was Paul Daneman. 'I was involved in a strike about cue scripts when I was at Guildford because they were so terrible to work with,' although Sir Peter Hall is not wholly in sympathy over this. He argues, 'Shakespeare's company weren't acquainted with his plays until they all sat down and read them together.'

Once the lines had been learnt, the moves decided upon and the nature of the characters established, the trauma of the dress rehearsal arrived, when the production and all its component parts, of scenery, costumes and props, came together for the first time. Nowadays it is customary to have a technical rehearsal first to iron out any hitches, so that the dress rehearsal can take place in performance conditions. This was not always the case. In weekly rep there was not enough time to separate the technical from the dress rehearsal, giving rise to an ordeal for the actor, as Alec McCowen recalls. 'Dress rehearsals were *hell* in weekly rep. Quite often one didn't finish them and the curtain would go up and you hadn't done the third act.' The alternative to this was equally ghastly, as Philip Voss says. 'When I was at Ipswich dress rehearsals went on until four in the morning.' Michael Simpkin's story gives an insight into the kind of wrinkles ironed out by a technical rehearsal: 'I was in a play at Southampton called *Hawks and Doves* and an actor had to come on during a scene when I was standing on these wind-swept hills. Without speaking to me he had to get from his bag a succession of bird whistles which he would blow and I'd say, "Owl", then he'd blow on another one and I'd say, "Woodcock", and so on. They sent for some bird whistles from a sporting gun shop in London. We were trying out this scene during the technical rehearsal and the actor didn't know what each of the whistles was. He got one out and it made a rather pleasant noise and so I said, "Woodcock". Then he blew on another one and I said something like, "Wood pigeon". Then he pulled out another one and it was a referee's whistle and he blew it and I said, "Foul".' Light relief is an essential mechanism if the company is to remain good humoured through what can be a long and gruelling day.

Daniel Massey voices what many think when he says, 'Acting requires an enormous amount of very detailed hard work to make it look simple.' Given this, it is astonishing that anybody ever found time to have a life outside the rehearsal room, but some people managed. Alec McCowen now marvels at what he managed to pack in. 'I have my diaries of that time [the 1940s] and I seemed to go to the movies at least twice a week, I used to read two books a week, I had my bike and I used to bike into the country. We only rehearsed in the mornings. I think they thought that was all you needed. I don't remember learning lines at all, I used to do that on the way to the theatre from the digs.' He may well have been the exception which proved the rule, for what most people cannot forget is a pervasive feeling of exhaustion. Among them is Philip Voss: 'I remember being so tired that I had to lie down during a session of notes from the director.' Judy Campbell was another who had difficulty staying awake. 'The work was so hard and we were tired all the time, once I went to sleep on top of an upright piano in the rehearsal room,' and Richenda Carey probably speaks for anybody who has ever survived the rigours of rep when she says, 'One was whimpering with fatigue. We worked thirteen hours a day, thirteen days a fortnight, for nine pounds ten a week.'

10

Scenery and Costume

*'The flats applauded far more than the audience, when you shut the door the
whole set went, "Clap, clap, clap, clap."'*

William Franklyn

WHILE THE ACTORS were busy in rehearsal, another central department
within the theatre was working flat out. The designer, who was sometimes assisted by a scenic artist but more often than not painted the
scenery himself, and the stage carpenter were faced with the challenge
of devising a new set for every production, be it weekly, fortnightly or
longer. Often they were working within parameters which meant that
artistic vision took second place to pragmatism, although there are
designers whose talent was such that both these flourished side by side.
Of the artists who stand out one is Tom Osborne Robinson, who regularly dazzled the audience in Northampton over many years (while at
the same time managing to design the window display for Liberty's
every Christmas). Another was Hutchinson Scott, who began his
working life at the Oxford Playhouse and the Bristol Old Vic before an
illustrious career in the West End. John Moffatt says of him, 'He was a
wonderful designer and he used to turn out these sets every week,
which were well up to West End standards.' Latterly, Philip Prowse
deserves special mention for his innovative work at the Glasgow
Citizens Theatre as well as at the National.

However, these examples are largely atypical and many of the
smaller weekly reps made do with the likes of Lewis Nanton and
George Dougal, who worked with Derek Nimmo in Bolton and
Clacton-on-Sea respectively. He says, 'There was a resident scenic

artist at Bolton called Lewis Nanton, who was also the character actor. I shared a dressing-room with Lewis Nanton, who smelt of size.' Of George Dougal, Derek Nimmo says, 'When I was in Clacton-on-Sea we had a proper scenic artist who didn't act at all, well he occasionally acted, he was called George Dougal, and he was Maltese and there weren't many Maltese scenic artists around and we were doing a play called *The Deep Blue Sea* by Terence Rattigan and one of the things we needed was a picture of Weymouth pier, a painting that was referred to in one of the acts or something. Anyway the dress rehearsal came and the set was built and there was a large picture of an old gentleman in ermine with a coronet and Lord Weymouth underneath it.'

The majority of reps had their work cut out for them, labouring against the clock and with very few resources. Speaking of his time at the Esplanade Pavilion on the Isle of Wight in the 1940s, William Franklyn declares, 'If I said the sets at Ryde were cornflake boxes with three-ply behind, over-painted by anyone who happened to be passing with a brush, that would be a fairly generous description. The budget down there could have been a hundred pounds a week for a set that now would cost eight or nine thousand.' Of more recent times Robin Herford says, 'At Scarborough between 1986 and 1988 we had a budget of three thousand pounds for sets and costumes for each production.' In neither case do the sums involved stretch very far, with the result that flimsy canvas flats were continuously recycled.

Vilma Hollingbery describes a standard rep set. 'The sets were usually boxed sets with a French window at the back and a grand piano somewhere. At the end of the week we had to turn the set around and paint the other side.' Timothy West remembers, 'If you were a well-set-up company you painted the spare set of flats during the week, to be brought in on the Monday. If not, you painted the same ones the night before.' According to Richenda Carey, 'At Derby they painted the flats until they buckled,' while April Walker describes the practice at the Civic Theatre, Chesterfield: 'We only had a certain number of flats, so they had to be painted over and over. When they couldn't take any more and the cracks in the paint were showing, they had to be hosed down. Either that, or they'd be covered endlessly in different wallpapers. Curtains were made out of lining material that could be got very cheaply, or from ends of rolls. They used to get in touch with material factories to see if they had any flawed material they were chucking out.' At Frinton in 1966 they coped with the same difficulties in a slightly different way, as Christopher Honer explains, 'They used the same set every week, but with the flats in a different order.' The effort of creating a set on demand every week or so was wearing. It is no surprise that Alison Steadman says of her time in Lincoln, 'I remember coming in on Monday mornings to find bodies lying everywhere fast asleep covered in paint, having just got the set up.'

By definition, the flats were temporary structures and not very robust. William Franklyn says, 'They applauded far more than the audience; when you shut the door the whole set went "Clap, clap, clap, clap."' Belinda Lang remembers being rather dashed during a season at Frinton, 'We thought we were doing really exciting work, really at the cutting edge, till a friend of mine came to see *Private Lives* and he said, "I don't know why you're so pleased with yourselves, the sets wobble."'

Once the hard work of getting the flats into position was accomplished, the set then had to be 'dressed' with furniture, ornaments, curtains, carpets and pictures. Enter the trusty ASM. Michael Kilgarriff describes his involvement in the process in this way. 'On Saturday night we struck the set and on Sunday mornings we had to come in to the scene store, which was about half a mile away, and move all the flats on a hand cart through the streets. I also had the hand cart to get the furniture on a Monday morning.' As with props, the furniture was usually borrowed from private houses or local shops. Kilgarriff says, 'On one occasion we turned up for the dress rehearsal on a Monday morning and we had put this great big wardrobe on the stage and it had gone! The furniture firm had an advert in the programme and someone in the audience had seen the wardrobe, gone along to the shop and said, "Can we have one of those?" and the firm had said, "That's the only one we've got," and they had come along and taken it off the stage.' He remembers a similar disaster occurring when a local hotel loaned the theatre some of their furniture. 'We were doing *Death on the Nile* and the producer said, "This play's set on a boat on the Nile and I think we should have some wickerwork chairs." I borrowed some from a local hotel, but on the Saturday morning at the end of the run I got a call from the hotel manager. He said, "I'm terribly sorry but we've got a function and we're going to need all our stuff back."'

Because so many items were borrowed, enormous care had to be taken so that they came to no harm. Harry Hanson was a stickler for that and Carmen Silvera recalls that he insisted on certain edicts being obeyed. 'One was that the flowers on stage must be right for the season in which the play was set and that every night they must be wrapped up in tissue paper and put in their boxes. All the lampshades that were used on set had to be covered in tissue paper every night, so that when we rehearsed on stage in the morning no dust would get on them and they would not be dirtied. Everything was protected so that his sets always looked good.'

Lighting played an important part in the visual concept of a play. No matter how much work went into showing the set off to its best advantage, the effort was wasted if it could not be seen by the audience. Ian Mullins describes the design process from the director's point of view. 'In terms of scenery you designed around your stock of flats. Nowadays, designers tend not to paint as well as they used to, in days gone by it did depend tremendously on the designer being a good painter because you couldn't afford three-dimensional sets. In areas of design and particularly lighting design, enormous strides have been made. When I was first directing, I used to do the lighting design and the electrician said, "These are the lights you've got and this is where they are." The director had to produce the ground plan with all the lights placed. On Saturday night when the previous set came down, the electrician would rig the new lights and on Monday morning we would do the lighting with the cues. By modern standards the lighting was fairly primitive, but on the other hand, we did achieve some remarkable effects – you can go far with little. These days you get catastrophes when the computer crashes and no one can do anything about it. In the old days it was hands on, it was human error.' Shaun Sutton remembers battling with fairly primitive systems as a director. 'We used to overload the switchboard. I used to light all my own plays, there were no lighting designers, you see. I used to do things like the sun going round from window to window. I was always overloading the whole thing and sometimes we'd blow the fuse.'

An account of the elementary apparatus available comes from Derek Nimmo, 'We had footlights and strips, occasionally we managed to get a couple of spots, but it was very flat and boring.' This inadequate equipment was sometimes operated by people with few qualifications and without rehearsal. Alan Bennion describes the conditions in Colwyn Bay, 'At the Prince of Wales Theatre . . . we never properly rehearsed the lighting. The actual switchboard was terribly old-fashioned. A lady from Rhos-on-Sea in a flowered hat would come in for the first night, but she wasn't available for the dress rehearsal.' In these circumstances it is hardly surprising that the effects created lacked subtlety. Alec McCowen describes the kind of thing that used to happen. 'You very seldom these days see actors with light switches, but then you had to be so careful, you put your hand on the light switch and left it there and there was a colossal noise while the electrician heaved on the handle and the lights came on.'

Once the set was up and lit, all that was needed was the actors, but they too required dressing. Under the terms of the Esher Standard Contract, which Equity had negotiated with all regional companies, the artist was expected to provide his or her own costumes for everything other than period plays, when the management would hire them from a costumier. The contract stipulates, 'All character and special costumes and wigs shall be provided by the Manager. No Artist shall be required to provide any costume that could not ordinarily be used by him in his private capacity. A male Artist receiving a weekly salary of £8 or less shall not be required to provide more than two ordinary walking suits and one evening suit.' Moray Watson describes what he was asked to supply. 'Just before I started my first job they gave me a list of what you should have in rep – a dinner jacket, a dark suit, grey flannel trousers, sports jacket, brown shoes, black shoes, patent leather shoes, shirts, ties. You didn't have to have riding breeches or plus fours.'

Often the number of costumes actors accumulated over the years influenced their employability, as Barbara Lott remembers. 'There was an agent in those days called Miriam Warner, who was famous. A great big fat lady with a broad cockney accent and when you went to see her and put your head round her door she would say, "Got a good wardrobe, dear?"' Just as the scope of one's wardrobe could be instrumental in securing a job, its depletion could spell the end of employment. Alan Ayckbourn says, 'Someone rather cynically suggested that actors moved on from a rep when they'd exhausted their wardrobe.' Vilma Hollingbery recalls a certain amount of intolerance on the part of the audience, 'If you'd been in the same company for two or three years, you'd make your entrance, and you'd get an entrance round, then you might just hear someone say, "I've seen that before. She wore that dress in such and such."'

Vilma also remembers, 'We didn't know what part we would play next week until Saturday night. When I got the script I didn't look at the size of the part, the first thing I looked at were the number of costume changes.' This could be considerable. Janet Whiteside has this daunting recollection. 'I can remember one play twice nightly in Bradford when I wore riding kit, tennis kit, evening dress, a cocktail dress and a bikini.' This was quite a feat when the Esher Standard Contract only specifies, 'A female Artist receiving a weekly salary of £10 or less shall not be required to provide more than two ordinary day dresses, one evening dress and one two-piece suit.'

The designer had only a minimal involvement in the selection and provision of costume, as Carmen Silvera explains. 'The set designer would provide a drawing of what the set would be like, they didn't have time to make a model in those days, and at the top of the drawing would be all the colours he was going to use. We had to make sure that none of our clothes clashed with the colours he had chosen. On Fridays we would have a dress call after the morning's rehearsal and the director would say, "Yes that's all right," or, "Have you got something else?" Or "Why don't you wear a scarf with that?"' Michael Stroud describes the self-consciousness evoked by these dress calls, 'There's always that moment when everyone sneaks out of their dressing-rooms in their costumes and meets in the corridor and people go, "Oh, get you!" or "That's not your colour, dear," and all that goes on and you have to pretend you're not in it.' Tenniel Evans recalls one piece of advice that he was offered, 'If you're playing comedy you must have your suits lined with silk so that you keep cool.' Beyond that, little help was given and actors had to use their wits to find clothes when and where they could.

Of all the sources discovered by actors, the strangest was found by Derek Nimmo. 'On four pounds a week you couldn't afford much, but I formed a friendship with the local undertaker, who was extraordinarily helpful and I got all kinds of garments from him, I don't know where they came from but they were still sort of warm when I got them. I got a smoking jacket for half a crown, in lovely blue velvet, which I still wear, actually.' From the ridiculous to the sublime – Nancy Mansfield, during her time in Scotland, used to borrow clothes from the local nobility. 'In Dundee I wore this wonderful negligée because the Countess of Airlie had this collection of period clothes from her ancestors and whenever we were doing a play that required something a little bit special, she would say, "Come and look in my box." On one occasion I was going to some very big ball to do a draw, it was some big occasion and she lent me a gorgeous Edwardian dress, but dressed up with modern jewellery it was heavenly. It was black and covered in jet. It was very beautiful.' Vilma Hollingbery had similar good fortune, 'The Ladies' Theatrical Guild used to send us parcels of costumes, they were cast off clothes usually from very grand people, even royalty,' but for Barbara Leslie, who was working in Buxton shortly after the war when rationing was still in place, the struggle to dress herself week after week was considerable. 'The awful thing was, just after the war, nobody had any clothes, we were all on coupons. Equity gave you some ridiculous amount of coupons, but also when the New Look came in – when you're on the stage clothes always have to be longer to adjust for looking up. That was all a pain. You just had to beg, borrow, get second-hand clothes.'

Costumes were assembled with varying degrees of success, as Richenda Carey remembers, 'In a production of *The Country Wife* we used the ugly sister costumes from the pantomime. We had no corsets, just a steel ruler shoved down our bodices to stop them bending.' Occasionally one struck lucky, as Carmen Silvera found. 'There was a cloth market in Warrington on a Friday in those days and the traders used to take pride in the fact that we would go and shop there. One day one of them said to me, "I've got just the thing for you, darling, a bolt of unbleached satin. There's eighteen yards on the bolt. There's a flaw at the very end, but you won't notice it and you can have it for eleven and six." That was a miracle. I took it to the theatre and cut it into three-yard lengths, six different die buckets in the wardrobe, I had my sewing machine in the dressing-room, we used to cut the patterns from news-paper and the girl I shared a dressing-room with used to pin them on me.'

A sewing machine could be vital for an actress working in rep. Vilma Hollingbery confesses, 'It was the dressmaking that finished me. On Sundays I used to go mad, making things to wear to open in on Monday. I used to have a tiny sewing machine and I used to make what were called sheath dresses, they were completely straight. You either wore a stole with them or you put big bows on.' If you couldn't sew yourself, it was helpful to have a friend who could. Sheila Reid remembers, 'I had a friend who was a dab hand with the needle and a lot of bedspreads were turned into dresses.' People were forced to be endlessly inventive. Peggy Mount says, 'If you had an evening dress in a play one week, next week you'd turn it inside out and use it as a dressing gown.'

As a last resort, if an actress could not beg, borrow, steal or sew, there was the expensive alternative of hiring something, although the splendour of the hired costume ran the risk of putting others in the shade, as Eileen Atkins discovered. 'In one production I remember spending a lot of money, because you had to provide your own costumes, my character came back from an evening out, so I went to Manchester and hired an evening cloak. I was only the juvenile, and when she saw me, the leading lady shouted out, "She looks absolutely ridiculous, she can't wear that, she looks as if she's doing a Shakespearean play or something." So they found this absolutely ghastly short red velvet cape for me, which, now I come to think of it, was probably more correct.'

Having assembled a basic wardrobe, which demanded a certain amount of inventiveness in the first place, actors were able to extend the range of what they wore in a way that Alec McCowen describes, 'Ringing the changes in your clothes was a terrible business at a time of clothes rationing, so we all borrowed from each other. You didn't want to wear The Suit two weeks running. The hectic invention of changing your clothes, changing the make-up. Looking back on it, it was more like impersonating than acting. Try and have a different walk or a different accent. It was a very visual approach,' but as Philip Locke rightly points out, for a man it was particularly limiting. 'I think women have a much easier time in rep becaue they can go out and buy a blouse or some artificial flowers or a scarf or something to put on their basic costumes. With two suits and a dinner jacket it's much harder for men to ring the changes.' This is certainly true; although finding costumes could be more challenging for women, there was often more scope for them to extemporize. Brigid Panet makes this point. 'You were always in evening dress for one act, whether it was a working-, middle- or upper-class play. I had a ballet dress I covered with different materials each week, I painted my shoes to match.' John Warner found that there were fewer possibilities available to him. 'You had two suits and you rang the changes, you wore the top half one week and the bottom half the next.' In one instance, Simon Williams was able to rise to the occasion magnificently. 'I had a run of parts that called upon a plain grey suit I'd left school in. After thirteen weeks wearing this, I thought I'd make it look like a pinstripe and I got some tailor's chalk and a ruler and spent Sunday making pinstripes. It did look very fine; fairly fine. The leading man clapped me on the back and a cloud of dust came up, leaving a hand print of un-pinstriped suit.'

Getting the costume was by no means the end of the story. Even as late as the 1960s, lighting was considerably less sophisticated than it is now, and before that the use of footlights or floats meant that the make-up used in a theatre had to be applied in enormous detail. Sticks of Leichner greasepaint, particularly the flesh tones of Nos 5 and 9, were prominent in every dressing-room. John Warner became expert in transforming his appearance. 'You used make-up every week even playing a juvenile because you had to look entirely different. In those days we put red in the corner of our eyes and in our nostrils and, of course, we used false noses. I can't tell you the number of tramlines I used to put on. I think the peak of my rep performances was Fagin, when I was twenty-eight. I remember playing Fagin at Dundee and I took two hours doing my make-up with this plasticine nose. You could get nose putty, but I think I used plasticine. I know one matinée I'd done my two hours' make-up and went to the washbasin to wash my hands and I rubbed them all over my face!'

Simon Williams was given a useful hint on tramlines by an older member of the company. 'Bertie Heyhoe taught me to do character lines not with a cocktail stick but with a coin, you get a non-solid edge to them and they look better.' Daniel Massey had a penchant for false noses. 'I used to try and mould noses and particularly if you were playing the inspector in the third act, they used to fall off and land with a terrible thud, but that's how you learnt and it's what drew the punters in to see the play in a lot of ways.'

Phyllida Law went to great lengths in pursuit of an effect, as she describes. 'I used to make my own false noses out of a mould with Copydex. I was always most interested in that, it was my best favourite, costume and make-up. I made my own false eyelashes. The actor who became my husband had very strong hair and I used to make false eye-lashes out of it. I used to pull a thread across two hatpins and blanket stitch this hair on to this thread, trim them, roll them round a knitting needle, then trim them again and then put them on with eyelash glue and mascara.' Clare Welch remembers using a substance called Hot Black. 'We used to use Hot Black on our eyelashes, which you melted. It coated each eyelash and left a blob on the end, so that your eyes looked stunning but if you cried, God help you.'

When ageing up, Richard Briers was aware of how easily his hands could betray his real age on stage and found an ingenious remedy, 'Playing out of my range, I used to wear gloves a lot of the time so that I wouldn't have to make up the veins in my hands. The things we used to do! We used to take an hour and a half to get ready – all these Lake lines, No 5 and No 9 [Lake was a plum-coloured greasepaint applied in lines to age an actor's appearance].' Vilma Hollingbery found good use for her eyebrow pencil. 'With a brown eyebrow pencil I used to draw the seam for stockings on the back of my leg because I couldn't afford nylons.'

Make-up was not restricted to a performer's face, particularly in an era when black actors were not generally employed and white actors used to black up to play ethnic roles. Taking short cuts over the black-ing up could prove disastrous, as Alec McCowen discovered. 'In the days when I was in rep there were very few if any black actors and I remember on a couple of occasions playing black roles. One was the servant in a play called *The Petrified Forest* and I had to serve dinner in a big dinner-party scene, and I was serving and I'd made up my face and my neck and my hands, but that was all because I was in a nice costume. But my trousers caught on the back of a chair and ripped wide open and it was revealed that I was not totally black.' John Warner recalls cutting up small lengths of rubber gas piping and inserting them into each nostril to capture the nasal characteristics of a black role he was playing.

Invention is all, though nobody went to quite the lengths of Lewis Nanton, who shared a dressing-room with Derek Nimmo in Bolton. 'If he was playing a red-haired Scotsman, he was totally bald, he had a bag of horsehair and he'd stick it all on his head and put red grease-paint on it and it stayed on for the week. There was no laundry, and a lot of parts required stiff shirts, but Lewis used to shave his chest and paint white greasepaint on and then studs and then just put a collar round his neck. You couldn't tell from the front because the lights were so dim.' Nimmo mentions the fact that there was no laundry, which presented quite a problem for actors who had to wear stiff collars as part of their costume. As with all things, a way round this was soon devised. Apparently the best thing for getting greasepaint off a stiff collar is sliced white bread!

On the subject of wardrobe maintenance, Evangeline Banks says, 'I can't think how we did our washing, we didn't have washing machines or anything. There were always knickers drying in the dressing-room.' It wasn't only knickers which were hung out to dry. In the 1930s when heating backstage at the Oxford Playhouse was negligible, Rachel Kempson remembers that the costumes got so damp in the theatre they had to have a coal fire in the dressing rooms to dry them before wearing them. Another minefield facing the actor was the difficulty presented by wigs and additional forms of facial hair. Often they did not stay on, as Lionel Jeffries reports of an incident which occurred in Lichfield. 'They only had one toupée, I used to try and clean the lace of all this terrible spirit gum, one night I stepped forward when it was my turn to make the curtain speech and I'd forgotten to put the little bit of elastoplast on the back of the toupée and it fell forward over my eyes as I bowed, like a dead mole. I couldn't see the audience.' Josephine Tewson had a similar experience with some runaway ringlets. 'We did a play called *Quality Street*, in which there's a line, "Phoebe, Phoebe of the ringlets." I was playing Phoebe as well as stage managing and I had to get ready in such a rush that as the line was said, the ringlets in question fell off.' Facial hair could come unstuck as well, as Paul Williamson relates. 'Half my moustache fell off during a Christmas play at the Birmingham Rep. My character carried a dagger and I used it to hack off the other half, to a huge round of applause.'

Keeping hair in place was not the only problem. There was also the join. John Warner remembers, 'The wigs were terrible, with a lace join and you used No 3½ to cover the join so it blended in with your make-up. I remember an actor at Liverpool, Larry Payne, playing an old man and taking hours with his make-up to cover up the join and his aunt was in front that night and he asked her, "Could you see the join?" "Yes, beautifully," she said.' As with their costumes, actors also needed to ring the changes with their wigs. When she was working in rep in Barnsley Barbara Lott recalls, 'The man playing the lead said to me, "How do you think my wig looks?" and I said, "It looks fine," and he said, "I wore it last week turned round the other way."'

Sometimes headgear could be nothing short of unpleasant; Sheila

Reid in particular had a terrible experience. 'At Colchester I played the little old lady with the parrot in the cage in *Ghost Train*. I had this wig with a lovely furry hat on top. During the interval I took my fur hat off in order to titivate the wig and sitting on top of my head was a mouse. It had been nesting in my hat. I got my hat on and it had been on my head for the whole of the first act.'

Wigs could be hideously inappropriate, as Malcolm Farquhar discovered to his cost when he appeared on stage in his first big part wearing a blond wig in a Scottish play called *Jeannie* and overheard someone in the audience say, 'That's that new girl Jane Hillary, that is.' Dulcie Gray was so appalled by a wig provided for her in one production at Harrogate, because it made her look like Harpo Marx, that she refused to wear it. When the management offered her a choice between using the wig or getting the sack, she chose the sack.

Once the actors had their appearance sorted out, their problems were not necessarily over. If the costume does not look right it can have an undermining effect on the artist's entire performance, as Suzanne Bertish testifies, 'It is very painful walking out on stage in a costume that you know is wrong, very, very painful.' Because of actors' vulnerability, if anything went amiss with their costume on stage, the result was mortifying. Virginia Stride recalls an oversight she made. 'When I was twenty-three I played an old woman in a play called *The Potting Shed*. I had gone to tremendous trouble to put on a false nose and a widow's hump, I was wearing an old tweed suit, an old tweed hat and a pair of shoes that were a couple of sizes too small for me and they pinched. I used to leave it to the last moment to put them on and wear my own shoes till then. One matinée I looked down and saw I was still in my high-heeled court shoes. Luckily in that theatre there were still footlights, so I don't suppose a lot of people saw them.' Donald Pickering came even further unstuck: 'When I did *The Little Hut* at Canterbury I played The Stranger, and I played the whole thing in a loincloth, and somebody pinched it. There was no other costume, so they had to get a pair of underpants for me quickly.'

Sometimes costumes disappeared altogether, on other occasions they came loose during a performance. Francesca Ryan had a sticky moment, 'When I was playing Lady Fidget at Lancaster I had this magnificent red silk dress with panniers, which came out to about the width of my arms, and the hooks that attach the skirt to the bodice came adrift and it started to drop, but I grabbed it. For the rest of the scene my movement was really limited because I had to keep hold of my skirt.' This little, localized difficulty pales into insignificance beside Sheila Reid's ordeal. 'I was doing a play at Carlisle and our leading man took fright after the dress rehearsal and ran away. Robert David MacDonald was directing us and he had to take over the leading role, which was rather a sophisticated gentleman in an evening suit, and I was playing his wife. I had managed to borrow from a shop in the town a strapless white evening dress. Robert was terrified, he knew the lines, but he hadn't acted since he was at Oxford. He had to kiss me, we had this great embrace, then he shot me and as I slithered to the ground in a dramatic dying fall, both my breasts popped out of the dress and there was nothing I could do – I was dead. He lifted me up and stuffed me on to the ottoman, hysterical with laughter, which meant he was completely relaxed for the rest of the show.' Decades earlier the veteran rep actress Marie Fontaine had to overcome an equally embarrassing moment, as Peggy Mount describes, 'My first part was playing the maid in *Hindle Wakes*. There was a wonderful woman in the company called Marie Fontaine, who had been in the original Court Players. She was a tall, very beautiful old lady. She walked on to the stage to a foul gust of laughter – I looked at her and she'd forgotten to put her petticoat on. She was wearing one of those see-through dresses and you could see her corset. You could understand the audience laughing. When she came off I said, "Miss Fontaine, you've not put your petticoat on," and she looked down, went into her dressing-room, put her petticoat on and walked straight back on that stage and, of course, she got an ovation, even in Keighley in Yorkshire. It was a brave thing to do.'

Minor hitches occur as Nicola Pagett found when her zipper became stuck as she was starting a striptease on stage in Worthing. Nudity in the theatre brings its own particular pitfalls, as Alison Steadman discovered. 'I remember doing *The Prime of Miss Jean Brodie* and I played Sandy. It was my first nude scene. I had my back to the audience – but my front to the actors! It was very embarrassing! They gave me this body stocking, it's kind of more embarrassing than having no clothes on, it's like having a pair of very see-through tights all over yourself. It hides nothing. I tried this thing on and I thought, "This is more embarrassing than having nothing on," so I just took my clothes off. The local journalist, who was well known in the town, got in through the stage door, climbed up into the flies and was watching me in this scene. It was rather nasty and he was actually caught and ticked off.'

The problems costumes can cause for actors are legion. Jean Anderson remembers appearing in Cambridge in an avant-garde play by Joseph Gordon Macleod, who was running the Festival Theatre there in the late 1930s. 'Joseph Gordon Macleod used to write plays himself, very odd, very modern, very episodic, very strange and we generally had to do one of those each season. In one I was a tree, I can't think why I was a tree looking back at it now, but I was. There was quite a lot of music in it. I was pregnant at the time and I was absolutely static playing this tree in a rather beautiful costume. Some dancers had to dance round me and the BO was so terrible when they were dancing that I passed clean out. It was such a strange play that the audience thought there was nothing wrong with a tree toppling over!'

Philip Voss says, 'When costumes were hired for period plays, often they arrived two sizes too small and that's how you ended up playing the part.' Shaun Sutton remembers a production in which 'the actors had to cut the collars off their shirts so that they were period, and I remember Patrick Cargill wearing the same shirt – it was one of those plays that went on for ever – for sixty years'. That sort of thing can puncture illusions carefully created for the audience, as can the incidents like the one Stephen Hancock describes. 'It was the depths of winter and we were doing *Queen Elizabeth Slept Here*, which is set in the summer with all the characters complaining about the heat. I had to do one of these exits on one side of the theatre and re-appear on the other and it was snowing and I came on with snow all over my costume.'

Sometimes the sheer size of the costumes can wreak havoc, as Jill Gascoine found out during her time at Leicester, 'At Christmas we did *Beauty and the Beast*. It was one of my greatest parts, I've never been quite as good as I was as that lady dragon! I made a dragon costume which was really quite spectacular for someone who couldn't sew, but I stuffed the tail with something that was too heavy and I dragged it on during the dress rehearsal and knocked down all the stand-up trees. Also I couldn't stand up in it, I had to kneel down.' Tenniel Evans was brought to his knees unwittingly by the costume he was wearing in a Northampton production of *A Midsummer Night's Dream*. His wife

Evangeline Banks takes up the story. 'Tenniel and I played Theseus and Hippolyta. We had the most terrifying costumes with sort of breastplates, I looked exactly like Britannia. Tenniel had a breastplate which had been made for an actor called Niall MacGinnis, who was enormous. Tenniel sat down and the breastplate hit the chair between his legs, forcing it up, and he was so small inside he could hardly see over the top. Then on the first night the designer said, "I'm sorry to spring this on you at the last minute," and he threw round Tenniel's shoulders a sort of gold lamé stole. Tenniel staggered on with this and we sat down and watched the Mechanicals' play, after which the Wedding March struck up and we had to walk out. Tenniel was getting shorter and shorter and shorter and I whispered, "What's the matter?" and he said, "I'm walking up my fucking stole!"'

The most grisly story about costumes comes from Michael Stroud. 'I remember doing *Mother Goose* at the Belgrade Theatre in Coventry and there was an elderly lady who spent the summers tap-dancing and tearing up newspapers on the end of the pier and in the winter she arrived with this huge skip with a goose costume – have goose, will travel – and on the first preview she had these new flippers and as she went on she tripped on her own feet and her hands were inside the costume so she couldn't do anything but just fall, on to her beak, and broke her nose, so we went on, we were playing Willy and Nilly, another actor and I, and we got her on her feet and she finished that scene, but as she was doing that obviously in great distress, all the front of her neck, all white feathers, started to go scarlet with blood. And all the children who were asked to do a project on it the next day, did drawings of this white goose looking like a red robin.'

Despite their potential dangers, costumes were of great value to actors, as Lynn Farleigh explains, 'Costumes were very important, you relied a lot upon your costume.' Actors would take great care to keep them looking their best, as Simon Williams recalls. 'Clarkson Rhodes, a variety artiste who worked at Worthing rep, used to come down to the stage with his trousers on a hanger, and sit in the wings waiting for his entrance. When his cue came, he put his trousers on and made his entrance. This was an old rule, to prevent trousers bagging at the knee.' Nobody could have been more diligent than Daphne Palmer, who took her concern for her wardrobe to extraordinary lengths. She was doing a play called *The Odd Couple* at the Intimate Theatre in Palmer's Green, which had a very suspect boiler in the basement. On the first night during the second act smoke started pouring out from beneath the stage. Suddenly the curtain came down and everyone was evacuated from the theatre, but instead of rushing out, she went straight downstairs to the dressing-rooms to rescue her costumes.

11

First Nights

'You have no safety net on stage, you really are doing a high-wire act,
hundreds of feet up.'

Sir Derek Jacobi

THE CULMINATION OF the work of all the many departments – the actors, the director, stage management, the scenic workshops and the electricians – comes on the first night, which in weekly rep was usually on a Monday. With contributions from so many different sources, as with any jigsaw, it can sometimes be difficult to fit the pieces together, particularly if rehearsal time has been short. Most companies rely on the technical and dress rehearsals to iron out any wrinkles, but it is not uncommon for these to be truncated if time is running out. The first night can occasionally become a disaster into which actors slip head-long, although most of the time they escape by the skin of their teeth. Either way, the moment of walking out in front of hundreds of people can be grim, as Derek Jacobi reveals, 'First nights were an ordeal, they always are. If you were under-rehearsed it was always worse. But the excitement was extraordinary, the buzz, the sense of job satisfaction was amazing.'

Ray Cooney tells a classic tale of the kind of crisis which can occur when the adrenalin is flowing in torrents round an actor's frightened body. 'When I was in Blackburn I witnessed my first case of stage fright. There was a play called *We Must Kill Toni*, which was a good old rep pot-boiler. It was the story of two brothers who are planning whether to marry or murder their girl cousin, whose name is Toni, because she's inherited all the family money. The curtain goes up in this baronial hall with these two brothers in dinner jackets smoking cigars with brandy glasses in their hands and there's a pause and one brother says, "Marriage or murder?" and the other brother says, "Murder or marriage?" and then there's a thirty-minute scene where they discuss what they're going to do to Toni. These two guys are never off the stage, they're really long roles. Come the first night, I went round to wish my fellow actor good luck and I knocked on the door of his dressing-room and there was no reply. I put my head in and there he was being sick in the sink. I said, "What's the matter?" and he said, "I cccccan't go on." "What do you mean?" I asked him and he said, "I don't know a word." I said, "Of course you do," but I thought, "God, I've got half an hour with this man." He was shaking, he hadn't got his clothes on or anything and it was five minutes before we were meant to go on. I said, "You'll be all right, we know it, we've been rehearsing it. You say, "Marriage or murder," and I say "Murder or marriage," and we're away." We gave him brandy and the ASM got him dressed and he was still shaking. We got him upstairs and into his chair and we stuck the cigar in his hand and the brandy glass and that's all shaking and I'm thinking, "God I've got half an hour with him" and I said, "You'll be all right, once we get over the first bit."

'The music starts, the curtain goes up, there's a hell of a long pause, the brandy glass is shaking and finally he says, "Marra or murdidge?" and all I could think of to say was, "Murdige or marra?" The audience were totally bemused and he didn't know he'd gone wrong. After that I was shaking like crazy and he was all right. The irony was that the local critic said, "Mr Travers (he was the other actor) gave a very good performance, but Mr Cooney seemed singularly ill at ease."'

'Singularly ill at ease' is an understatement for the kind of trauma that a performer puts himself through on a first night. One comparison often quoted in a terrified whisper in the wings before the curtain first goes up is that it is equivalent to the shock induced by a minor car accident. Picture that every Monday night! Nerves can play terrible tricks on an actor and often lead him to commit unforced errors, as William Franklyn shows in the following account. 'A story was told by Leonard Rossiter about the first night of a rep production and one of the cast was playing Inspector Mainwaring. It was an old-fashioned three-act play and he was due to come on at the end of the first act to interview a family where a murder had taken place. By the end of the first act all the members of the cast had been on and given their performances and they came into his dressing-room and said, "Look, it's going terribly well, they can't wait for you to arrive." And then someone else would come in and say, "By the way, the murder was a great success, it's all going very well." In the meantime, the man playing the inspector would be turning his collar up, turning it down, thinking which was the most appropriate, looking in the mirror, putting his hat on, turning the brim up, turning the brim down, taking the hat off and putting it under his arm. Again somebody came in and said, "They can't wait, it's really going beautifully, it's all set up." By this time the man was getting even more nervous. He came to the moment when it was time to go down to the stage. The cast were all onstage, the doorbell rings, the lady of the house goes to the door and opens it centre stage and there is our man, who says, "You are Inspector Mainwaring, I am Mrs Chapman." And with that the curtain slowly came down.'

Ways of dealing with stage fright are described by Malcolm Farquhar. 'The worst thing about weekly rep was the unbelievable nerves of every Monday night. People went to the loo four or five times. They said, "Don't look at the script or you'll dry." Between the end of the dress rehearsal and the start of the performance, I used to go to the cinema. I've seen no end of films halfway through because I used to come out at half-past six, because it was the only way I could cope with forgetting the whole horrible thing.' Jocelyne Page remembers being so scared that she felt she could not go on at all. 'At the Oxford Playhouse I did a music hall production with Peter Hall playing the piano, Ronnie Barker and Maggie Smith, and we all did these numbers and I was so frightened on the first night that I couldn't go on. On the second night Peter Hall left the piano and pushed me on and I got an encore!' Philip Voss remembers being gripped with terror. 'In weekly and fortnightly rep I never dared to listen to the other actors during a performance until possibly the Saturday matinée. All one knew was, "Now I speak, now I speak, he's stopped, now I speak." By about the Saturday matinée one thought, "Oh, that's what you're saying to me." Truly.'

Another actor afflicted by Monday nights was Rosemary Harris, 'I was terrified on the first nights, terrified, but only terrified of not remembering my lines. I remember making my little bed on Monday mornings, kneeling down and saying a little prayer as I smoothed the sheets and tucked the blankets in. It was almost a superstition, saying, "Please God, let me get through this without too much disaster," looking longingly at the bed and thinking it will happen, I will be back in this bed and all will be well.' Jan Francis was so frightened she would not remember her lines on a first night in Cheltenham that she resorted to a desperate remedy. 'On the first night I had the most appalling fit of nerves. Luckily it was a small part and I wrote it out on the palm of my hand, but I got so hot and bothered and agitated that when I turned my hand over to look at it, it was just a blue puddle. It was a pretty nightmarish experience. I went back later on and did a couple of plays and at one point they asked if I'd like to play Juliet and I looked at my hand and said, "I don't think I've got enough space to write the lines."'

Peter McEnery believes that the fear which drives actors in this situation is not that they will forget what they have to say, but something more deep-rooted. 'You hope you'll remember your lines, but you don't fear forgetting them because you'll get yourself out of it or your fellow actors will get you out of it and the audience never knows anyway. What actors fear, and this is true in rep as well, is failure in front of their peers.'

To be judged by one's peers and found wanting, or worse, to let the rest of the company down, is something an actor cannot quickly forget. Peter Meakin describes an excruciating experience which has been branded into his memory. 'I was in *Our Day Out* by Willie Russell at the Belgrade Theatre, Coventry. It's a real problem for me doing musicals because I can't sing. God knows why they gave me the part. During rehearsals we just had the piano accompanying us. At the dress rehearsal we had the full band, but between that and the first performance they moved its location. When I came out to sing my awful solo song I couldn't hear them. I thought, "Oh bollocks, this is just what I need," and I came in on what I thought was the right beat and hoped was the appropriate note, but I started on the third beat instead of the first. There were hundreds of people out there. I felt like a kid who is made to stand up and sing to the whole school to show how bad he is. The band didn't stop playing, so I carried on and they played on. It was awful.'

Faced with the prospect of ordeals such as that, it is not surprising that performers suffer as they do. Alec McCowen admits, 'I used to find Mondays very terrifying. I was quite often literally sick. I remember doing a Noël Coward play called *I Leave It to You* and I had to leave the stage several times and throw up in the wings. They gave me a bucket because I was so churned up. Yet by the end of the week I was quite stale, looking forward to the next one.' Richard Pasco underwent similar torture, although he was helped to overcome his feelings of nausea by the manageress of the Birmingham Rep. 'H. Nancy Burman cured me of my nerves. She would knock on the door and say, "Richard, have you been sick yet?" "Any minute now." "Well, we're going to take the curtain up in five minutes so you'd better get on with it."'

The impression of being ill-prepared frequently permeated every area of the production. Simon Williams remembers, 'On the first night there was often an announcement made to the cast, "Ladies and Gentlemen, will you be careful not to touch the back wall during Act One until it's dried off."' If this announcement wasn't made there could be terrible consequences, as Peggy Mount describes. 'We were doing *Twelfth Night* and Johnny Myers went straight on to the stage, sat down, and the paint wasn't dry on the seat so it all came off on his trousers.'

The scenic artists were slow on this occasion, on others the stage management hadn't quite got their act together, usually because they had not been given the opportunity to practise the scene changes. Michael Simpkin says, 'I did a season for Alan Ayckbourn in Scarborough in 1987. We did a new play called *Tapster*. But because the theatre is in the round at Scarborough, it means you can't set any props in advance. There's always a little delay after the house lights go down when the stage managers come on and set props before the play starts. At the start of *Tapster* a coal bucket has to be set and on the first night, the world première of the play, I'm standing at the side of the stage, there's a full house, we're all very nervous. The house lights have gone down, the stage manager runs on with the coal bucket in the dark, she trips, falls and showers the audience with great lumps of coal. She went down with the noise of a whale being beached. Her glasses were broken. She got up and ran off the stage. I had to come on and I was shaking with laughter, the stage was festooned with coal and people were being led from the auditorium to have first-aid treatment.

'The next play we did was *The Importance of Being Earnest* and exactly the same thing happened there. On the very first night the actor who was playing Lane the Butler had to go on stage during the blackout, to be discovered when the lights went up. He was carrying a plate of sandwiches that one of the characters, Algernon, was meant to spend the whole of the scene eating. The actor tripped while making his entrance, and the house lights went up to find Lane on his hands and knees, trying to pick up bits of cucumber and bread that were all over the carpet. He managed to make some sort of attempt at putting the sandwiches back together again, but they were the most appalling mess, covered in wood shavings and bits of fluff. The actors had to carry on eating them throughout the act and they kept on coughing up gobs of old staple.'

Vilma Hollingbery recalls that on her first first night in the business, a dangerous combination of enthusiasm and lack of experience nearly resulted in her losing her job. 'I was a student understudy ASM at the Boltons Theatre in South Kensington. I was understudying Dinah Sheridan. I felt that I was very important, although all I had to do was to stand in the wings and ring a cowbell before her entrance. It was my very first night in the professional theatre. So I rang this cowbell and it all went wonderfully well, and on she came, and the play proceeded as it should and I stood in the wings with my mouth open watching her and when it was time to take the call, I took the curtain up and every-one went on in a line and took a bow. Then as the curtain came down and went up again I ran on and I also took a bow because that's what I'd done in the amateurs. I ran on and expected the lighting men and everyone else to come on too and I did a huge curtsy behind her and then went off the stage. We had a hair-raising stage manager called Robert Henry and I found myself being lifted up by the scruff of my neck. He roared at me, "What do you think you are doing? Never do that again. Never come back in this theatre," and I was squeaking, "Don't give me the sack, please don't give me the sack, I thought every-one took bows." Dinah Sheridan, bless her, was hysterical; she saved me, she saved my job. But I thought that was what you did – I'd done the cow bell, so I took my call.'

Dramas on the first night were not confined to the stage or behind the scenes, as Peter Howell remembers. 'We did the first night of *This Happy Breed* by Noël Coward at Windsor in the presence of Coward, the King and Queen and the entire court, all wearing long dresses and dinner jackets. Someone gave the wrong signal so that the lights went down with the Royal Family desperately trying to find their seats in the dark. Noël Coward said to the Queen Mother, who was then Queen, "Ma'am I think it would be a good idea if you were to move forward," to which she replied, "I would like to move forward, Mr Coward, but you are standing on my frock."'

In Scotland, the royal family did not come to the local rep, the local rep came to them. Nancy Mansfield was working in Dundee when the theatre received an invitation to give a command performance at Balmoral. 'When I was at Dundee, Richard Todd was in the company and we did a Royal Command Performance at Balmoral. The royal household at Balmoral rang up and said that the King and Queen would like us to give a performance for them and their guests at Balmoral and would we like to submit a list of plays? We gave them a list of about six plays, most of them very good, but one was appalling. It was called *At Mrs Bean's*, all about a boarding school and they chose that. We opened it at Dundee and played for a week. We went in a coach and we got to Balmoral and we had a wonderful day. They took us round the grounds and they took us to the stables and they showed us round the castle, though not to the private apartments. They gave us a lovely lunch and after they gave us some headed notepaper so that we could write letters to go out on the Balmoral plane – a mail plane left Balmoral every afternoon. So that was rather fun. Then we had a rehearsal in the ballroom. They'd mocked up a stage and put up some funny old curtains. There were only a few feet between the front row and the stage. And in the front row were the King, the Queen, the King and Queen of the Netherlands, the Princess Royal, the Duke and Duchess of Gloucester. On the other side was Princess Margaret, sitting next to a handsome young man and quite obviously they were very close, heads together and lots of giggles. I wasn't in the first scene of the play so I watched them through a slit in the curtains and afterwards I asked someone, "Who's the handsome young man with Princess Margaret?" and they answered, "Oh, that's the new equerry, Peter Townsend."

'After the performance we went into a wonderful reception room – one side of it was just a bank of flowers, fresh flowers, and there we met the King and Queen, the two Princesses, and the Duke and Duchess of

Gloucester and we chatted for about twenty minutes. They were very kind, very interested. All the staff and all the estate workers were in the audience as well. Then we had supper and then we went home. It was lovely, it was really great fun.'

On rare occasions the agitation and exhilaration which combine to propel the performer into a state of high excitement can end in anti-climax, as Michael Stroud discovered during a season at Dundee. 'We did a first night of a play called *Wise Child* by Simon Gray that Alec Guinness made famous in the West End. This character is in drag, an escaped convict who hides in someone's house and finds women's clothes in a cupboard and I was standing in the wings at seven-thirty all dressed up and ready to go on and it sounded very quiet and at twenty to eight I said, "What's going on?" and nobody had turned up at all, not one single person, so we all went home. It caused such a fuss in the paper next day that it perked up no end and it did really quite well.'

The cast was rarely let off the hook in this way. Generally, not only were they dealing with their own nerves, but they were having to cope with the panic of their colleagues as well. Peggy Mount remembers an incident which occurred when she was in rep at Wolverhampton. 'Johnny Myers was the leading actor and we had an actress come into the company who was religious. She was a pain in the arse – "Oh please don't blaspheme in front of me!" Johnny didn't like this a bit. She got herself a big lead and the one thing you mustn't do in rep is go round saying, "Oh I'm so nervous," because it makes everyone else nervous if you've got the lead. She comforted herself – "Never mind, never mind, God is with me, God will help me," and Johnny said, "Well don't depend on Him too much in the third act because He's helping me with my quick change!"'

12

A Test of Memory

'Once an actor, drying, asked the prompter, "What's the line?" And the prompter replied, "What's the play?"'

Maurice Denham

ONE OF THE hazards of a first night was the actor's fear that he would dry, or forget his lines. Indeed the whole repertory experience, particularly if it was weekly rep, was characterized for actors by the horrendous business of cramming the script into their heads. Tom Conti says, 'People dried all the time. With only two weeks' rehearsal there was hardly any time to learn the play – people sat with their books at lunchtime, they went home with their books at night and did an hour, an hour and a half after the show. You knew it when the curtain went up on a Monday night, but some people would muddle through and invent bits and cut bits out.'

Over time people developed their own methods of working and even became expert at learning lines. Carmen Silvera had got her method of study down to a fine art. 'I used to learn my script against the clock. If it was a French's Edition I'd allow myself two minutes per page, in an hour I'd learnt an act.' Vilma Hollingbery discovered that it was a wise precaution to have a working knowledge of other people's speeches as well as her own. 'The strain was enormous. I used to make sure I knew the gist of all my scenes backwards. I knew my own part and the gist of the other speeches in case someone dried. I gave myself a kind of safety net. I knew my own part, we used to call it DLP – dead letter perfect. If anyone dried on me I would be able to start ad-libbing or jump.' Malcolm Farquhar also had his own particular approach to the task. 'I used to get back after the evening show, have a quick meal, dive into bed and start to learn the next act. I absorbed as much as I could and then did the old actor's trick of getting the script under my pillow so it would sink into your brain the next day. It worked!' By and large actors were grateful for any help with their learning and many were indebted to tireless landladies, who took them through their scripts play after play, but Elizabeth Bradley remembers being rather put out when she was given the following tip! 'When I was at the De La Warr Pavilion the chairwoman of the entertainments committee came up to me and said, "Let me give you some advice. I do a lot of amateur dramatics, I'll tell you how I set about learning parts. I read it and I put it away for five weeks." You thought yourself lucky if you got the script a week before, let alone put it away for five weeks!'

After a long season the discipline of study became entrenched and learning was something which an actor did automatically, as Alan Ayckbourn discovered. 'I can remember at breakfast reading a cornflakes packet and remembering it. You learnt as you went.' Indeed, the regime of learning a new part every week can become difficult to throw off; Timothy West cites the following example. 'There was one old actor that my mother knew, she was in rep with him years and years ago. After years of working in rep he got a part in the West End. She went in to see him one Monday night and he was looking at the script. She said, "Come on, Charlie, you must know the play by now, you've been on for four months." He replied, "I've trained myself all my life to forget a play a week." He had to re-learn the play every Monday.'

People who were less than thorough in their preparation, either through their own fault or because they were called upon at short notice, often paid the price for not knowing the text well enough. Richard Bebb recalls when his wife Gwen Watford was working at the Palace Theatre in Watford. 'In order to save a salary very small parts used to be played by the director. On the Thursday night of one partic-ular play, when the whole company was waiting in the wings to go on, there was the director with his French's Acting Edition, going through the part and he looked up and said in all seriousness, "The trouble with winging a part is that you have to learn it every night!"'

When it comes to drying, there are varying degrees of offence. Stage fright, a fractional lapse in concentration, momentary preoccupation if a prop is missing or wrongly set, can cause an actor to come out with the wrong line. Nickolas Grace found that the rapid turnover of plays could lead to confusion. 'The horror of it was having to learn eight parts in eight weeks because I was their so-called in inverted commas "Lead Actor" on the eleven guineas a week contract. I can remember in *Spring and Port Wine* opening my mouth and lines from *Chase Me Comrade* coming out, and just hoping for the best.'

It was not only plays which became muddled up. Shaun Sutton found that he had enormous difficulty in remembering the name of his own character or of the one he was playing opposite, as he explains, 'I was always getting names wrong. That was a very difficult thing in rep. One week you were Sir Henry, then you were Charles and the next week you were Geoffrey or whatever, and it was quite often difficult to remember who you were or who everybody else was, particularly if you'd been rehearsing with them with a different name all day long and then suddenly you looked at them and thought, "God! What is he called?" Gwen Watford and I were playing husband and wife in a play at Buxton and I was accusing her of adultery and she was hotly denying it and we were coming up to the end of the second act talking a bit louder and a bit faster to bring the curtain down, until I came to my immortal line, "It's no use trying to deny it, I happen to know you've been unfaithful with Max." There was a pause and Gwen said, "You mean John," having just spent a whole scene denying it! And I said, "Yes, yes, yes, yes, with John," then I put on a sneer and said, "I see, you've been unfaithful with Max *and* John!" and Gwen, who was getting fed up with this, whispered, "Shut up about Max, *you're* Max!"' This was not the only incident; he goes on to say, 'I also remember calling Joan Sanderson Lady Thing because I couldn't remember her name, and was rewarded with one of her beautiful faces.'

Sutton's tendency is confirmed by his wife, Barbara Leslie. 'I played Miss Marple once when I was about twenty-eight and Shaun was playing the detective and he said, "This is marple, Miss Murder!"' Shaun Sutton was by no means the only culprit, as this anecdote from Tom Conti shows. 'There was a wonderful moment during a play called *Chips with Everything* by Arnold Wesker, which is about some youngsters doing their six weeks' training for the RAF and there's a section in it where the corporal – there's always a rotten corporal – came in and worked us all up. And he had a line to an actor called Roy

Hanlon, the line was, "You, Seaforth," that was his name, I'll never forgot that the man was called Seaforth. He said, "You, what's your name," and the actor couldn't remember, couldn't remember what his name was, so there was a terrible pause and we all turned upstage with heaving shoulders, and he said, "Aaahb aaahb aaahb." Then he remembered his first name, which was Wilf and he said, "Wilf, Sir", and the other chap said, "Not that, your surname, you dolt." His name was Seaforth, but the best he could do, the worst thing he could possible have said, was "Seaman, sir." As you can imagine the action stopped for about five minutes, nobody could speak.'

Single words could often be a sticking point. Donald Pickering recalls an actress who had difficulty with foreign words. 'At the Penguin Players Dickie Burnett's wife Peggy Paige used to play the lead in everything, even principal boy in the pantomime. She had marvellous legs and had sort of assumed this grand persona. There was one thing she could never do, she could never pronounce foreign names, ever. We were doing a play called *Sabrina Fair* and she had to sing this little French song in it and she used to make us hysterical every night. In another play during an argument scene her character had a line, "All you do is try to humiliate me, I suppose you think I'm so ignorant I don't know the difference between *La Traviata* and *Il Trovatore*." And every night she used to say, "All you do is try to humiliate me, I suppose you think I'm so ignorant I don't know the difference between Trovatorty and Trovatarty."' Tenniel Evans describes a similar occurrence at Northampton, 'We were doing *The Merchant of Venice* and the acting ASM, who was playing either Solanio or Salerio, had the line, "What news from the Rialto?" He dried completely and came out with, "What's on at the Tivoli?"'

If individual words did not present a problem, then sometimes phrases or whole lines did. Mary Kenton recalls an actor at Northampton coming unstuck. 'I did *Romeo and Juliet* with an actor who never quite knew his lines. He closed the play with "Never was a story of more woe than this of Juliet and her Romeo." One night he said, "Never was a story of more woe than this of Romeo", searching pause, ". . . it's one we shan't forget".' Tom Conti agrees that, 'The funniest experiences were always in Shakespeare where an actor would dry on something like, "I know a bank whereon the wild thyme grows," then he would stop dead and sixty children would shout out the next line.'

Because of his wordiness, Bernard Shaw was another writer whom actors sometimes found difficult to learn. John Warner remembers an incident: 'We were doing *You Never Can Tell* at the Little Theatre in Bristol. The last line was the old waiter saying, "You never can tell, Sir, you never can tell." And one night he stepped forward, there was a long pause, and he said, "Well one never knows, does one?"'

Certain writers seem to be easier to commit to memory than others, with plays in a foreign language being hardest of all, according to John Moffatt. 'A translated play was much more difficult to learn, it didn't flow naturally. You got to know who the good writers were. With Rattigan you barely had to learn it at all, even after just blocking it you almost knew it because it is so beautifully written. The only way to reply to something that has just been said to you is what he's written.' One author whom he remembers presenting a particular challenge was William Congreve. 'We did *The Way of the World* at the Oxford Playhouse. It is the most complex play ever written, at first sight almost impossible to understand. It's well known as a play that is immensely difficult to learn, it's so convoluted. We had one week to rehearse it, it was directed by Christopher Fry. I've never seen such a bunch of frightened actors. I can remember people shaking with fright, drying and forgetting. In Act Two one of the actresses dried stone dead and the line that she dried on was, "If she should flag in her path I should not fail to prompt her."'

Agatha Christie can present the actor with altogether different demands, as Annette Crosbie found out. 'At the Citizens we did *Ten Little Niggers* by Agatha Christie and in the cast we had Roy Kinnear, who was a terrible corpser. I can't play Agatha Christie, I don't know anyone who can get through those plays, you'll find if you watch carefully in a production of Agatha Christie that no one is ever meeting anyone else's eyes. At one point there was a scream off-stage and it was only Roy and Fulton Mackay and myself who were on stage at the time and Roy had to run off, leaving Fulton and me on stage registering horror etc. The minute he had gone off we could see him in the wings banging his head against a flat trying not to laugh because he knew that when he came on we were going to say, "Is he?" and he was going to say, "Someone must have got him as he bent over the wood box." We never got that line, for a fortnight he would come on to the stage puce in the face, shaking.'

A small amount of laxity or inaccuracy with individual words or phrases is unavoidable, but if a performer consistently blunders through whole speeches it places an enormous burden on fellow members of the cast, as Tenniel Evans can testify. 'There was one chap who worked at Northampton who can remain nameless, he was maddening to work with because he fluffed his way through every performance right through the week, we'd come to the end of an act and he'd say, "I thought we did that rather well," and you knew that every single effect you'd thought of had been wrecked. Those were the things that mattered terribly.' An example of this kind of difficulty is provided by John Newman, who was faced with a tricky moment when he was doing a play by Somerset Maugham with Malcolm McDowell, who suddenly dried completely. In an attempt to jog his memory, John Newman said, "What were you saying?" McDowell replied, "I don't know old boy, I'll leave it all to you."

Some artistes, because of their advanced age, were more susceptible to drying than others, and in extreme cases emergency procedures had to be used, with varying degrees of success. Tom Conti remembers one occasion. 'We were doing a play called *The Carmelites* and an elderly lady was playing the mother superior or something. This was a play of such immense tedium it's hard to imagine. There was some section of the play that she could never remember. She was sedentary throughout and so it was decided that she would go on and there would be a lectern by her side and the script would be on the lectern disguised as a bible. She went on with this and because it was there she couldn't take her eyes off it, she read the whole play every night, it made it impossible for anyone to act with her, but there was just no getting round it.' Simon Williams admits that if a lectern isn't handy, then even more desperate measures have to be taken. 'An actress called Edie Stephens was brought out of retirement to play a clairvoyant in a play by Philip King. She could not learn the lines, so I sat under a table with a torch and the script and when she rapped on the top and said, "I wonder what I can see now?" I'd whisper the line for her. She tipped me 2/6d.'

When an actor dried and no help was available, he would have to start ad-libbing. This happened to Geoffrey Davies. 'I can remember opening in *Out of the Crocodile* and I had had a terrible week and done the get-out on the Saturday night and tried to learn Act Three on the Sunday, but I couldn't get the lines in and on the Monday I said to

Charmian May, who was playing opposite me, "I'm afraid I don't know Act Three very well." She said, "Never mind darling, we'll make it up." Well, of course, you could do this if you knew the story. She said, "If you get in a state, just put a cushion on your head and I'll know that you've gone wrong." So we got to Act Three and up came a bit I had no idea about, so I picked up a cushion and started playing about with it a bit, then I put it on my head. "Ah, right!" said Charmian and we were off, making it up, the audience had no idea.' Even more peculiar than seeing an actor with a cushion on his head was the sight of the leading character in *Charley's Aunt* suddenly embarking on a music hall turn, which happened to Barbara Lott during her opening night in Barnsley. 'The man playing the Aunt, Charley Fancourt Babberly, whose name was Paul Courtney was brilliantly clever, a little man, a chameleon. On the opening night he dried in the first act and as there was no prompter, nothing happened for a bit and then suddenly on came Eunice, his wife, who was playing Donna Lucia, who doesn't come on until the last act. On she came and they went into their variety act, which they used to do on Sundays at working men's clubs. And I just sat there with my mouth hanging open watching, and then this went on for about quarter of an hour, and he then trotted off and she sang a bit of a song and he went to look through the script and then came back on and the play continued.'

Doreen Andrew recalls an equally fraught and perplexing occasion. 'I once had an actress faint on stage, I never quite knew why, I think she dried and the best way out of it was to fall in a heap, but she came round very quickly and remembered the rest of it.' Robin Ellis found a different sort of refuge for himself when exhaustion began to hit home at the end of a long season in Salisbury. 'I remember doing *She Stoops to Conquer* in the June of a year which began in October. I was playing young Marlow, but I was so tired by this time I had great difficulty learning the lines. Luckily he had a stammer, so I could stammer away while I thought of what to say and everyone thought I was acting.'

When actors, for whatever reason, are unable to help themselves, they are thrown on to the mercy of their fellow performers. Sir Alan Ayckbourn remembers one actor who never failed him. 'Peter Byrne was a cornerstone at Worthing, he always knew everybody else's part, it was extraordinary. I remember drying once on stage and he said, "I think I know what you're going to say, Jim. You're going to tell me . . ."

He gave me the whole of my speech, wrapped it up neatly and then gave me his reply.'

While some actors are expert at rescuing their colleagues, others seem to have a knack of sabotaging them, as Alec McCowen discovered to his horror. 'I found I had a terrifying power, and I'm sure I didn't make it up, but I used to be able to make another actor forget his lines. If I thought ahead to the line he was just going to get to, it seemed to go out of his head. This was an actor who was pretty neurotic anyway. It was a terrible power to have and I had to really discipline myself not to do it, but then I'd think, "Surely he won't?", and I'd think ahead to his next line and sure enough he'd go to pieces.'

The ever-present threat of going to pieces on stage meant that performers became dependent on the prompter, the member of stage management who sits in prompt corner with the script and runs the show. Lionel Jeffries remembers being lost for words: 'There was a wonderful moment when I dried stone dead on the opening line of a whole play. Dead mutton, I was. The wings were blocked off for this show, so they couldn't prompt from the wings. But there was a fireplace with a big cowl in the middle of the stage up centre and somebody prompted me down the chimney.' Maria Charles describes an actor in Oldham who dried so horribly that even when the prompter threw him a lifeline, he was unable to make use of it. 'There were three of us on the stage and somebody dried and nobody else knew what to do and the stage manager in a panic rang the phone and this actor picked up the phone and went, "Yes? Hello?" and then he handed it to one of us! "It's for you!" '

Prompts did not always arrive seemlessly, as Lord Rix, the actor Brian Rix, explains. 'On one first night when I was out front watching, Elspet Gray dried very badly. She crossed over to the fireplace and got the script handed through to her, saying, "I'm awfully sorry, could you tell me the page?" I nearly died.' Elspet Gray herself reports the following incident. 'I remember doing *The Giaconda Smile* and in the first act the other actress and I just looked at each other and we knew – we kept on talking – but we knew that we weren't doing the first act we were doing the third act. In the end we paused and I looked at the prompt corner, nothing. Eventually I heard a voice say, "Sorry," so I walked over and said, "George!" And he said, "Which act are you in?" ' Maurice Denham describes a moment of even greater confusion.

'Once an actor, drying, asked the prompter, "What's the line?" And the prompter replied, "What's the play?"' The most unhelpful comment of all to come out of the prompt corner was heard by Mary Kenton, 'Someone dried and waited for help from the wings and nothing happened so they started to ad-lib rather frantically, then came a voice from the prompt corner – "Wrong!"'

Although actors occasionally grumble about the support they receive when they forget their lines, inept assistance is better than no assistance at all. Moray Watson describes how disconcerted he felt when he went to the Pendragon Theatre at Reading in May 1951. 'I'll never forget going up on the Thursday to do my entrance in *Outward Bound* and I noticed there was no prompter there in the prompt corner. I went on feeling slightly nervous without the prompter and I happened to mention this to one of the other actors when we came off and they said, "Oh we never have a prompter after the Wednesday night." I said, "What happens if you dry on Thursday, Friday or Saturday?" and they said, "Tough."'

Brian Rix recalls another occasion on which help from the prompt corner was unforthcoming. 'There was an actress on stage with Jimmy Haggart in *The Young Mrs Barrington*. They had a big scene coming up and they both dried totally. Eventually he ran off stage to the prompt corner and she shouted after him, "Jimmy, Jimmy, come back you rotten sod, it's my best scene!"'

To obviate the need for rushing off stage to check what came next, Clive Francis recalls that actors used to plant little crib notes for themselves around the stage. 'The set used to be littered with bits of script in drawers and under magazines and if you had a long speech you used to be able to work the moves around the room. "I've got the first part of the speech down there, then I can do a circuitous route to the bowl of fruit because I've got another bit planted there." Before I realized what was going on I used to go round and tidy all these bits of paper up. These poor demented actors used to be on stage frantically searching for these bits of paper.'

April Walker says that if the stage management were not busy moving these cribs, then sometimes other members of the cast were. 'People never knew their lines so it was invariable that there would be bits of paper stuck all over the set on the first night. By the end of the week people were playing tricks – moving the bits of paper so that the wrong speech was at the wrong place on the set.' Brian Murphy confesses, 'Sometimes there were so many cribs hidden on-stage it was a bit like a paperchase.' He became a master of concealment, as the following anecdotes reveal. 'A handy place to hide your lines was in your cigarette packet, but one night someone else picked mine up from the props table and my lines ended up in his pocket.' He remembers another incident which had equally dire consequences. 'I had a pouch sewn into my Iago costume just big enough to hold my Temple Shakespeare and I used to rush off into the wings to check my lines and have a quick fag. Once I stubbed out my cigarette and tucked it behind my ear for later, but it was still alight and my wig started smouldering. Othello cuffed me rather more than usual to put it out.' Belinda Lang favoured the back of the set door on which to keep her script for handy reference in an emergency. 'We did *Chase Me Comrade* by Ray Cooney at Frinton. It was one of those farces where you're jumping in and out of wardrobes all the time. By the time we got down to doing it we were totally exhausted and we couldn't stuff another line in, so we hung script on bits of string inside the doors and every time you left the stage, with some relief, you grabbed the script to see what was coming next.'

In spite of the help available from the prompt corner and from other members of the cast, let alone the strategies that individuals developed for learning their parts and for jogging their memories if they forgot them, the stage and the audience beyond it were still capable of filling artistes with panic and dread, particularly if the performance in question was on a Monday night. Paul Williamson sums the situation up. 'At the end of the rehearsals for one play the director gathered us together for notes and he gave one to me, "Don't pat the vicar!" We all had a terrible need to touch each other at times, in fact, to hold each other how ever inappropriate the holding was, because of the terror of not knowing what the hell the next line was. You just reached out and held on to their forearm for dear life.'

13

Deaths and Entrances

'*Maria? Mayhap she has gone bear-baiting.*'

Peggy Mount

FORGETTING A LINE or even a speech is nothing compared to the heinous crime of entirely omitting an entrance, known in the profession as 'being off'. This often happens when the actor, instead of concentrating on the moment in hand within the play in question, starts to think ahead. Paul Bradley allowed his concentration to lapse in this way. 'I was playing Bottom at the Contact Theatre in Manchester. I wasn't happy with it, wasn't settling down, so I was determined to make my next entrance really something. I sat down near where my next entrance was and went through it all in my head, thinking it out, and one of the mechanicals was hissing, "Come on, come on," and I said, "No, no, don't disturb me," and I'd jumped a cue completely and was waiting by the wrong entrance and had to run on stage and get to where I should have been.'

Another terrible trap to fall into occurs when an actor gets too involved in what is going on in his dressing-room, as William Franklyn says, 'This story concerns John Fernald's production of *The Cherry Orchard* at the Liverpool Playhouse. My job was putting on what was called the panotrope for the sound effects of the Jewish orchestra and the cutting down of the orchard. As well as that, I had to go and call people for their entrances. Harold Goodwin was playing Firs, who is the ninety-year-old, very aged retainer. At some point they realized that Harold was not down in the wings and he was due on stage in about thirty seconds. I was sent up to his dressing-room, which was on the third floor. He was sharing it with Brian Wilde. I knocked on the door and they were playing poker. I said, 'Mr Goodwin I believe you're off,' which was such an under-statement that Harold Goodwin, who was then about twenty-six but playing this old man, tore downstairs and he had to go under the stage to make his entrance on the other side. He made his entrance, which was a little late and Eric Berry, who was playing one of the leads, had managed to do a little Chekhov ad-libbing, this frail little old man then came on panting and very short of breath.'

Michael Kilgarriff describes another problem during a performance of *The Ghost Train* at Stockton-on-Tees. 'The play is set in a waiting-room and all the characters get locked in. I went up to my dressing-room after the first act. There was no PA system in those days and, instead of coming up to my room and knocking on my door, the ASM just shouted my call up the stairs. I didn't hear it and I remember think-ing, 'It's rather long, this interval . . .', so I went down and, of course, they'd started the second half. They'd run a couple of pages skipping over my lines, but of course the thing was the door was meant to be locked. They must have been crapping themselves on stage thinking how are we going to get through the rest of the act? I went on stage and said, "There's nobody out there," and closed the door behind me, then I rattled the handle and said, 'It's stuck again!"'

Howard Attfield was another actor who was caught on the hop. He remembers, 'I was playing an inspector, I forget the name of the murder thriller, and it was a matinée day and very hot and I remember standing in the dressing-room and I was having a shave, and I thought I had all the time in the world because my first entrance wasn't until the ending of the first act. The inspector comes in, says his lines and ends the first act. So I was standing there quite happily in my boxer shorts having a shave when I heard my call, which I could not believe, and I went absolutely wild. My costume was a suit, an inspector's suit, and a sort of a trench coat and a hat. Anyway, I thought I'd best put on some-thing, the least possible, so I put on trousers and I remember putting on shoes without socks, then I put on the trench coat, did it all up as I'm flying out the door, grabbed the hat and went charging down the stairs, saying, "I'm coming, I'm coming, I'm coming," and I made it on to the stage just in time, but as I went on someone in the wings said, "Shaving foam, shaving foam!" and I realized that I'd got halfway through this shave and I hadn't wiped it off. Luckily it was on the upstage side, as I was coming on from stage right. So instead of looking at the audience, I did everything looking from stage right to stage left, and the upstage bit was foam in my ears and right round my face. I delivered the line and the curtains came down and I collapsed on the floor half naked and half shaven.'

Attfield was fortunate that the shaving foam remained hidden. Simon Williams was not so lucky when he played the genie in *Aladdin* at Worthing. 'For my first entrance there was a puff of smoke and a clash of cymbals. I was chatting to people in the wings, wearing my brown cardie because it was the dead of winter and the theatre was so cold, I heard the cymbals, leapt on stage, and landed beside the Dame, still wearing my cardie.'

A performer can be so thrown if he does miss an entrance, that his concentration becomes fatally impaired and the original mistake is compounded, as Gemma Jones describes. 'I remember being in a play, playing a maid and my part consisted of coming on every now and then and saying, "His Lordship's at the door, Ma'am." That was about it, but I think I approached it as if it were the most important part in the play. I took it very seriously and rehearsed very hard and I was sitting in my dressing-room, not gossiping, but listening to the tannoy and think-ing about my next entrance, when I had to say, "The post has arrived, Sir." I heard my cue on the tannoy, but I was listening so hard that I forgot to go down to the stage. So I threw myself down the stairs and threw myself on to the stage and John Neville just raised an eyebrow and said, "We know, the post has arrived." I was so mortified. I left the stage and stood shaking behind the flats thinking, "Oh no, this is the end of my career," taking it all far too dramatically, and I missed my next entrance! I can tell it now, but at the time I think I was in shock.'

Maids can be fiendish to play, as they often have countless entrances with very little to do or say once they arrive on stage. Judy Campbell suffered in a similar way to Gemma Jones. 'I played the maid in a play called *Storm*, my brother was backstage making the storm sound effect, and I was downstairs trying to decide whether to put on emerald green eyeshadow or gold. I heard the cry go up, "You're off," and I went pounding up the stairs, but I missed my first entrance. I felt so bad that I kept my hand on the doorknob so that I wouldn't miss the next one and I was thinking how angry my uncle was going to be, how angry everyone would be, and I missed the next one. I was standing backstage listening to the actors thinking they were talking gobbledeegook and I was off again. My grandfather was so angry. It was like being back at school. I had to apologize to everyone, to the leading lady and the leading gentleman especially.'

On rare occasions not only does the actor fail to make it to the stage on time, he does not turn up at the theatre either. Tony O'Callaghan was in a production of *The Long, the Short and the Tall* when this happened. 'The Japanese soldier isn't on until near the interval, so the actor playing him didn't have to be there at the half, he came in at curtain up. He liked a bit of a gamble and on Saturday matinées he'd have a couple of bets on the horses. One matinée he wasn't there, but the stage manager decided to take the curtain up anyway. The play started and during it there is a lot of standing at the window acting and the stage manager was in the wings shaking his head and mouthing, "No, he's not here yet," and we were getting quite close to the Japanese actor's entrance. I went up to the window and looked out and the actor was there, but in his black slacks, Gucci shoes and black silk shirt, with all his medallions and rings. I thought, "He hasn't got his gear on but at least he's here." He saw me at the window and then he came over to say hello. I thought he was going to come on as he was. If he had done, we'd have been finished. A Japanese tourist in the middle of the Burmese jungle!'

When Nancy Mansfield worked at the theatre in Guildford they were doing plays in rotation with Amersham, a system which could lead to terrible mistakes. 'We would open a play in Guildford, play it for a week, then take it to Amersham, where we would play it for another week. It was, in effect, fortnightly rep because we played it in two centres. There was one occasion, one of the nightmares of my life, it was a matinée day and I had to go to London for a costume fitting. I went up and did it, then I went to Victoria to get the train. The train started and I realized I was on my way to Guildford and the matinée was at Amersham. We were doing *Wuthering Heights* and I was playing Kathy. I didn't know what to do. I jumped off the train at the first stop and rushed to the station master's office, then explained my situation and he held the departing train back to London so that I could race over to the platform and catch it. I got a taxi from Victoria to Marylebone, then rang the theatre to say that I would be half an hour late. I can't tell you what the train journey to Amersham was like. I was pacing up and down the carriage, I couldn't sit. They were waiting at the station for me with a car. They'd given the audience a cup of tea each and told them there would be a slight delay due to the indisposition of Miss Mansfield. I just threw the costume on and went on without any make-up. It was awful.'

William Franklyn remembers being caught out when his car broke down on the way to the theatre in Windsor. 'I was doing a play by Somerset Maugham called *The Happy Prisoner* at Windsor and my car broke down on the way. I had my dog with me. I'd been playing cricket at Lord's in the afternoon as we had a seven-thirty curtain up. The car broke down where Heathrow is now, there used to be a police station on the left and we broke down about fifty yards from the police station. I went into them and I said, "Look I'm in terrible trouble, I'm supposed to be on stage in Windsor in under forty minutes, can you help me?" And the policeman said, "Well, Sir, there's not very much we can do about that. We can call you a taxi." In the play I was not on until the end of the first scene. The curtain had been up about twenty minutes when I was due on as a squadron leader. I asked the police to ring up and explain what had happened, which they did. As I hadn't arrived by curtain up, the management decided to cut the scene in which I first appeared and all the cast knew that and had mentally rehearsed it. In the meantime the police had thought, "This poor sod, he really is in a bit of trouble, we'll run him to the theatre." When I got there I went straight through the stage door so fast I don't think anyone saw me, went up to my dressing-room, changed into my costume, went down on stage and entered on cue when they all believed I wasn't coming. I said my lines and nobody could speak a word. I was meant to look like a cool squadron leader and I was sweating so much I must have looked as though I'd just parachuted out of a blazing bomber.'

When an actor misses an entrance it leaves the cast on stage in a bit of a pickle and when the crisis is over feelings can run high, as Peggy Mount remembers. 'We were doing *Twelfth Night* and I was playing Maria and they said, "We've got to top and tail because the play is too long," so they cut all sorts of things. I came off after one scene and sat down in a chair and someone said, "Peggy, you're off!" I didn't know where I was, they'd cut the following scene. As I came down I heard one of the characters saying, "Maria? Mayhap she has gone bear-baiting!" When we eventually came off stage he said, "If you ever do that again in Shakespeare I'll kill you!"' Beryl Cooke remembers hearing an equally barbed remark when a member of a pantomime cast was late for an entrance. 'During a matinée an actor was off and one of the comics, who was stranded on stage, called out, "Comfortable up there in your dressing-room is it?"'

Actors developed strategies for coping with the dreadful pause which indicates a late arrival on stage. Michael Kilgarriff says, 'If people missed entrances, which was not infrequent, there were a couple of tricks you could always do. You could pour yourself a drink because there was always a drinks' table and if they still didn't come on then you went out of the French windows and smelt the air. I was stuck on stage once and I couldn't do any of these because I was about to have a knife stuck in my back and it was already fixed between my shoulder blades.' If an actor fails to appear and his colleague has poured the drinks and smelt the air as much as he is able, he may have to go and look for him, as Peter Bowles did. 'I was in *The Beaux Stratagem* with Ian Hendry. I was on stage and whoever I was on stage with was supposed to go off and Ian Hendry was supposed to come on. Ian didn't come on . . . and he didn't come on . . . and he didn't come on and I made some excuse to the audience – "My companion is delayed" – and I went into the wings and said, "Where the fuck is Ian?" I went haring off to his dressing-room, but he wasn't there, so I came back and I could hear him ad-libbing on stage. He'd gone on as I'd come off. By the time I reached the stage he'd made his excuses and gone to look for me so I then had to go on – it was a whole new play.'

If the errant actor cannot be found in his dressing-room or even in the building, the stage management may be called on to step into the breach, as this incident in Harrogate described by Geoffrey Davies illustrates, 'In another play we did one of the older actors always used to nip off during the interval for a drink. He'd put on his coat and whip round to the pub for a whisky and be back in time for Act Two. But one night he thought he'd finished the first act, he'd forgotten he'd got another scene. He wasn't there for his entrance. None of us on stage knew what was going on, but the ASM realized and she gave the stage manager the book. He knocked at the door and said, "I can't come in, the door's jammed, what did you want?" And he played the rest of the scene shouting the lines from off stage.'

Des Barritt received no help from the wings, when he found himself deserted in the middle of a scene, as Michael Simpkin explains. 'Des was playing a detective in a murder mystery in Bridlington and in one show the actor he was playing opposite failed to come on. For a while Des wandered around the stage picking up props and having a look at them. Still no sign of his colleague. In the end he turned to the audience and said, "I'm so happy I think I'll sing a song." Which he did.' If performers are not so confident of their singing voices, there are alternatives. Malcolm Farquhar says, 'One actress who was left alone on stage when an actor missed his entrance, stood there and recited, "I wandered lonely as a cloud"! She said, "I got two very good laughs as I went to the sideboard and back."'

The opposite of missing an entrance is making one too early, which can be just as confusing for the poor actors on stage, who are not expecting anyone to appear for several minutes. Michael Simpkin was guilty of this in a production for Alan Ayckbourn's company. 'One evening during *Tapster* at Scarborough I was chatting in the green room when suddenly the tannoy went quiet and I realized I was off. I grabbed my props and ran on to the stage as fast as I could and Christine Kavanagh and Russell Dixon looked at me as though to say, "Where the hell have you been for the last four minutes?" When we got to the end of the scene, we came off and I said, "I'm most dreadfully sorry about that, how long were you waiting for me to come on, then?" And Christine said, "There were still five pages to go before your entrance!"' Simon Williams remembers a similar incident involving the actress Hazel Bainbridge. 'Hazel came on too early during *George and Margaret*, in the middle of the juveniles' love scene. "Oh don't mind me," she said and started tidying up the set.' John Newman recalls an early entrance which had more drastic consequences. 'When Caryl Jenner was running her repertory season at Amersham, there was a pub next door to the theatre and the stage door there led practically on to the stage itself. They were doing a thriller in which one of the characters was killed during the first act. The actor playing him had to hang around until the end of the show to take the curtain call, so he used to nip into the pub for a drink. At the last performance the audience were very enthusiastic and they gave the leading actor a round of applause on his final exit. In the pub next door the actor heard the clapping and thinking he was late for the end of the play, hared through the stage door and straight on to the stage in the middle of the final scene, bright eyed and bushy tailed, ready to take his bow.'

The cast, not to mention the audience, must have been nonplussed by an incident which Derek Nimmo describes. 'I remember doing one play in Bolton and the stage-door keeper had been there for years. The stage door was next to the Hen and Chickens and the stage doorman used to pop in there quite a lot. We were doing an Aldwych farce, I can't remember which one it was, but suddenly the door opened and he came on to the set, saying, "Quarter of an hour please, quarter of an hour," and then he walked off again.'

Nothing can be more startling for an artiste than the appearance on stage of someone who has nothing whatever to do with the performance, but on rare occasions this happens, as Frank Middlemass remembers. 'When we needed music for a production, a trio would play in the pit and a little old lady who played the violin came to discuss the music for the next week's show. She chose her time badly. There was no stage doorman and only a couple of chaps backstage and she found her way on to the stage in the middle of a performance. She carried on a brisk conversation with the manager Frank Barnes, who was appearing that week. I was sitting in a corner of the sofa and it was a tense scene – he didn't know I was there because he was blind. He was trying to persuade this little old lady to get off the stage and she was quite unaware of what was happening.'

Dulcie Gray remembers a wartime incident which left the cast in open-mouthed amazement. 'We were doing a production of *Queen Elizabeth Slept Here*, which was one of those plays where people run on and off stage and there is a lot of laughter. I had just come off and Michael [Denison] was acting away looking upstairs, when a woman in a long brown dress arrived and sat down on the sofa. She was nothing to do with the play and it turned out that she was an escaped German lunatic who had strayed into the building. They finally caught her in the gents' loos two floors up.'

As all these stories demonstrate, the capacity to think on one's feet and, at times, to think extremely fast, is a prerequisite for anyone contemplating a career in repertory theatre.

14

Not Good with Props

'Don't worry about me, dear, you go to the ball.'

Mimi Whitford

HUMAN ERROR CAN cause actors problems during a performance, but whereas the fluffed line or the mis-timed entrance can usually be incorporated into the action by a quick-witted performer, the predicaments posed by inanimate objects are much harder to overcome.

Because the scenery was often flimsy and usually put up in a hurry, the actor frequently faced hazards caused by the set, with doors being the main culprit – they stick, they open when they shouldn't, the handles come off, they keys get lost, the locks jam – the door itself may even come off in the actor's hand. The permutations are endless. Michael Stroud had to deal with at least two of these difficulties in a production of *The Ghost Train* at Salisbury. 'In one scene we were all stuck on that railway station in the waiting-room and one of the characters is saying, "Oh dear, we'll never get out," and at that moment the door just swung gently open and the stage manager pulled her jumper over her hand and reached for the door and slowly shut it. And another moment a person went off stage to go to the ticket office, and he couldn't open the door to get back, so he did the rest of the scene with his head through the ticket hatch.'

Tony O'Callaghan went through an ordeal of cataclysmic proportions in Cheltenham during a production of *Signpost to Murder*. 'I was playing a male nurse in the local asylum. One of the inmates had escaped, he was the husband of a woman who had had him put away because he threatened to murder her. There had been a murder at the hospital. It all comes out at the end that I'd been having an affair with the wife and the policeman accuses me of the murder and there's a scuffle and I run up the stairs. I remember getting to the door at the top, and the top half of the set, which was a country cottage, was gauze painted to look like a wall, but the minute you turned the lights up on stage you could see straight through it. The door into the bathroom had gauze in the middle of it and what had happened was that during the technical rehearsal and the dress rehearsal under the lights it had warped ever so slightly. When I got to the top I couldn't remember if I was supposed to pull it or push it. I tried to pull it towards me and it made a funny sort of creaking sound, so I pushed it, got through it, got to the window, where I was to try and escape and there's a stage manager standing in the wings with the book saying, "Get away from the window, you know you can't get away with it." So I go back to the door and a lot of policemen are waiting at the bottom of the stairs and I couldn't remember if I'd pushed it or pulled it. I tried to push it and it made a funny noise again, so I tried to pull it. With all the pushing and pulling and warping it got stuck behind the door jamb. When I tried to pull it the set started to come as well. I thought, "What am I going to do?" So I started walking around and the rest of the cast were at the bottom of the stairs looking up at me, thinking, "What is he doing?" and I went back to the window, thinking, "Shall I climb out of the window?" but it was too great a drop, so back to the door I come. I had a huge adrenalin rush, thinking, "I've got to get through the door, I've got to get down the stairs." I pushed it with all my might and it came right off its hinges and I let go of it and it tumbled right down the stairs. At the curtain call I took the door in with me!'

If the door is not co-operating, finding a way on to the set can be a real challenge, as Anna Carteret discovered when she was appearing in *Gaslight*. 'The door has a practical lock. The heroine is trying to gas herself and the leading man comes in. She's supposed to open the door, but I couldn't open it because I'd lost the key, it had dropped and I couldn't find it. I was just about to say to the audience, "Look, I really have lost the key," when he appeared through the fireplace! I quite like a bit of adversity, I like being sharpened up.'

A bit of adversity is one thing, but Nancy Mansfield had rather more than her fair share during a season at Dundee. 'We were doing a play called *The Cat and the Canary* and I was lying on the bed, it was a wonderful four-poster and I had a necklace round my neck, then a panel opens and a hand comes in and takes it while I sleep. I wake up and get out of bed and scream and carry on and the rest of the cast rush on and the play goes on from there. On this particular night the hand came on and took the necklace and I got up and screamed and screamed – and screamed! And I thought they ought to be coming on and I went over to the door and someone whispered, "The door's locked, we can't get on." The lock on the door was practical and the door was locked and there was no key. I went on screaming and making up a bit of dialogue and then I thought, this is a bit daft, so I went down to the floodlights and I said, "Ladies and gentlemen I'm terribly sorry we shall have to bring the curtain down briefly because the rest of the cast should come on now, but unfortunately they are locked outside the door." The audience thought this was hilarious and I turned round only to see the others streaming on through the fireplace. The audience cheered loudly and we went on in fits of giggles, of course.'

Brian Murphy also remembers how likely this sort of accident was. 'Sets were made out of canvas, they weren't the solid things you now see on the stage. You had to be careful not to lean too heavily against them and sometimes during a scene change the door might be put on the wrong way round, so you couldn't open it. Many times I've been locked out on a set and had to appear through the fireplace.' If there is no fireplace, other means of entry have to be found, as Clare Welch relates, 'Athene Seyler, a wonderful actress, was appearing in a play in rep and during the second act she was in her bedroom on her bed in a negligée and every member of the family had to come in and have a scene with her about why she shouldn't marry a certain young man. One night she was sitting there and the curtain went up. She heard her mother coming along the corridor, she heard the door handle turn and the door rattle, but the door didn't open. She heard her try again and then go back along the corridor. She heard more footsteps and more rattling and in the meantime she started combing her hair and so on, then she heard more footsteps and the sound of sawing – they were sawing out the back of this enormous wardrobe that was on-stage. It was one of those wardrobes where the doors open over a very deep drawer, and her mother threw open the doors, climbed two and a half feet down on to the stage, shut the doors behind her and had the scene, knowing that the only way out was a two and a half foot climb up back through the wardrobe.'

Geoffrey Davies remembers yet another surprise appearance. 'Once in a production of *Black Chiffon* an actress was due to come on stage, but the door handle came off in her hand, she couldn't get on, she couldn't get through the door and so she came in through the window instead. But she didn't open the window, she climbed in through a closed window.'

Once an actor has negotiated his entrance he is still prey to all sorts of dangers while he is on stage, as Anna Carteret's story shows. 'At Lincoln we did *Cinderella* and I played Cinderella and Penelope Keith was an Egg Head in the panto. I remember going off to do my trans-formation scene into my ball dress and all the fairies were dancing about. When I came back on my cardboard horses were on their side: a flat had fallen over squashing the fairy godmother, played by Mimi Whitford, and she was peering out from under the flat with her broken wand, saying, "Don't worry about me, dear, you go to the ball."' Cherry Morris had a similarly narrow escape. 'I remember once there was the most tremendous thunderstorm and the water started coming through the roof. In those days it was all flats, we didn't have solid sets. The water started pouring on to these flats and they fell on to the stage. One flat fell behind me and one flat fell in front of me. I'd have been clobbered and might not have been here if I had been standing further up-stage or further down-stage. I stepped over the flat and carried on. The audience loved it, they love it when a tragedy occurs.' Stephen Hancock was also hit by falling scenery. 'I was in a production of *Salad Days* and there was this huge safe on stage, about seven foot high and made of wood. One night I opened the door to put in a secret docu-ment and the safe overbalanced and tipped over on to me. I was enveloped in this huge thing and I managed to push it back and the audience saw that I was in trouble and I made some silly remark and then it was over.' Paul Greenwood says, 'The scenery was insubstantial and very flimsy. I remember when I was playing Romeo, as I climbed up to the balcony I kicked over a tree and it landed cardboard side up on the stage. I said, "Whoops", and it got a big laugh.'

If danger did not come from the doors or the flats, it could come from the floor. Philip Locke remembers the peril of the rug. 'At Oldham we were doing a Frederick Lonsdale play set in an old baronial hall that had suits of armour round the walls and a tiger-skin rug on the floor. One night the leading lady tripped over this rug and knocked her teeth out. Then during Act Two the legs on the chaise longue broke so that it tipped up like a see-saw.'

The floor can be even more treacherous if the revolve is in use and a section of the stage turns around to reveal a new scene. Julian Fellowes recalls a bitter experience with one in Northampton. 'I remember they did a musical called, *Cowardy Custard* and they decided to use a terribly expensive revolve that was hardly ever used. The stage manager didn't really take the trouble to acquaint himself with it. There was a moment in the play when I was supposed to finish a speech, step back on to the revolve, join the chorus there and start to sing. I said my lines, glanced back and there was the revolve going past me like the clappers, this flying set spinning round, and from a very, very long way away I could hear the chorus starting to sing. I was alone on stage with this whirling set behind me, I started to sing. Finally the stage manager realized there was this solitary soul singing on stage and he speeded up the revolve, they whizzed into place behind me and he stopped it dead, all the chorus fell over and I then had to pick my way across the bodies.'

Last but not least, the curtain which divides the stage from the auditorium can sometimes cause havoc for the cast. Anthony Tuckey recalls another production of the accident-prone play *The Ghost Train*, this time in Perth. 'The curtain up on Act Three was quite sensational. The stage manager, instead of raising the curtain, lowered it vigorously to the floor, suffocating the prostrate heroine and leaving the rest of us peering over the top of it like coconuts in a shy.' Donald Pickering also found himself uncomfortably revealed by a malfunctioning curtain. 'On tour with the Strolling Repertory Company in *It Won't Be a Stylish Marriage* I was the juvenile playing the policeman. The director never really rehearsed us, so I just played it straight. We did a show at RAF Cranwell in front of three thousand men and all they did was take the piss out of my accent. At the end of the play we went on to take the curtain call and I was on the end. They were huge curtains like you have in cinemas and there wasn't anyone pulling them, someone just pushed a button. They opened and we bowed and they closed, they opened and we bowed again and when they closed again this time they came right off the runner, they came loose from the anchor point in the prompt corner and came across obscuring the others and disclosing only me and I got the bird from all three thousand air crew, they were jumping up and whistling.'

Vilma Hollingbery had an exceedingly narrow escape in Leeds, 'I went up with the iron curtain in what used to be the Theatre Royal, Leeds, but is now Schofield's department store, I think. In the interval the big blue curtains came down and then the iron [safety curtain] came down and there was a hole in it, a little peep hole. My mum and dad were in the audience. I wasn't playing, but they were on their way to Scotland and they stopped off to see the show because I was on the book. I wanted to see them because I hadn't seen them before the show. The iron curtain had got a sort of ridge along the bottom and two crossed braces. I jumped on to the ridge at the bottom and held on to the braces and I was looking out through the peep hole to see if I could see my parents, not realizing that in front of that was the heavy curtain. All I could see was blackness. I found a little chink open and I could see people through it, then I could see people going down. Of course, it was me going up. I was getting further and further towards the grid, where I would have been crushed because there's no room, the iron just goes straight through. I thought, "What am I going to do? What am I going to do?" I don't know how high I was, but I jumped off and as I jumped off the blue curtains were going up so what the audience could see, and, of course, the front-of-house manager could see, were these funny little legs running about. I didn't know whether to come out of the front and run across the stage, or duck back out of sight, so all they could see were these panicking feet.'

Even if the various components of the set behaved as they should, the other inanimate objects, the props, could prove to be a severe headache for performers. The most common form of adversity was experienced when something vital was left off stage. Stephanie Cole remembers a moment of crisis in Salisbury. 'This play had the usual set, French windows, fireplace, telephone. The telephone was supposed to ring and there was a terrible, terrible pause – a) it didn't ring and b) it had not been set. There was this pause, and we improvised around and suddenly from the wings we heard the young ASM making telephone sounds: Brr Brr, Brr Brr. We all started to laugh and then of course we couldn't find the telephone. We were all lurching round the set pretending that we weren't looking for anything, when suddenly a hand appeared through the fireplace holding the telephone. At which point we just fell apart.' Maurice Denham also suffered from an absent telephone. 'In one play the phone rang, but there was no telephone there, it had not been set on the stage, so they brought the curtain down, set the phone, raised the curtain and started again.' Michael Stroud was in the audience when a similar oversight became apparent. 'I once went to see a Tennessee Williams thing at Cheltenham, and the second act went up and the actors were sitting on a wooden veranda rocking backwards and forwards, fanning themselves, as they do in those plays, in blue overalls and big hats, and nothing seemed to happen for what seemed like several minutes and suddenly a stage-hand appeared with a telephone under his arm and he walked on and said, "Evening", and he put the wire on the end of the phone under the rug and the phone immediately rang.'

Doreen Andrew recalls having to think fast when she was confronted by – a missing telephone! 'I was at Cheltenham doing a dreadful play called *Love with a Stranger* and in one scene the phone rang and I went to answer it and it wasn't there and I thought, "Oh my God, what will I do? This phone has got to be answered." So I said, "I'll go and answer the phone", and I went off stage and they hunted round and found a phone and I backed on holding the phone as though it were on a long flex because I had a lot of plot to deliver and we sort of got through that and later on I found that they'd put the actual phone in a drawer on the set and then forgotten to take it out.' In another production Doreen had to cope when a revolver was left off stage. 'There was a wonderful time at Salisbury when we were doing a play called *The Ghost Train* in which everyone is locked in a waiting-room and then the lights go and a train rumbles through and in the end somebody produces a revolver. It's a very funny play and I spent it all half asleep under a table because I'd had too much to drink. I was happily asleep under my table and all the lights went out, then I heard this whisper, "Pass it on, pass it on." And the villain had forgotten to bring the revolver on with him and he couldn't go off to get it, he was trapped on the stage, and in the blackout we had to pass this revolver round from hand to hand until it reached the right person.'

Tim Woodward describes a moment during a production of *Twelfth Night* at the Glasgow Citizens in 1983 in which he hurried to the wings, thinking he was late for his entrance and in doing so forgot to take on a prop purse. To cover his mistake he mimed handing it over to his fellow actor. 'He looks at me strangely. Did I detect a smile? Pause – LONG PAUSE – then I hear, "See yer," and he walks off stage left, leaving me with half the scene completed. Alone on stage, feeling sick, I suddenly shout, "At the Elephant!" and exit stage right. A nightmare, but I've been "Good with Props" ever since.'

Patricia Brake had a moment of crisis with some missing paintings, but she rose to the occasion magnificently. 'In one play we did, someone on stage has to open this chest and find some paintings inside it and they weren't inside the chest. In those days you never really knew the plays well enough, two weeks wasn't long enough. Without the props the actors were stuck, so I remember shooting round in a panic and stuffing these paintings through the letter box.'

Paintings and guns are easy enough to smuggle on, furniture can be more tricky, as John Newman discovered when he was an ASM at York doing a play called *Housemaster*. He left off the armchair, a vital piece of furniture, and one of the actors had to wheel it on at the start of his scene so that he would be able to sit down on it. Malcolm Farquhar recalls a similar moment. 'I remember being in a production of *Time and the Conways* and stage management forgot to set a pouffe on stage and when the two visitors arrived in the course of the act, one of them came on carrying it with her.' Donald Pickering must have been even more disconcerted when the sofa, which stage management had set all right, appeared to have a mind of its own. 'At Canterbury we did a dreadful play called *Ambrose Applejohn's Adventure*, all set in flashback. In the third act, which was the present day, I was playing a newspaper reporter. Of course, we hadn't had enough time to rehearse it. There was a scene which was the culmination of the whole play and I was saying my lines looking out of the French windows, which were down right with a sofa set in front of them, to see that no one was coming up from the cliffs. And while I was saying my lines, the sofa with me on it started to roll and it went straight out through the French windows. And I had to pull the sofa back on while going on with my lines.'

Lionel Jeffries reveals that his wife, Eileen Walsh, had great difficulties with a chair during a performance of *Pride and Prejudice* in Lichfield. 'Eileen played Elizabeth and I played the father. On the opening night on the Monday, she had to sit down at one point, and she fell through the wicker seat, it was so old, it was a terrible prop chair. Her arse hit the stage, her legs were up round her ears and she went like a "U". I had to get up, go over and try and pull her out. There she is, bent like this in the chair, and Mrs Bennet and I are trying to pull her out. On that night she stepped forward, in rep it's your turn if you're the lead to tell the audience what the play is next week, thank the audience very much and then next week we are going to do so and so. She steps forward, it's her first big leading part, there was this big round of applause, and she said, "Ladies and Gentlemen, thank you very much for my wonderful performance." That got another round!'

Guns can be very problematic, usually because they do not fire properly on cue and, even with a standby gun in the wings, performers can still find themselves in serious difficulty, as Paul Bradley indicates. 'At Contact in Manchester we did *The Comedy of Errors* and we did it cowboy style. We all had guns, in the duels we used guns. The gun would go off at the wrong time and people would feel about them and say, "Missed". Or when it was supposed to go off it wouldn't, so you had to have stage management on standby waiting in the wings with a gun.' Even with back up from off stage, the actor can feel very helpless at times, as Tony O'Callaghan describes. 'I did *The Long, the Short and the Tall* at Worthing. It's about a lot of soldiers stuck in the jungle during the Second World War. This Japanese soldier wanders by and they grab him and hold him in the hut they are staying in. They don't know what to do with him, it's a dilemma. They can hear on their crackling old radio that the Japanese army are closing in, so the young lad in the company grabs a gun and shoots the prisoner. Then they all run outside and they all get killed. In the prompt corner as a standby there was a starting pistol. One night the gun didn't go off and the actor playing the young lad made much of shaking the bullets back down into the chamber, but nothing happened and the Japanese soldier is looking at us and we're thinking, "Somebody do something." The woman in the prompt corner grabbed the starting pistol and went click, click. The guy on stage was going click, click, click. In the end the Japanese soldier grabbed his chest and fell to the ground and that was it. Then there was a lot of deliberation about how he died. He smoked all through the play and we talked a lot of gibberish about him dying of lung cancer!'

Paul Williamson remembers in a similar situation, that the stage management in the wings opted for an extreme remedy. 'A friend of ours went to see a melodrama being done by her local rep, during which the heroine, who was being menaced by the villain, had to draw from her bosom a derringer, which is a tiny pistol, and shoot him. She pulled the trigger once – click. She pulled it a second time – click. There was no standby gun fired from off stage, but they had been doing *Journey's End* the week before, which is set during the First World War, and there was a maroon left over in the wings. The third time she fired the gun they let that off and there was a huge explosion, with smoke pouring over the top of the flats.'

Even without a large explosion firing a gun can be alarming for those in the vicinity. Donald Pickering says, 'I remember doing *The Eagle Has Two Heads* with Peter Wyngarde and I played a deaf-mute Negro. There was a scene in the middle of the play which had someone shooting at a picture and the Negro servant is standing on the stairs reloading the gun for the leading lady and I found that every time they shot the gun I jumped out of my skin.' John Warner found himself with a gun which fired perfectly, but it flew out into the auditorium. This happened in the same production of *The Cat and the Canary* at Dundee in which Nancy Mansfield was locked on stage, and on the same night! 'The next scene was in the library and the two crooks had been revealed by this time and were fighting over a revolver and Nancy is on the sofa in the middle and one of them drops the gun and the other picks it up and holds him up. But what happened was that when he dropped it, it hit his heel and went out into the audience and they couldn't find the revolver and there was this hunt under the chairs. And they had to say, "Ladies and Gentlemen, please can we have our revolver back?" and somebody threw it up to them.'

Lionel Jeffries and Eileen Walsh were reduced to near hysteria in Lichfield by an errant lettuce leaf. Lionel begins the story. 'We had the curtain brought down on us in *Laburnum Grove*. I was playing the old character man and I was growing lettuces in the greenhouse at the end of the garden in the play and I presented this lovely fresh lettuce for tea and I had to take a leaf of this lettuce and shake the water off it, and I let go of this lettuce leaf, which had got salad dressing on it, it flew out of my hand across the plates and landed on the head of a man sitting in the front row of the stalls and he took it off and handed it back to me. We never got laughs like it in the ordinary play, it was what went wrong. I'm sure most of the time the audience was there to see what a fuck up there was going to be.' His wife Eileen takes up the narrative. 'We were all sitting at the table. In a situation like that if something goes wrong, you are really hysterical anyway because it's quite difficult to do. The director really lambasted us.' Lionel continues, 'We couldn't get the audience back. Mrs Calvershall, the manager, was in the wings, screaming at us, "Pull yourselves together, you're all sacked, I mean it, pull yourselves together, get on with it, get on with it." And we were convulsed, everybody had gone, so she pulled the curtain down, came on to the stage and bollocked us, pulled the curtain up again and as soon as the curtain went up we all started again. There was one actor who was the nephew of the Bishop of Lichfield, who had been a stalwart in situations like this, but he put his teeth through his bottom lip and drew blood, to try and stop laughing.' For the rest of the week they were hostages to this moment, as Eileen says, 'Every night of that play, when Lionel got near to that lettuce leaf, we all went. On Saturday night we had a packed house – they had to come and see the lettuce leaf!'

Less dramatic, but trying in its way, was the moment faced by Patrick Ryecart. 'My first part was an African butler called Sabu, not exactly type-casting, although they did make him English, but they kept his name, Sabu! I had to come on stage and offer the leading actor some cucumber sandwiches. I came on and realized that I had left on the clingfilm covering the sandwiches. I didn't know what to do, I was carrying a tray as well, so I turned upstage and sort of bit the clingfilm off. Everyone on stage came to a standstill, shaking with laughter, it was the most noticeable thing I could have done.'

Food and drink can often create pitfalls for the performer, as Angela Thorne demonstrates. 'I was ASMing, but I was also playing the lead because the leading lady had had a neurotic fit and decided she couldn't go on. I was playing the lead in *Spider's Web* and it was the most fiendishly difficult thing to learn. There's a tremendously important section of the third act when she discovers that this man who she's in love with is the murderer and she has to go off and get this tray of coffee that she has laced with poison and she brings it in and he drinks it. There was this tiny little area in the wings where the tray was set and I walked off and I don't know what happened, but something occurred, but somehow I sat on the tray and broke the coffee pot. I had to go back on stage and say, "There – is – no – coffee," while they scrambled around back stage and eventually found a mug. In the end I

HARE PRODUCTIONS LIMITED
present

MONDAY, OCTOBER 30th, for one week

J. B. Priestly's Comedy Drama

L'ABURNUM GROVE

MONDAY, NOVEMBER 6th, for one week

By Public Demand—Revival of

WHITE CARGO

MONDAY, NOVEMBER 13th, for one week

George Bernard Shaw's

PYGMALION

MONDAY, NOVEMBER 20th, for one week

The funniest play for years

GEORGE & MARGARET

1. Forthcoming attractions at the weekly rep in Aylesbury, 1939

2. The Liverpool Playhouse, the oldest surviving rep in the country

3. The Theatre Royal in Bristol, pictured here in 1954, is the home of the
Bristol Old Vic Company and has been in continuous service as a theatre
since 1766, a record unequalled anywhere else in Britain

4. Without books by Friday – Nigel Hawthorne, Joan Sanderson and
Nigel Arkwright at work in Buxton, 1950

5. Makeshift dressing-rooms: the Perth Repertory Company on a tour
of the Highlands and Islands in 1948

6. The lure of the footlights: Perth Rep preparing for a performance on their tour
of the Highlands and Islands

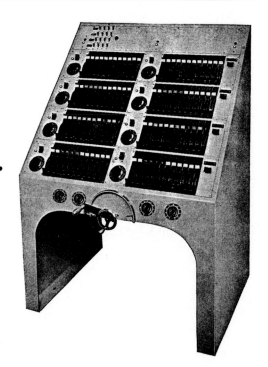

7. A revolution in stage lighting control was much needed. At Derby, Richenda Carey says, 'We had to wear plimsolls and rubber gloves to avoid getting shocks.'

8. The Penguin Players, based at the De La Warr Pavilion in Bexhill-on-Sea, were typical of the numerous weekly rep companies which flourished well into the 1960s

MURDER AT
THE VICARAGE

A Thriller in Two Acts by

Agatha Christie

Characters in order of their appearance

THE VICAR (the Rev. Leonard Clement)	ROBERT HOWARD
GRISELDA (his wife)	MARGARET LATIMER
DENNIS (his nephew)	DAVID BEAUMONT
MARY (the maid)......	JENNIFER WOOD
RONALD HAWES (curate)	MICHAEL NAPIER-BROWN
LETTICE PROTHEROE	CAROL HADDON
MISS MARPLE	VALERIE DUNLOP
MRS. PRICE RIDLEY	BEATRICE BEVAN
ANNE PROTHEROE	JEAN McCONNELL
LAWRENCE REDDING (an artist)......	PETER RUTHERFORD
DR. JOHN HAYDOCK	ROBERT WOOLLARD
INSPECTOR SLACK	OLIVER FISHER

The Play Produced by Robert Howard

Scenery constructed and painted by John Carter and Bathia Saye Macgregor

9. Vintage weekly rep fare at Tunbridge Wells in the 1960s

Synopsis of Scenes

The action passes in the study of a vicarage in the country.

ACT I SCENE I A Tuesday in Summer - Afternoon.

SCENE II The following day - 6.45 p.m.

SCENE III Thursday morning.

ACT II SCENE I The following Sunday - Late Afternoon.

SCENE II An hour and a half later.

Acknowledgments:

Telephones kindly loaned by the G.P.O. Modern furniture by Chiesman's
Antique furniture by Strawsons China by Phillip Peters
Hardware etc. by Timothy Whites W. H. Smith
Hollambys Nurseries Ladies' hairstyles by Josey
Electric light fittings by E. Powell Ltd. J. S. Tidby & Son
Fowle, Optician Boyds, High Street
S. E. Haward & Co. Ltd. Kent and Sussex Gold Refiners

Director of Productions		RICHARD BURNETT
General Manager	**For**	KATHLEEN WILLIS
Producer	**Burwil**	ROBERT HOWARD
Stage Director	**Productions**	DAVID BEAUMONT
Stage Manager		CAROL HADDON
		PETER RUTHERFORD
Asst. Stage Manager		JENNIFER WOOD
Stage Manager for Tunbridge Wells Corporation		B. J. WHITE
Front of House Manager		R. E. KNIGHTS

10. *Charley's Aunt* in Buxton, 1952: *(left to right)* Prudence Williams (the author's mother), Gwynne Whitby (the author's grandmother), Robin Hunter, Dennis Ramsden, Nigel Arkwright (the author's uncle) and the young Nigel Hawthorne

11. *Charley's Aunt* has always been a favourite with rep companies. This production was staged at the Wolsey Theatre in Ipswich in 1984

12. *Charley's Aunt* – again! The Penguin Players had to contend with extremely cramped conditions at the De La Warr Pavilion in Bexhill-on-Sea in 1960

13. At the Arts Theatre in Ipswich it was impossible to exit on one side of the stage and enter on the other without going outside and round the back of the building

Oldham Repertory Theatre.

Telephone MAIn 2829.

THE COLISEUM,
OLDHAM.

January second 1943.

Bernard Cribbins Esq.,
33, Smith Street,
Greenacres,
OLDHAM.

Dear Bernard,

In reply to your letter to the Committee of this theatre, I am instructed to offer you a position here at a commencing salary of fifteen shillings weekly.

You will understand, of course, that as there will not be a part for you in the play always you will be required to make yourself useful in helping with the stage-management as requested.

I should like you to commence at ten o'clock on Monday morning next, the fourth of January and I hope you will have a long and happy association with us.

Yours sincerely,

PRODUCER.

14. 'When I was a child it was really slave labour, because I used to work a seventy-hour week and I used to get fifteen shillings for it.' Bernard Cribbins's first offer of employment, from the Oldham Rep

15. In rep at Hayes in 1950, Joss Ackland *(second from right)* in *The Happiest Days of Your Life* – for many actors an apt description of their time in rep

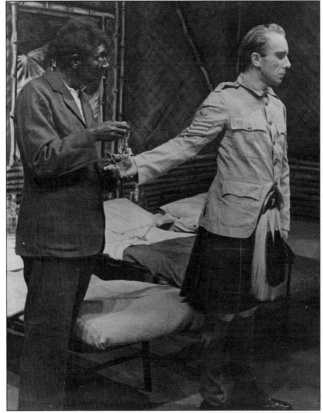

16. *The Hasty Heart*, Buxton, 1948. Actors were sometimes required to 'black up' in the days before integrated casting

THE LIVING THEATRE

Vol. 1   OCTOBER, 1948   No. 7
MONTHLY.   Price—ONE SHILLING.

17. Some weekly rep companies managed to find the time
and resources to produce a magazine for their playgoers' club.
The Living Theatre was published monthly by the Darlington Rep

18. Nigel Arkwright, pictured here in Buxton in 1948, had his nightcap whisked off his head by a piece of invisible fishing line in a bid to corpse fellow company member Barbara Leslie

19. Richard Todd *(right)* and Dennis Ramsden were often partners in crime at the Dundee Rep in the 1950s

20. The Penguin Players in pantomime

went back off stage and returned with this mug of coffee for him to drink.'

Terrible things can happen out of the blue, leaving the performer thrown and sometimes even injured. Julian Fellowes was a victim of such an incident in Northampton. 'I was playing the Wicked Witch of the West in *The Wizard of Oz*. The two other witches had to come and visit me for tea and I had to say, "Would you like something to eat, girls?" They fired a gun into the flies and these dead bats fell down and we had to pick them up and start to nibble them. Stage management had cut them out of cardboard and in order to make them fall they had put weights in the top. I picked one up and the weight fell forward and shattered my front tooth, which fell into my lap. Mercifully I was playing the Wicked Witch of the West, it would have been terrible if I had been playing Romeo. Afterwards I went and saw this perfectly strange dentist and I said, "You've got to do something about this, help me!" and he came out of his private house and fixed me up!'

With crises such as this occurring in the normal run of things, it is astonishing to think that actors would dare to risk playing tricks on each other, but the brave few do. Nickolas Grace recalls that when he did *Macbeth* at Theatre 69 in Manchester, 'someone put a goldfish in the goblet which is passed round during the banquet scene, corpsing everyone'. Barbara Leslie remembers appearing in a production of *A Christmas Carol* at Buxton when the ASM Penelope Williams played a trick on her, with the help of the actor Nigel Arkwright, who was playing Scrooge. 'I was playing the Ghost of Christmas Past and I had to appear through the bed curtains and Nigel was terrified, and on the last night Penny and another ASM were up on the fly rail and they attached some fishing line to Nigel's nightcap, so when I burst through the curtains his night cap shot into the air. It made me roar with laughter.'

There is great sport to be had in deliberately making someone corpse. Paul Williamson remembers working with a man who was a master of this. 'Geoffrey Lumsden was a terrible joker. By about Thursday in weekly rep he was getting bored. In the first act he'd announce himself as Mr Macaulay-Leighton instead of Mr Smith, knowing that we all have to go on introducing him as that later on. Or if he was playing a forty-year-old, by Thursday he would come on playing seventy, he wouldn't do much make-up, it would just be bloody

good acting, and where you had been clapping him on the back, he'd
be far too old for you to do that and you'd have to change all your reac-
tions.' By this own admission Geoffrey Davies used to be a terrible
corpser and because of that he was the butt of many jokes, 'Once in
Rebecca, I was standing warming my hands with my back to this enormous fireplace when someone from stage management leant forward
and put a sausage in my hand. It was awful, I didn't know what to do
with it, I didn't have a pocket to put it in. I had to hold on to it for the
rest of the scene.' Gabrielle Drake remembers another moment of
indiscipline during a production of *Edward II* at the Birmingham Rep.
'It was John Harrison's experiment with theatre in the round. The
action took place centre stage and all the actors sat around watching
when they weren't performing, the clothes were on racks behind us. It
was during Test cricket time and somebody would creep off and bring
a transistor radio back on to the stage and the Test score would be
going round.' It is rare but inevitable for actors to become involved in
escapades during a performance. Philip Voss recalls, 'I went to
Cheltenham to do a season and by that time I'd bought a flat in
London and used to try and get back at weekends. I remember one
awful time doing an Agatha Christie when everyone wanted to catch
the nine-eighteen to London and we cut down to the basic plot. Of
course, it made us laugh, we were standing up as soon as we'd sat
down.'

Even the best jokes can backfire, as Dennis Ramsden proves in the
following anecdote. 'At Dundee I was in a production of *The Importance
of Being Earnest* playing Algernon and Richard Todd was playing Lane
the butler. The first act ends with Lane presenting Algy with several
letters on a silver salver, which Algy, after looking at them, tears up.
Dickie Todd was dreadful, on a couple of nights he brought on
Littlewood's pools, things like that. I thought he was going to do something dreadful on the last night. Algy has a long wait before the end of
the act, so I went down to the props table and there was the salver with
all the letters and I checked them, they were properly addressed, but I
thought they looked a bit thick. I opened them and he'd put wood
inside them. I rushed down to the workshop, took out the pieces of
wood, cut them all in half and put them back. I just made my entrance
in time and then Dicky came on. He'd come down from his dressing-
room, checked the props to see if I'd discovered them, assumed that I

hadn't and came on, killing himself with laughter. I picked them up and tore them all without batting an eyelid. He couldn't believe his eyes. They had to bring the curtain down early because we were all laughing so much.'

The purpose of staging a play is to create an illusion of reality for the audience, but all this effort can be wasted by a single gesture, the simple mishandling of a prop, as Christopher Luscombe explains. 'My favourite rep story was told me by Josephine Tewson, who was appearing in *Johnny Belinda* at Morecambe. She was playing a deaf and dumb girl who has a baby. At the end of the play she is cradling it and she says its name and this represents a breakthrough. The audience was in floods of tears and the curtain came down, but it came up a bit too fast for the curtain call and they caught her chucking the baby into the wings. The audience were absolutely horrified; having been emotionally wrung out, they were aghast.'

15

Cry Havoc!

'She let out a piercing scream before going back to the dialogue.'

Frank Middlemass

TECHNICAL HITCHES COMMONLY occur when actors dry or mistime their entrances, when props are not set correctly or when the scenery fails to function, but misadventures are not confined to these areas. Some happen if an actor ignores the old theatrical adage, 'Never work with children or animals.' From the evidence available, children do not seem to be the cause of too many problems, but animals are. On some occasions it is clear that they should not have been in the theatre in the first place, as Frank Middlemass says of an incident which happened when he was appearing in a play in Cornwall. 'In Penzance a seagull got into the theatre during a performance of a drawing-room comedy and flew back and forth across the stage in a panic. The leading lady, who was terrified of birds when they were close, did admirably well and kept the scene going, except when the bird came near her. Then she let out a piercing scream before going back to the dialogue.' Brigid Panet was taken by surprise during the last act of *Othello*, 'At Guildford I played Desdemona and we never had time to rehearse all of the last act. I went on for the first night completely unprepared, and found the theatre kitten asleep in the bed.'

Pets belonging to company members have a habit of making impromptu appearances, as Richard Johnson records, 'The leading lady at Perth had a little dog which she kept in her dressing-room and one night the dog came on through a burning fire in the fireplace. We all took it in our stride, God knows how.' Maria Charles had a similar problem in Buxton: 'We had a wonderful actress called Beryl Measer, who had a great bull mastiff, who was terribly, terribly good, except that sometimes he would decide that he would just come up and see where Beryl was. It was the early Fifties and the particular play we were doing took place on a boat, it was called *Clutterbuck*, by Ben Travers. I spent most of the play in a bathing costume. The dressing-rooms were under the stage and I came up the stairs to go on for an entrance, just in time to catch hold of this dog, who had decided to go on. There was nowhere I could put him, so I went on with him. I got him by the collar, he was a big dog. One of the actors went, "Gosh, you've swum a long way." We all collapsed.'

Even animals who were scheduled to appear could sometimes behave capriciously, just to keep the cast on their toes. Pauline Yates was acting in a special week in Richmond, playing a murderess who was intent on suffocating the young heroine by locking her into a huge safe at the back of the set. In order to test the efficacy of this method, she first tries it on the girl's dog. With much ado, Miss Yates locked the dog in the safe, then proceeded with her next speech, only to be interrupted half a minute later when the mutt trotted back on to the stage through the French windows.

Brian Cox was flummoxed during a performance in Dundee, as he explains. 'In certain productions during the performance the only way from one side of the stage to the other was to crawl underneath it along a three-foot tunnel. One night I was crawling through with a live chicken I had to set on the other side. The bloody hen escaped and it suddenly popped up at the back of the stage.' Even once the animal is safely where it should be, there is no guarantee that it will stay there, as Barbara Leslie found to her cost when she was ASM for a production of *The Barretts of Wimpole Street*, in which the character of Elizabeth Barrett has a spaniel called Flush. 'As stage manager as well I had to borrow everything and I couldn't borrow a spaniel to play Flush, I had to borrow a bloody great dog that could hardly go on the sofa! On the Saturday the owner was in the audience and Miles Rudge was playing the doctor, he was giving a touching performance at Elizabeth's bedside and suddenly the dog recognized its owner, leapt over the footlights and into the stalls and Miles, playing an old man at the age of nineteen, suddenly became a very young man and leapt after him to bring him back.'

Animals can do far worse things than jump into the auditorium, as Michael Stroud learnt during a pantomime in Scotland. 'I had a terrible time in Dundee when we were doing *Cinderella* and we had two little ponies, rather gnarled, spavined old things, and they were in the wings one night and we suddenly heard a terrible thud and a very rude word rang out and I was skipping and hopping around as one of the Ugly Sisters and looked off stage and one of the horses had had a heart attack – it had fallen down in the shaft, which made the other horse go down, so the coach had shot up in the air to counterbalance it and Cinderella, who shouted the F word round the theatre, had her wig to one side, and this horse had to be taken out and it died in the theatre workshop shortly after. Taken off to the knackers' yard.'

Awkward though this must have been, it is John Warner who probably endured the most embarrassing moment while on stage with an animal. 'I remember we were doing *Tobias and the Angel* and Tobias has a dog called Toby, and we could not get a dog to play this part, and my landlady had a very obvious bitch, with dugs that hung down to the ground and she went to the theatre, "You'd better borrow this," she said, "but please don't let her get anywhere near water." So I didn't tell her I had a scene bathing in the River Jordan. This River Jordan was a duck bath behind a cut cloth with some tea boxes arranged around it. I had this rope round the dog, which I put under my knee, splashed about making swimming noises in the duck bath and of course some of it went on the dog, which leapt through the cut cloth, shook itself in front of the audience, got a round of applause because the audience had never seen such naturalistic acting in the Playhouse, ran off and I didn't know what was happening because I couldn't see. So I climbed up on to the tea boxes in just a loincloth, grabbed on to the canvas tree, which ripped from top to bottom, and fell right down upside down on to the stage. There was a lovely actor called Bernard Warwick who was playing the archangel Gabriel and he had a line something like, "You mustn't think this happens often." The next day I got a notice saying, "John Warner as the clumsy Tobias carried realism rather too far." Years later at High Wycombe I did *Tobias* again and travelling down on the train I was reading a horoscope and it said, "People born under Capricorn smell slightly of goat." On the first night I had a dog again, and there were some goatskin bags and this dog started doing very embarrassing things on stage to the goatskin bags. So the next night I put the goatskin bags much further upstage and had him with me and of course he did the unmentionable things to me instead.'

Sensible companies opt to use sound effects to suggest the presence of an animal rather than risk letting one loose on the theatre, but even these are not infallible. Alec McCowen recalls, 'I did a version of *Little Women* at Bromley. At the first or second act curtain one of the little women, Beth I think, has died, and the noise of birdsong is heard off stage and in my character I had to say, "Don't you hear her message from the other side?" and one night they'd lost the record with the birdsong on it and I saw the stage manager in the wings trying to whistle and make bird noises. I couldn't say the line I was laughing so much.' April Walker remembers a similar incident, in Chesterfield in 1952. 'I was on the book for a play called *The Gazebo* and there was one particular moment when the sound of Alsatians barking could be heard. Just as the cue was due, I realized there was no record on the panotrope, and I thought, "What can I do?" So I jumped up and walked round the back of the set barking myself.'

Where rep is concerned, the old theatrical adage should read, 'Never work with children and animals and on no account attempt to fly!' It is when small companies become over-ambitious in their staging that accidents tend to happen, as the following anecdotes reveal. Anna Carteret suffered a baptism of fire during her first-ever pantomime at Windsor. 'On the first night the fly man who was flying me on overshot, he was a bit over-eager, so I went right up in the air and right down and started to speak and then I was whisked up again in the air and off. The audience started to clap and they brought the curtain down and we had to start all over again. In the second act another time I never came down at all because my wire was tangled in the chandelier for the ball scene. I just slowly spun in the air and spoke every time I faced the front.' Leslie Lawton remembers similar chaos reigning in York: 'We were doing *The Hunchback of Notre Dame* and Donald Bodley the director says, "Right, at the end of Act One Esmerelda is tied to the stake and Quasimodo is in the belfry saying, "Sanctuary, sanctuary," and he swings down the rope, picks her up and swings back up with her." He kept saying this and eventually I said, "Please Mr Bodley, how are you going to do this?" He replied, "It's none of your bloody business but, if you must know, Kirby's Flying Ballet are coming in." On the Sunday Kirby's Flying Ballet arrives and Esmerelda is wearing a harness and when she's tied to the stake there's a rope waiting and the rope is attached to her harness. Quasimodo is also in a harness and he's on a wire and she's on a different wire and he's on a rope as well. The idea is that he goes, "Sanctuary, sanctuary," the flying man pulls his wire and he swings across the stage and as he swings back he drops him and as he touches Esmerelda the other guy pulls her wire for her to fly up. That's how it was meant to be. We had a dress rehearsal and it was superb, absolutely superb. On the first night the Kirby's Flying Ballet chaps were as nervous as everybody else and when they got the go from the prompt corner to pull Quasimodo's wire, they both took the same go. Esmerelda rose miraculously up into the air and Quasimodo swung straight past her. When he swung back his wire got twisted in her wire and by this time they were both spinning together about ten feet up in the air. I was on my knees screaming with laughter and the curtain came down.'

Even without the hazards of flying, the fly door in a theatre can be a dangerous place, as Tom Conti says. 'There was a flyman at Dundee, I think his name was Joe, who was awfully fond of the bottle, and there was this tremendous thud one night and he had climbed up the ladder to the fly rails, which are about forty feet above the stage, the flies themselves are another thirty feet above that. He was on the fly rail and when you are letting a backcloth down you belay it on a belay hook so that you don't take the whole weight of the cloth, and he was standing on the coiled rope and he didn't belay it he unhooked it, and the cloth immediately started to descend at a great rate and he was lifted up over the fly rail and he fell over forty feet on to a pile of blacks. He was so drunk he didn't really know what had happened. He was completely all right and just climbed back up the ladder.'

Joe was lucky because accidents do occur which have more serious consequences. Francesca Ryan had to halt a performance of *Peter Pan* at the Birmingham Rep when it became apparent that all was not well with one of the actors. 'In the first big family scene with the Darlings the chap playing my eldest son suddenly lurched forward and lay on the ground making peculiar noises on the rug, choking, hysterical noises. This was a morning matinée. It became apparent that these were not noises of mirth, they were noises of deep pain. He'd dislocated his shoulder, it just came out, I don't know what he'd done. I had to say, "Can we have the house lights up please, I'm terribly sorry but we're going to have to stop the show for a little while." This we did. We got him off into the wings and somebody who knew what they were doing put his shoulder back and we continued five minutes later.'

Christmas shows seem to be particularly dangerous. Eileen Walsh nearly came to grief during a pantomime. 'One night I cut myself, not too badly, but I cut myself and I got some Elastoplast and as I was doing it, I cut myself dreadfully on the Elastoplast tin and I couldn't do anything about that, I was spurting blood and it was the finale, so I rushed on and I was in such a panic that I knocked over the fire extinguisher in the wings, knocked the top off it and it shot up underneath my costume, right up my knickers. I did not go on to the stage, I *shot* on to the stage and landed in amongst everybody, covered in foam and bleeding.'

Stephen Boxer was involved in an incident which was altogether more serious, 'I played twelve parts in a production of *Macbeth* at Lancaster – young Siward, the doctor . . . I remember having a broadsword fight with Macbeth on the first night and splitting his head open. I felt very remorseful.' Many superstitions surround *Macbeth*: no actor worth his salt will quote from it inside a theatre building and it is always referred to as the Scottish Play. Its reputation for bringing disaster may well rest on the fact that there are a number of violent moments in it in which the possibility of an accident occurring is high. Barbara Jefford was told of an accident in Oldham which ended in tragedy for the actor involved and only adds to the ill omens associated with the play. 'In *The Giaconda Smile* the character I was playing had to slap the juvenile girl. I remember going into the green room having rehearsed that scene saying, "Oh my God, I've hurt her. I'd so much rather be slapped than slap." And Anthony Oakley, who was an actor in the company, said, "I should think so, I killed someone on stage once." And he had; he'd been doing a production of *Macbeth* in Oldham and he killed the man playing Macduff during the sword fight. That was because they'd had too little time to rehearse. You should spend more time rehearsing a fight than you would choreographing a dance. There had to be an inquest – Was it revenge? Were there feelings involved? I think there was something – the blade was dirty or rusty or something. He was exonerated.'

If an actor appears in *Macbeth* at his peril, he would also be wise to avoid working with colleagues who wear false teeth – misadventures with these can also bring performances to a standstill, as Vilma Hollingbery remembers. 'I remember working with an actor once, and we were having a terrible row on stage as father and daughter and suddenly his false teeth shot right out of his mouth. He caught them in his hand, turned upstage and put them back in again in one. It was like a conjuring trick. I was finished, I cried with laughter, I was beyond help. By that time the audience had joined in and it was terrible, we had to bring the curtain down. I was finished, I was rolling about.' Tom Conti had his own dental crisis during a moment in a play by Dylan Thomas called *The Doctor and the Devils,* which is about Burke and Hare. 'I played a character called Daft Jamie, who was a documented Edinburgh local at that time. He was sixteen when he was murdered by Burke and Hare, but he had a mental age of about four. That was my first really smashing role in life. Some crazy dentist had removed one of my front teeth when I was about sixteen and I had a tooth on a plate, which had to be gummed in, it was the most horrendous thing. One night I was playing this scene with Roy Hanlon, who was playing Hare, and it was he who lured Jamie with gin and suchlike to their lodgings, where they suffocated him. We were playing this scene and one of the features of Jamies's character was that he laughed a lot. And in one of these bursts of laughter the tooth on this plate came out and dropped into his glass of gin. Oh my God! It was terrible!'

The use of any technical equipment seems to increase the likelihood of hitches. Alec McCowen remembers that a fault with a projector in a melodrama called *The Bat* rendered him speechless with mirth. 'The Bat was actually a cripple who was terrorizing the neighbourhood. At the first-act curtain a silhouette of the bat was projected on to the curtains of the set during a dinner party and I had to turn round and one of the women screamed and someone else said, "What is it?" and I had to say, "The Bat!" But the back projection of this huge shadow hadn't worked and the silhouette at the back was like a tiny butterfly or a moth. It was terribly difficult to get the words out in that sort of situation.'

It is not often that it can be said of a theatrical performance that 'Rain stopped play', but this was the case in Hornchurch during the early 1980s, where Michael Simpkin experienced nothing short of calamity. 'I played Tony Wendiss in *Dial M for Murder.* One night we were doing the classic scene at the end of the first act when I think I've killed my wife and my friend comes round to see how I am. The act finishes with the friend saying, "I'm going home now, look after yourself, I hope you'll be all right, I'll call you in the morning." He leaves the flat and the curtain slowly descends with me looking vaguely villainous. Just as Michael Irvine, who was playing the friend, made his exit, the stage manager, instead of pulling the lever for the curtain to come down, pulled the lever for the sprinkler system! This meant that the smart Maida Vale flat in which the play was set was suddenly engulfed in rain water. I'm standing there with my Brylcreemed hair slowly losing its sheen, wondering what I was going to do, with this torrent pouring down on me. Michael Irvine realized what was happening as he went through the door; he waited six or seven seconds then popped his head back round and said, "By the way, I'd get that roof fixed if I were you." The curtain was then indeed brought down and the interval extended by an hour and a half to dry everything out. The audience had to be given free drinks.'

Peggy Mount recalls a situation in Leeds when the audience doubtless had to be mollified because the play went off with more of a bang than the stage manager had intended. 'I went to Leeds, which was Harry Hanson's top company, I went as an ASM. The director at Leeds was retiring and he wasn't doing his job as well as he should have done because he had a madman as the stage manager. We were doing a play in which the sound effect of a bomb exploding was required. The stage manager went to the director and said, "I've only got a small amount of ammunition for the bomb in the play, so do you mind if we don't use it at the dress rehearsal?" The director said, "OK," which was madness to this madman who had no idea of anything. What he'd got was a small Mills bomb. On the first night he took the pin out and threw it in a dustbin and it exploded and went right through the roof. They couldn't find the lights for the auditorium and the audience was charging about in the dark.'

There is one final theatrical adage, which says that, 'The show must go on.' In repertory companies, where there were no understudies, this required a special kind of valour from those struck down by illness and the poor unfortunates who sometimes went on with the script in their place. Tim Pigott-Smith says, 'I remember the bucket in the wings when everyone had gastroenteritis because there were no understudies. You never didn't play, somehow it always got on.' An actor had to have an illness as serious as smallpox before he was let off a performance, as Derek Jacobi recalls. 'There was a smallpox scare in Birmingham, everybody was innoculated, and I got it. I was the one in two million who got it, just for a week. The stage manager had to go on for me as the Beast in *Beauty and the Beast* with the script, and he had these big paws on as part of the costume, which meant he couldn't turn the pages of the script so he had to keep taking these paws off.' In Bristol Anna Carteret succumbed to the flu, but soldiered on regardless. 'I remember doing *The Beggar's Opera*, in which I played Polly. I remember having gastric flu and doing the matinée – there were no understudies – I was sick in the wings and then went on and sang opposite Amanda Barrie, who brushed me down and said, "Get on that stage, I'm not singing that duet alone." Dorothy Tutin was in front and she came round and said, "I thought you had a wonderful ethereal quality" – I was completely spaced out with flu.'

16

Acting

'To me, versatility is all.'

Eileen Atkins

DISREGARDING ALL THE hazards which could confront an actor during
a rep season and putting to one side the gruelling nature of the
rehearsal schedule, the demands made on an actor performing in
repertory were considerable. Vilma Hollingbery describes the regime.
'In Harry Hanson's company we did two performances a night, at five
o'clock and eight o'clock. Not only that, the first performance was cut
and for the second we put the cuts back in. We wanted a bit of time for
tea after the matinée. The plays were snipped all the way through so
you didn't cut anything important. In the first house you were remembering all the bits you'd snipped out and in the second you were putting
them back.' Surprisingly, Richard Bebb found that there were benefits
to be derived from this testing routine. 'I found twice nightly in
Bridgend far less tiring than weekly rep. By the second performance on
the Monday you had sorted out the technical hitches, after the first performance on the Tuesday you had sorted out the rest of the problems
and by the second house you were running on railway lines, and could
give greater concentration to the play you were working on in the day.'

The constraints of time and money seem to have resulted in performances with a kind of basic simplicity, which possibly made some
plays more accessible to their audiences. This is a theory put forward
by Tenniel Evans, 'If you were good, what you did get in rep were the
bare bones of the play. Very often people would say, "I saw the play you
did in rep, and I saw it in London and I didn't understand it when they

did it in London." They'd had four weeks' rehearsal and had been able to explore it and so had made it a bit more complicated.'

By definition, live theatre performances are ephemeral. In the days before video or even ciné film records were difficult to keep and, although newspaper reviews survive, it is hard for a modern theatre-goer to imagine what the standard and style of acting were like at the Penge Empire in 1952. Talking about her days in rep, Stephanie Cole refers to 'that terrible improvisatory quality of it all', and in some cases the audience must have had the impression that members of the cast were busking their way through the play. However, for every actor who questions the quality of the work carried out, there are scores who maintain that in the circumstances the standard was high.

Leslie Lawton gives a possible reason why this was the case. 'It was miraculous what we did and in fact the standard was not as bad as some people might think it would be. This was because we never really knew it well enough and therefore we were very considerate to each other. Bad actors don't work with other actors, they tend to work out front and there's no eye contact – well, you had to have eye contact – you had to keep your eye on the other person and hope that he would say something that would give you a clue as to what your next line was.' Peggy Mount echoes his opinion, 'I don't know how I did it, I don't know how we did it, but the fact is that some of those performances were really rather splendid,' while Alec McCowen maintains that, 'There were some wonderful performances, particularly a lady called Enid Staff, whom I saw play Hedda Gabler in Colwyn Bay. She was a knockout, I've never seen a greater performance by an actress.' Sounding a note of caution amongst these paeans is Paul Daneman. 'I worked with John Gielgud, after which I was out of work for a while, and I asked John if I should go back and do some more rep as I'd been asked back to Birmingham. He said, "No, no, no, don't do any more, stay with what you've done, it gives you a kind of spurious authority" – which is the best description I've ever heard of repertory acting.'

It is possible that the experience of being a big fish in a little pond, while initially gratifying, can have a detrimental effect over time and lead to what Sir Alan Ayckbourn describes as 'not quite coarse acting'. He goes on to say, 'To be honest, the attraction of a good rep or the good actors who were doing it, I think, was that they were the same in what they did, they didn't bother to change that much. They sort of brought themselves to the character and this is what the audiences liked. We were like *Coronation Street*, a lot of familiar faces the audience would see every week.' Bernard Cribbins echoes this, 'I think there was a certain facileness about what one did, you did look for a stereotype and jump on that. You went for a short cut, I suppose. Some actors invariably gave the same performances every week, with different frocks and different lines and were totally adored by all the old ladies with teacups on a Tuesday afternoon.' Trying to sum up the style of acting required during her days at the Marlowe Theatre in Canterbury, Lynn Farleigh says, 'Rep demanded a more conventional style of acting – charladies were over sixty and fat.' Belinda Lang agrees that the approach was largely traditional. She says of her stint in Frinton, 'We did plays very traditionally and very fast; in many ways it's an excellent way of working, providing the material is solid and you're not hopelessly miscast. Some people were terribly good under those circumstances, I'm not saying you're going to get anything brilliant, but I've been in much worse productions since when we've had a little too much time and no ideas. It is a very honest rendition of a play that you get that way.' This is reminiscent of Tenniel Evans's comment that what rep achieved was the bare bones of the play, which his wife Evangeline Banks puts down to the fact that forty years ago the style of acting was very different. 'I think in the 1950s acting was much less complex, it was much less inward-looking.' Indeed, Lynn Farleigh described it as, 'eyes, tits and teeth, out-front kind of acting'.

There seem to be two schools of thought about the foundation of the work carried out in rep and possibly in the theatre as a whole. Some actors rely on technique to put over a performance. They know that the use of certain skills and tricks will create a powerful effect, but they are often at odds with actors trained using the Method, developed in the United States by Lee Strasberg and his disciples. This school of thought believes that discovering the psychological and emotional truth which motivates a character will enable the actor to give a more profound performance. Certain artistes think that it is possible to use elements from both these approaches in their work. Paul Williamson suggests, 'There is a happy medium between utterly motivated people who look down on technique and people who are totally dependent on technique. It's both – you find the motivation, you find the truth and then you put it over with technique, but technique is not a dirty word.'

Among those who put less emphasis on technique and more on the emotionally creative aspect of the process is Rosemary Harris. Talking about her earliest days in the theatre, at the Roof Garden in Bognor Regis, she says, 'I didn't know about anything, I was literally flying by the seat of my pants. The thing was to learn the lines and sing out Louise – just get out there and do it loud enough to be heard. By about Thursday night you began to feel a nice feeling of confidence, but by then next week's play was already crowding out everything else. By concentrating on learning next week's play you might have been using the right side, the creative side of your brain to act with, because the left side, the logical side was very busy learning next week's script. The artistic side would be given a free rein. I think quite often one felt very free, there wasn't anybody editing you.' Peggy Mount describes a dovetailing which occurs when an instinctive approach gives way to more technical mastery of a part. 'What you had to do in rep and I'm being vulgar now, is to play as your belly guided you until about Wednesday, when you knew it and you knew where the laughs were and you could give a performance, a thinking performance.' For Daniel Massey, 'All acting is character acting. Imagination and emotion are what count, not technique.' Gabrielle Drake believes that levels of energy are crucial to performing in a theatre. She says, 'It's not to do with vocal power, it's to do with creating an energy around you to communicate with the audience, and the audience's response will show you whether you're getting through to them or not.' While Tom Conti says that as a fledgling actor in Dundee, 'I didn't know very much at all, just instinct, but what I always felt was right and still do, was not to act, to be absolutely real.'

Conti's faith in the importance of a performer striving towards realism in his work is probably attributable to the influence of television. The intimacy and immediacy of the medium make redundant the amount of projection required in even a modest-sized theatre and it is possible that acting has become less stylized and more naturalistic as a result. Television has raised the public's expectations of realism. Whereas in rep part of the fun for the audience lay in watching an actor in his twenties play a character aged sixty or more, a similar stunt would not be tolerated on television. This has had a profound effect on the method of casting within the profession, as Sir Alan Ayckbourn notes, 'Accurate casting means actors don't often get the chance to act.'

Robin Herford, who worked as a director at Scarborough for Ayckbourn, amplifies this idea. 'So much of the pressure now, and I find casting directors hugely responsible for this, is "Find me someone five foot eight and a half inches with blue eyes and orange hair who has a lisp." And they go and find five people who fit that description and say, "Right, here you are, take your pick out of these," instead of saying, "So and so's a jolly good actor, he could do that." Actors are not given the opportunity to expand, they are expected to be the people they seem to be and those are the parts they are given to play.'

When the embodiment of a character becomes so literal, much of the creativity from the actor's point of view is lost. Peter Hall points out, 'A degree of what a casting director would call mis-casting can be very creative and very valuable.' Eileen Atkins mourns the fact that actors are now expected to conform exactly to the roles they are to play. 'My memory of rep is the delicious freedom of being cast apparently against type and then finding out that you can do it. You're not given the chance now to see what you can do because everyone is thinking in types.' Sheila Reid agrees: 'Quite often in a company you had to play parts that you weren't suitable for, but that sort of strange casting could produce glorious results. Nowadays it seems that behaviourism is what is required, not acting. It can be a wonderful kind of adventure story, discovering why somebody is the way they are, what their eccentricities might be; using yourself, your imagination, your observation, because that's all you have. It's so thrilling rather than just going and behaving.'

The more creative casting which used to take place may have meant that in some cases people were given roles for which they were frankly unsuited, but Stephanie Cole believes that to be miscast can be beneficial. 'One was in plays with the most wonderful actors, now household names, giving amazing performances in the sort of parts they would never be called upon to play now. For instance, Penelope Keith, who is now only asked to do one thing, which she does superbly well. She and I were at Lincoln Rep together when we were both about nineteen. Penny played a huge range of parts extremely successfully, which she would never be asked to do now because there is a lack of vision. Some parts she was completely wrong for and not very good in, the same was true of me, but that was one of the things that made it wonderful.'

An example of this kind of miscasting is offered by Frank

Middlemass, 'I was never a leading man, I was always what is known as a character man except in one play at Oldham, about a lifeboat crew, in which I played the romantic lead, Jem. The stage directions for my first entrance were, "Jem stands in the doorway, a Greek God." And there was I, in my oilskins!' And Julian Fellowes recalls his excitement at being allowed to play against type for once. 'I remember we did *Day After the Fair* and the juvenile lead in it was bald and the director said to me, "Well, you'll have to play it." I was thrilled, I never got to play the juvenile lead, I was always the sporty cousin or the young policeman. I got absolutely carried away with the glamour of the whole thing and I loaded my face with mascara. The other characters talked about me all the way through the first act, "Oh he's got such lovely eyes, did you see his eyes?" so I put more eye make-up on than a Lancôme model and when I made my entrance a woman at the back said in a very loud voice, "Oh, how disappointing, it's the funny one."'

The challenge of being cast in a role for which one is not obviously right is invigorating for performers, who are infrequently able to display their versatility. Eileen Atkins declares, 'To me, versatility is all,' a statement corroborated by Barbara Jefford, 'You had to be versatile, much better for a young actor than going into a soap and playing the same character all the time.' Occasionally an actor's scope was tested to extraordinary limits, as Patricia Brake discovered during a season at Salisbury. 'In the pantomime I played the front end of Lulu the cow with a back end who suffered from claustrophobia. I played a carrot in the vegetable ballet and as I looked rather plump in the costume I kept hiding behind bits of scenery. I didn't really feel I was very well cast as a carrot!' With some understatement she adds, 'Rep taught me versatility. I don't think that's much admired now, but thirty years ago it was.' Lynn Farleigh remembers her range being tested too. 'I remember playing a charlady in one of those corpse-type plays and I was meant to be fat and sixty. I was appalling and giggled a great deal. I remember playing a schoolgirl in an American thriller, I expect I was dire, even my mother went silent after that performance. I also doubled as the Fairy Queen and a merry man in *Babes in the Wood*, I heard someone in the audience say, "Oh God, here she comes again!"'

Alec McCowen worked in weekly rep at York for eighteen months, and when this is added to the time he spent elsewhere in the provinces, he reckons he appeared in more than a hundred plays. This more than qualifies him to speak on the subject of versatility. 'My chief ambition was for audiences not to know it was me, so that one tried to look as different as possible. If you were playing the straight juvenile, of course everyone knew, but for the audience not to say, "Oh, look, it's our Alec!" was a great victory. Or for the local reviewer to say, "Alec McCowen was unrecognizable as the American gangster."' He laments the fact that, 'Nowadays you have three weeks' rehearsal and you are cast to type. Youngsters wouldn't play a fat American gangster wearing three jackets and God knows how many shirts and things and a huge overcoat on top.' He recalls the greatest test of his ingenuity came in a play called *A Hundred Years Old*. 'At York my biggest claim to fame was on the week of my nineteenth birthday I played a character who was a hundred years old and it was the leading role. There was a character actor in the company who was seventy-six who had to play my son. He went into a terrible sulk. The director thought it would be a good selling point, to have me, aged nineteen, playing the hundred-year-old man.'

Talking of his time in rep, Brian Rix says, 'I played every sort of part you could think of.' An opportunity like that gives the performer the chance to reap the benefits of rep, which Caroline Blakiston refers to: playing many roles within a wide range, discovering different sides of one's own nature, learning how to feel beautiful if that's what a part required, testing out one's comedic skills and improving one's natural sense of timing.

The audience also benefits when actors are given their heads and allowed to show how multi-faceted they can be. Dorothy Tutin believes that the public derives pleasure from witnessing the full gamut of a performer's talent. 'In rep the excitement of comparing the range of one actor against the range of another was part of the thrill of it.'

To demonstrate their versatility actors were frequently asked to play older or younger than their actual age. Wendy Craig says, 'The first part I played was in *Waters of the Moon* and I played a very old lady, which was way out of my range.' They used these opportunities with varying degrees of success, as Alison Steadman admits. 'I did *The Plough and the Stars* at Bolton and I played a character in her eighties. When I think about it now it was absolutely hilarious. My mother said, "When you walked out you looked at though you had thrown a bag of flour over yourself."' Michael Kilgarriff recalls a bizarre occasion.

'I had my nineteenth birthday the summer that I went to Jersey and in one of the plays we did I played the brother of an actor called Lance Percy, who was eighty. He had a black wig on and rouge all over his cheeks and I had lines everywhere and grey powder all over my hair.' Looking back, Leslie Lawton now sees his attempts at ageing up as rather over-zealous. 'I'm fifty-five now and I remember when I used to play forty, I'd grey up and talk in a very slow voice. When I was playing fifty it would come over as about ninety, I think. But it was a wonderful experience and nowadays kids don't get to do that.' Shaun Sutton recalls similar difficulties: 'The hardest thing to do is to be forty, when you are in your twenties. What's forty? All those lines you put on, wigs, all that lot, it was ridiculous. Old was easy, but forty! I used to play forty and then I'd think, my father's in his sixties and he's still running up and down mountains, why am I playing this man in an old doddering way?' On the subject of wigs and lines, Vilma Hollingbery remembers, 'When I started in the theatre I remember going into the leading lady's dressing-room, she was possibly thirty-two and I'd got to play the same age and I said, "Could I look at your lines because I've got to play your age next week?" She flung me out, she never spoke to me again for the whole season. I thought you had to put all those lines on, I didn't know how to play young middle aged.'

With actors ageing up and ageing down, often looking, as Alison Steadman said, as though they'd been hit by a bag of flour, the potential for corpsing or laughing illicitly on stage is enormous. The urge to giggle may be exacerbated by nerves or boredom, but whatever provokes it, the effect can be lethal, as Sheila Reid explains. 'Keeping a straight face was always quite hard because you were so tired, you were on the edge of an emotional chasm all the time. I think it was Athene Seyler who said that was how one should always be, certainly to act comedy, just on the verge so that you can tip either way. It's a dangerous place to put yourself, but it's quite exciting if you can do it.'

Most actors regard their time in rep as an opportunity to learn. Anna Carteret recalls a number of skills she was obliged to acquire during her time in Bristol. 'I played Anita in *The Green Woman* and I had to learn to do a belly dance, that was something way out of my ken. I had to play the piano in *Let's Get a Divorce* at Bristol again; I had to be drunk and play the piano at the same time. That was quite difficult.' Maria Charles remembers being daunted by what was sometimes expected of her in rep. 'We did a straight play, then a modern play, then a classic play, every week we were stretched. We did a play where I was supposed to be a Welsh maid and I couldn't do the accent, I hadn't got a clue and I went to Douglas Emery the director and said, "Can I not do this, please? I can't do the Welsh accent." And he looked at me and said, "Oh yes you will." "But I can't do the Welsh accent." And he said, "I don't care, this is where you are learning your craft." He was right. Everything he taught me, it all came to fruition.'

One theme which emerges when actors recall their days in regional theatre is the degree to which they were able to develop as performers. Barbara Leigh Hunt speaks of mistakes that she made on first entering the profession, 'Over-playing things, under-playing things, not knowing when to hold back, being too obvious,' which her experience in rep helped her to overcome. Similarly, Philip Voss admits that in weekly and fortnightly rep, 'All one cared about was looking all right, sounding all right, trying to get laughs, how to time a line.' These are matters which actors need to come to terms with before they can really mature in their work, and again rep provided them with the opportunity. Alec McCowen ponders whether a long spell in rep was beneficial and concludes, 'I don't think it made one a good actor but it did stretch you,' while his colleague John Moffatt believes that there are advantages to be had. 'You're finding so much out about yourself – what you can do, what you'll be able to do one day, what you don't ever want to do.' Belinda Lang summarizes for them all, 'I played right out of my range, that was the bliss of it. I suppose it was quite stretching, but the thing about it was that at the time one didn't feel one was being stretched enough, but you don't realize that you are.'

17

A Training Ground for Actors

'You found out very quickly what you couldn't do and rather more slowly what you could do.'

Derek Nimmo

REPERTORY THEATRE HAS always been regarded as an important component of the British theatre and Ian Carmichael provides an insight into its significance within the acting profession. 'I always feel rather ashamed to admit that I have never worked in a rep company. Ashamed because I feel that, in some ways, I never served an acceptable form of apprenticeship in those bygone days.' Certainly, as late as the 1960s, the esteem for the practical training which rep gave actors was such that most novices were recommended to do a stint in a provincial theatre. Brian Cox says, 'I remember going to an audition with Laurence Olivier in 1967 when I'd just got into Birmingham Rep. What Olivier was offering me was walk-ons and understudies. 'You don't want to come here,' he said, 'go to rep, go to Birmingham, you'll have a much better time. Go and do that, there's no better substitute for it.' To emphasize this point Peter Bowles says, 'Doing rep was regarded as an opportunity to hone your talent. Albert Finney famously turned down *Lawrence of Arabia* in order to go to Birmingham Rep. He said, "If I do *Lawrence of Arabia* I will become a star and it will be too soon. I want to go into rep." We were all advised and recommended after drama school to go to rep; it was like a university after your drama school.' As Richard Pasco says, 'The value of rep was audience hours': what it gave inexperienced performers was considerable, solid experience of being on stage in front of the paying public.

Hilary Mason puts it this way, 'Doing weekly rep gives you a tremendous idea of the English theatre, you go through dozens of parts, lots of writing, it gives you a great craft,' while Liza Goddard explains, 'Rep helps you understand how everything works. I understand the problems of the costume department, the props department, stage management, from having to turn my hand to everything. It gives me more tolerance if things go wrong now.'

As an apprenticeship for the theatre a period spent with a repertory company is unrivalled. Among the numerous things which actors feel that they were taught, high on the list is the discovery of their limitations. Lionel Jeffries declares, 'I learnt what not to do. I learnt what an audience would not accept. I learnt what I wasn't good at. So I played character men. At the age of twenty-one, twenty-two, I actually got the grounding for what made my living once I left – a series of old farts, funny people.' Jill Gascoine echoes him, 'In rep I learnt my limitations. When you're very young, you think you can do everything. If you're plunged straight away into being a star, which nowadays so many people are, then, if you go on and you're bad, you've ruined your career. I knew my limitations and if somebody offered me something I would say, "No, I think that's a little out of my line." Rep taught me what I was very good at and it taught me what I was very bad at; it taught me that I'd have a go if necessary.' As far as Derek Nimmo is concerned, 'It was a very hard discipline with low financial reward, but a tremendous amount of artistic reward. You found out very quickly what you couldn't do and rather more slowly what you could do.'

The teaching was rarely formal, people learned from experience, by making mistakes themselves, through watching seasoned members of the company at work and sometimes by picking up scraps of advice from their elders. Stephen Hancock describes how the process worked. 'When I joined the Darlington company I was sixteen and I didn't know what I was doing, I just thought I'd like to do some acting. I went along and they said, "Oh yes, we need some young people." I didn't know what I was doing, but there were two or three old hands who didn't resent me at all and said things like, "When you do that you want to face the audience," and, "Just speak up or they won't be able to hear." Basic things. They gave me the rhythm of a line, there were so many things I learnt in those few shows with those old hands. They were so kind. That tradition has gone now, which accounts for so much of the bad acting one sees, because there's nobody to learn from.' Richard Briers also believes he was the beneficiary of specialized knowledge passing from one generation to the next. 'I was aware of working in a tradition that was being handed down. William Roderick was the oldest actor at Liverpool and he realized I was terribly highly strung. He always used to say, "Even if you're playing a small part, always think of it as the leading part." He used to say, "Don't rush it," because I always used to rush my speech and rush everything.' For Philip Voss, going to the Oxford Playhouse and into Alan Badel's orbit was a revelation. 'I was at Oxford Rep with Judi Dench and Nyree Dawn Porter. Alan Badel came down to do *Othello* and *Kean*. He taught me that there was more to acting than I'd ever attempted before. I might have smelled it in the air, but he started to ask me why I was doing things and that's the revelation. One had never had time, it had never cropped up, to ask why you did something. You just did it. You were told to move down right. But with four weeks' rehearsal and with people of that quality – for example, Leo McKern played Shylock – one began to see that there was a lot more to acting.'

The service which older actors can perform for beginners is acknowledged by Joss Ackland, who says, 'The great thing about rep was that if you were able to advance from weekly to fortnightly to three weekly and to work with good people, you could learn. You had your mentors, but unfortunately today this is a thing that doesn't exist. Today people resist all knowledge of anything that's gone before.'

If advice was not forthcoming, then the fledglings soon learned from the mistakes that they inevitably made, as Daniel Massey says, 'When I was at Worthing with Jean Anderson, who was the leading lady, I jumped up to get a Scotch and ruined her laugh. I got the most appalling dressing down, but in a way that's what the learning curve is.' Maria Charles also discovered how slippery the learning curve can be. 'The play was called *Mrs Moonlight*. In dress rehearsals there was no stopping, if you made mistakes, you made mistakes. On the first night my entrance was through a door at the back of the stage and I had to come on and trip down to the front, where Mrs Moonlight was sitting in a chair, and say, "Good evening, Mrs Moonlight." I opened the door, closed it, straight down to the front, looked at the chair, which was very empty, looked around and the leading actress had put herself right at the back against the flat by the door, so I said, "Oh, good evening," and I played the entire first scene with my back to the audience. She wouldn't move, she wouldn't, she glued herself to the back of the set. So I just stood there. And when we came off, I said, "Did I do something wrong?" and she said, "No." I didn't know anything. Nobody ever did it to me again. It taught me such a lesson.'

Mark Lambert describes his early days in the profession and the benefits he derived from watching more experienced people at work. 'I left the Bristol Old Vic Theatre School in 1979 and was brought into the Bristol Old Vic company by Richard Cotterill, along with Daniel Day-Lewis. As young naïve apprentices we were able to witness the same excellent actors – Peter Postlethwaite, Lindsay Duncan, Jack Klaff, Miles Anderson and Jonathan Kent – being terrible in one play and quite superb in the next. We were also understudying and at one moment after we had returned from the Edinburgh Festival with *Troilus and Cressida* and had played the show for many weeks, one of the actors asked his understudy to perform the "piss-take" that he had heard about. Within minutes and only a quarter of an hour before curtain up, all of us young brats did a floor show in the green room, demonstrating some of the terrible actions and performances of our senior actors. To be fair, they at least pretended to laugh. That night all the performances radically changed for the better, but it never saved the show. Having said that, we had huge respect for these actors, who as I say were excellent. The point of the story is that I learned more watching in the wings and seeing good actors being bad and then good, than I did at theatre school.'

Comparisons between what can be learned at drama school and what rep can teach crop up inevitably. Lionel Jeffries believes, 'Rep is much better training than drama school. You don't learn acting, you can't learn it. You may have it and it can be developed, but you've either got it or you haven't.' Derek Jacobi finds himself in some sympathy with this view. 'Rep completed my training for me. I had some voice lessons at Cambridge which helped me, but I had a naturally strong and flexible voice. I had something that has sometimes been in my favour and has sometimes been against me – I had a natural grace, I didn't bump into furniture, I walked well, I stood – I presented myself physically well and that was something I had. I learned fencing at Cambridge from John Barton, who was at that time Dean of King's. I didn't in all honesty miss drama school. They could have taught me a lot of things, but what they couldn't have taught me, and what they can't teach anyone, is how to be an actor. You either are or you aren't. And I thought I was, something inside me told me I was, and all I needed was to learn through experience. In rep I had three years of something that I thought was of infinitely more use to me than a drama school.' In tribute to repertory theatre's passing and its heyday, Annette Crosbie strikes a balance between its function and that of the formal academies. 'Drama school hands you the tools and then you have to use them and now there's nowhere to do that.'

Rep was particularly good at creating a climate in which purely practical tips could be passed on. Josephine Tewson says, 'I can remember at those matinées in Morecambe an old actor called Graham Armitage saying that all I would have to do is to shout the last line before I went off, bang the door and I would get a round of applause and he was quite right.' Malcolm Farquhar says, 'From watching the artists in the Rapier Players in Bristol, I noticed they played three-quarters out front when there was a laugh line, which I did, and I got away with it.' Alec McCowen learnt not to let the other members of the cast down either by unseemly behaviour such as corpsing, or by allowing the audience to sense how nervous he was. 'They were very funny times and I laughed so much. There was a very respected character actor in the company at York and during the run of *The Bat* I laughed so much, I came off stage weeping with laughter sometimes, and he said to me in the wings, "You are a fucking disgrace to the profession," and my blood ran cold because I knew he was right. I often think of that now when I laugh or if I see any youngsters laughing.' McCowen describes what else he learnt, 'The audience is worried if you're worried. If the actor seems nervous, they're nervous. If you didn't learn to become a great actor in weekly rep, at least you learnt to control your nerves. Despite all the throwing up on a Monday, one seemed to be ice cool on stage, because you knew you mustn't give anything away and you mustn't make your fellow actors look bad.'

Geoffrey Davies also acquired what McCowen describes as the ability to remain ice cool on stage. 'Doing rep meant that you learnt to get on and do it, you were not fazed by anything, whatever happened you would make a go of it, you had to.' From Bernard Cribbins comes the following tribute, 'Working in rep gave me muscles to begin with from carrying furniture. It gives one confidence and an enormous capability for learning lines. You get a very good brain muscle, doing that week after week. It gave me enormous discipline in the theatre which was quite essential.' Tim Pigott-Smith believes that his time in rep helped him learn how to retain a sense of spontaneity on stage. He maintains, 'What you really learnt was the fundamental craft of the theatre, which differentiates it from any other medium, which is the job of fresh repetition. That's really what you get exposed to. You suddenly discover what you do in the middle of the second week. Accidentally you imbibe craft and acting is a craft that happens by osmosis when you're working with other people. That's why repertory holds such a strong place in the profession's psyche and soul because it was that place where people were taught without being taught.' Jenny Seagrove agrees, 'You learn your craft, you watch other people and you just learn. I think it is terribly important and I find it really sad that nowadays actors don't get to fall on their faces in a provincial rep theatre and learn what works, and what doesn't work.'

For Caroline Blakiston, 'Rep was an energizing experience. Actors are athletes of a kind and rep is good phsyical training. It puts iron in your soul. One needs to find great resources of willpower sometimes in order to go on.' Jonathan Cecil is one of many actors who say that rep not only helped them hone their work in the theatre but that the benefit was translated into other media as well. 'Rep quite definitely gave me a basis to start from. It takes away self-consciousness to quite an extent because you've got to do it, and it takes the edge off the nerves and certainly things like television comedy series, which I then did an awful lot of, where you only have a week for each episode, there too you needed to get it done in time and get it ready. I think learning professionalism as actors was absolutely invaluable.'

Richard Johnson highlights the contact with classical works that rep provided for young actors. 'One's stagecraft was honed in rep; one's sense of professionalism and of being a member of a company was established. Also, I got experience of Shakespeare very, very early on there. Young people nowadays don't get the grounding in the classics which we got because nobody can afford to do them now. Now it's all one set and four characters. The handing down of traditions of how you get a show on and the ordinary basics of professionalism are not as easy to acquire for the young today. I still think, in this country anyway, that theatre is the basis for one's life as an actor. Television doesn't make a basis for a career and many people nowadays have to base their careers on television, which chews them up, spits them out and you never hear of them again.' Johnson's evaluation of the training in Shakespeare which rep provided is one which Sir Peter Hall talks about with passion. 'When I first worked in Stratford-upon-Avon in 1956 there were all different kinds of actors in the company, but they were united by an understanding of Shakespeare's tune – I don't say his verse. If you asked them how to speak his verse they wouldn't be able to tell you, but they could do it because they'd heard it so much in rep, and now they don't and now they can't do it. If I'm doing a Shakespeare play now I have two weeks' extra rehearsal just to work on the text before we start.'

The gratitude articulated by so many actors for the time they spent in various repertory companies is not only based on the training it provided: many were delighted to have the opportunity to play a wide range of differing roles. Among them is Timothy West, who admits, 'My support of regional theatre isn't just altrusim, I've played a lot of parts in the regions which I would never have been offered in the West End.' Roger Ostime describes its benefit thus, 'Rep provides the same function for an actor as a sketchbook does for an artist. Numerous parts, quickly done, some of which you're not quite suitable for, nevertheless give you a sketchbook of characters that you've had a go at.' Liza Goddard found that her range was extended beyond her wildest dreams by her early apprenticeship. 'As an actress having done rep, I feel I can play any part at all, literally any part at all. I even went on for one of the men when they were off. That was the wonderful thing about it, that you could play every single part,' while Maurice Denham laments the fact that, 'One never got the opportunity for playing such parts again.'

The theme which crops up repeatedly when actors contemplate the contribution working in rep has made to their careers is that it provided them with the opportunity to fail. With less at stake than on television or in the West End and a wider variety of parts to have a go at, they could take risks. Richard McCabe makes this point very clearly. 'The great thing about rep was that you could go and fail. You weren't aware of that at the time, you gave the best that you could give, but you could experiment more. I'm sure if I'd given the kind of performances I gave then at somewhere like the RSC with the nation's press there, the pressure would have affected me, it would have hemmed me in. I'd have been scared about committing myself to more adventurous choices, which actually I had no compunction about doing, so in that sense it extended my range. I found out what I could do and I was allowed to do that.' Bernard Hepton agrees, 'When I was at York and Windsor people used to talk about rep as the place where actors learnt their craft and I used to fight this and say, "No. I know my craft." But I was young and foolish. There's no doubt about it, that is where the actor learnt his craft because he failed most of the time and you actually learn by failure. Nowadays there are very few places for actors to fail. I think it is very unfair on young actors.' Gemma Jones feels very differently, however: 'I would deny the fact that rep gave you a chance to fail. For myself, I always felt I had to be a hundred and twenty per cent. I don't think I have a comparative conception that it would be easier to fail in Nottingham. I don't think I ever felt that it didn't matter because it was only rep.'

Whether or not actors felt that their prospects in the profession would not be irrevocably damaged by a bad performance in a play in rep, they did recognize that it was possible to pick up bad habits by staying in regional theatre for too long. Joss Ackland says, 'I think too much weekly rep can be disastrous because you pick up tricks. There was an actor in the company when I was at Wolverhampton. He was absolutely wonderful. He was brilliant, he would turn in the most fantastic performances. Eventually, after about seventeen years in rep, he went to the West End to do a play and they rehearsed and after the first week everyone thought, my God this is extraordinary, then the rehearsals went on and there was nothing there. He had got into this habit over the years and it was sad because there was no development.' Ackland explains what he means by bad habits: 'With rep you develop mannerisms and tricks, you know that if you walk towards the exit then turn your head a little, you can get the audience to applaud, really cheap tricks. The danger, particularly in weekly rep, is that you are inclined to over-emphasize. I don't think I started to act until I stopped acting, stopped going for effect. In repertory what you have to learn is to get rid of the false noses. I always used to cover myself up in noses, great lines under the eyes and hide. Now I do absolutely the opposite, but it can take a long time for somebody to learn that.' In contrast, John Moffatt says, 'You used to hear people say, "God it's so bad for actors to stay in rep for a long time because they learn such bad habits, they take the easy route and just trot out a lot of old tricks," but it was nearly always actors who hadn't done it.'

Most actors remain upbeat about the advantages to the young of working in rep, among them Wendy Craig: 'Unless rep experience is available to young actors they don't learn how to project, how to be disciplined.' Stephanie Cole is evangelical in her belief: 'I really worry about young people leaving drama schools now. Rep was the most amazing training ground. I did pantomime, I did music hall, I did revue, I did Shakespeare, I did Restoration, I did Agatha Christie – literally everything, so you stretched every muscle of the actor's being. You learn about so many plays and so many writers. You learn what you can do and what you have to work on.' Speaking of her own experience, Liz Crowther lists the indispensable assets she gained from rep: 'I learned how things went too far, how to play comedy, how to be subtle about things, how to hold yourself on stage, what make-up looks like backstage and how it looks from the front, the importance of pace, of coming in on time, the chemical balance between the audience and what's happening on stage.'

Undoubtedly Annette Crosbie strikes a universal chord when she says, 'I'm thoroughly of the opinion, and I think most of us are who have done rep, that it's the best time of your life, there's simply nothing else like it because your entire concentration is on doing these plays, you're not aware of anything else, you're enclosed in this family and that's what you do. You get to know the audience and the audience gets to know you. It's the best training, it's a real apprenticeship and the things you learn, you learn without realizing you're learning them. Amongst the most valuable things you learn is the energy you have to sustain from curtain up to curtain down. It's up to you and the rest of the ensemble to keep the play up off the ground. You realize very quickly that it only takes one person to drop it for a second and then you've lost it. There's no other way to get that kind of knowledge and it saddens me that it's gone. I don't know what will take its place.'

18

The Audience

'Most actors will tell you that the audience is the maker of the play.'

Daniel Massey

WITHOUT AN AUDIENCE a performance has no meaning and one thing which separates repertory theatre from other forms of dramatic understanding is its symbiotic relationship with the local community which it serves. In many cases a rep evolved from amateur groups within a town, or was established as a club for enthusiastic playgoers, as Bob Eaton, director at the Belgrade Theatre in Coventry, explains when he talks about, 'that initial impetus from those people who were in the amateurs in the Forties, Fifties and Sixties, who created places like Derby Rep. That's how the reps started out, the amateurs hired the occasional professional director, then the occasional professional actor, so in a sense the reps came out of their communities.' For some towns the fact that they have their own theatre remains a cause for pride, as though a community is somehow dignified by such an amenity. When theatres are under threat it is often local activism which saves them, as Harriet Walter illustrates, using her experience at the Duke's Theatre in Lancaster as an example. 'There were times when the funds were being cut back by the Arts Council and we had to be laid off and re-employed later. There was a lot of hoo-ha in the local paper about not wanting to lose their theatre. I have noticed that nationwide there is a tendency for a town to invest a great deal of civic pride in their theatre. People would hate to lose the building, even if they seldom go inside.'

Through their general support and the specific contributions which they offer, the audience is a sine qua non for any theatre. In rep,

209

perhaps because the relationship between the two is often particularly intimate, members of the public can adopt a high profile. There are times when the drama in the stalls or dress circle is greater than that on the stage, as William Franklyn remembers. 'This story took place at the Esplanade Theatre, Ryde, during my first rep season in 1947. We were doing *French for Love* and it was a municipal auditorium, two hundred seats in two blocks and windows on either side with the curtains drawn. It was a pavilion in every sense, with the sea on one side. During one act I was in the middle of a longish speech and a nude lady appeared down one aisle at a sort of steady trot. She was completely naked, very white skin, and I just kept talking, kind of mesmerized as if a cobra had just appeared in front of me. The audience looked at me as if I'd seen a cobra! I thought, "The best thing I can do is to keep talking because this is not an everyday occurrence." As she got nearer and nearer to the footlights, I saw two men in white coats appear at the back of the theatre and follow her down. As she got to the footlights, she didn't pause or react, she just looked slightly panicked. She turned to the right, went across to the windows, drew the curtains, opened a window out on to the esplanade, by which time the two men in white coats had dashed down. She was out of the window, the esplanade was about ten or twelve feet wide and she was up on the wall about to jump into the sea. I don't know whether the tide was in or not. The two men followed her out of the window. The audience didn't speak, there was a wonderful stunned silence. I went on talking, obviously getting a little slower in my speech, then I turned to my partners on the stage to give them a cue and they were a shaking mess. We carried on, very slowly and in rather a low key, while the audience assembled themselves and then they suddenly burst out in applause. It transpired that the lady had escaped from a local asylum.'

Lionel Jeffries recalls a similarly disruptive incident from his days in Lichfield. 'In the middle of the balcony scene in *Private Lives* there was a commotion in the front three rows and I looked up to see what the hell was going on. There was some talking and laughing, and there was a six-foot-four Irishman peeing against the wall of the theatre, in the middle of the play, with his old dick, totally pissed. So I said, "Sir, what do you think you're doing?" And he said, "You carry on Lionel, you're doing well." He finished his pee, rolled it up, put it back into his trousers and went off. It took nearly ten minutes to get the audience back.'

Members of the audience can also cause the ultimate inconvenience by dying during the afternoon performance, as Chris Harris recalls. 'At Worthing I seem to remember there was a particular matinée when somebody died. The turn-round was very quick and there wasn't time to get her out, so they just moved her along to the end of the row.'

This sort of occurrence is rare, although members of the audience do make their presence felt in ways that are sometimes lacking in subtlety. Timothy West says, 'I was in a new comedy recently and in the first house on a Saturday a mobile phone went off. This happens quite often nowadays, but on this occasion the fellow answered it and proceeded to have a conversation. We all just stopped and waited. The audience gave him a round of applause when he finally rang off.' Sir Derek Jacobi recalls an instance of audience intervention which, although it was less abrasive than the telephone call, was no less distracting. 'Usually in matinées the old ladies would be sitting there and they would have to walk across the front of the stage to get out and many times if their bus was leaving before the end they'd go a bit early, but they would always thank you for your performance. It was very cosy in that sense.'

Clive Francis remembers a similar cosiness pervading the era of the tea matinée, when afternoon tea was served with the performance. 'There was a wonderful link with the audience, they used to talk to you sometimes, they'd put their tea trays on the stage, which was always a nuisance when the curtain came down.' Alec McCowen claims that the rattle of the teacups at the Leas Pavilion in Folkestone used to drown out the dialogue on stage. Cherry Morris says when she worked at Folkestone, 'In the summertime we did tea matinées three times a week. They rearranged the seating so that there were tables and chairs. In the middle of a dramatic pause you'd hear things like, "No, you have the éclair, Ivy. I had it last week."'

If members of the public had any idea how audible they were from the stage they would be more circumspect in their comments. Jocelyne Page appeared in *The Applecart* at the age of twenty-one, playing the Queen, who was about seventy-four. In one scene she had to knit and on the Monday night she overheard from the audience, 'She can't knit, she may be the Queen but she hasn't got a clue.' Tenniel Evans says, 'We did a production of *As You Like It* at Northampton and when Lionel Hamilton, who was playing Jaques, reached the "All the world's a

stage" speech, a voice from the audience said, "Here we go, Mabel."'
Sometimes such comments can be directed at the actors themselves, as
Clive Francis again recalls. 'An actor I knew was in a Harry Hanson
play at Hastings and he was playing the policeman. He was standing
by the footlights and somebody tugged at his trouser leg; he pretended
nothing was happening, but there was still this tugging and in the end
he looked down and this woman said, "Oh we did think you were so
good last week."' Bernard Hepton remembers a moment in a production of *Julius Caesar*. 'John Whiting was an absolutely brilliant farce
actor, like I've never seen before, but his Shakespeare wasn't very good,
and he was playing Cassius, and when he got to the line, "Today's my
birthday," there was a great shout from the gallery, "Many Happy
Returns!" It was all in good part.'

Some audience interaction can be motivated by the best of inten-
tions, as Rupert Frazer describes. 'I was playing Alcibiades in another
Glasgow Citizens jock-strap production and I had to make an entrance
ostensibly with my army, but I had no army. The best note I ever had
was when the director said, "I want you to swarm down this net." I've
got this mole on my back and as I came down backwards I caught it on
the net and I could feel this warm blood and an old boy leant forward
and said, "Excuse me, your back, it's wounded." And it was the word
"wounded" that I really loved because it was clearly so much in the
show.' Frazer was untroubled by this well-meant remark, but Lucy
Fleming remembers an incident in Farnham, when the audience
wasn't so tolerant when a man intervened in the action. 'During the
show someone from the audience climbed up on to the stage and put
out a fire which had started in an ashtray. When he sat down again the
audience all went "Sshhh!" at him.'

The audience may interrupt a performance to congratulate an actor
on his work, but they may equally show their displeasure. Both Brigid
Panet and Marjorie Yates remember having pennies thrown at them
by bored children during schools' matinées, but in Michael Cochrane's
case someone took a more formal option and wrote down their criti-
cisms. 'I played the Welsh boy in *Night Must Fall* for the Penguin Players
and during a mid-week matinée an old lady in the back of the stalls got
up, walked down the aisle and put a note on the front of the stage. I was
on stage with this wonderful actress called Annie Dean, who was
playing the character of the woman in the wheelchair. I walked down

to the front and picked this note up, turned upstage, unfolded it and read – "Will the Welsh boy shut up and the woman in the wheelchair please speak up." That finished me, absolutely finished me.'

David Horovitch remembers being taken aback by the response of a woman who came to see him in a play in Cheltenham. 'We did a production of *Zoo Story* by Edward Albee and I think people came to see it expecting an innocuous play about animals, but it's really a very harsh play about alienation. The audience hated it, they just hated it and I felt waves of the most personal kind of animosity coming at me, particularly from matinée audiences. During the play my character had a long speech which went on for about twenty minutes, I think that it's one of the longest speeches in modern drama and it says that you have to establish a relationship with something, even if it's only a dog. He describes in great detail how he tries to make this dog love him. I used to play it very close to the audience and there was this woman who kept getting up and going to the loo and eating chocolates all the way through and suddenly in the middle of this speech she leant forwards and said to me, "I hope you die." And then she got up and left. The thing about audiences in Cheltenham was that if you stepped over a certain line they would give you no quarter.'

Most people in the audience would be able to restrain their comments until after the show was over. Of course, actors expect to come in for harsh words from theatre critics and the regional press are no exception, as Anna Carteret discovered. 'I remember the Rotherham critic saying, "And as for Anna Carteret, Lincoln Theatre Royal seems to dredge her up every week as their sex kitten."' Remarks like that are par for the course, but repertory audiences were often keen to voice their opinion as well. 'When you were out propping, the townspeople would all give you their tuppence-worth about your performance,' Simon Williams says. 'You had to listen to their critique because you wanted to borrow props from them.' Alec McCowen reminisces about his landlady in York, Mrs Lythe. 'I was doing a play by Mary Hayley Bell called *Men in Shadow*. I was playing a young airman who crashed in France and was being hidden in a loft. I think both my legs were broken and they had to be set on stage. There was a lot of gasping and screaming and of course they gave him a cigarette while this was going on. I thought I did wonderfully well on the first night. My landlady Mrs Lythe always came on a Monday and I went home to her house to have dinner after the show very pleased with myself and she said, "Well you made a proper fool of yourself, anyone can see you can't smoke!" She was a good fierce critic, Mrs Lythe.'

Many theatres have playgoers' clubs to increase contact between the company and its community. Often there are small receptions on the first night and John Warner remembers them well. 'The playgoers you'd see on the first night would always say how so and so's amateur production was so much better than yours.' Harriet Walter's recollections of similar encounters with Lancaster audiences are more positive. 'After the show you would go and mix with the audience in the bar and talk to them so you got direct feedback, which continued and influenced me in the other jobs I did after. It set a standard for what a theatre occasion can be. The material can be entertaining or provocative or whatever, but then you get a chance to follow it through after the performance, which becomes almost a means to an end. Obviously there were times when I wanted to block that off and be private, in a small town like that people can get into your pocket a bit too much, but on the whole at that age I was very happy to do that.'

Another veteran of the theatre club get-together is Stephen Hancock. 'At Ipswich there was a theatre club that met every fortnight to discuss the play. We were part of the community definitely, not as now, where you just go to a so-called repertory company for one show. That means nothing to the community, it's a touring show as far as they're concerned. You were seen about and people came to see you. You got the rough with the smooth, "Saw you in that and you weren't very good", and you knew you weren't but you made the best of it.'

Eileen Walsh remembers that the loyalty of the regulars did not blunt their critical faculties. 'The audience were very faithful, but if they didn't like you they let you know: "I did not like you this week and I don't expect you to play a part like this again." They were theatre-goers. They loved the theatre. They used to pack in, Friday and Saturday night.' Maria Charles describes how she was cut down to size by one Buxton playgoer. 'The audiences would come every week to see you and they got to know you quite well. In Buxton I was in a play called *Pick Up Girl*, which was set in the early Forties in New York, about two young girls who become prostitutes and one gets VD and has an abortion. It was quite harrowing. We had this middle-aged couple who used to come every Monday night and sit in the front. I was really quite pleased with what I'd done, in a weekly rep, and we were all having a drink in the George and this particular woman came up to me and she said, "Oh, you were good. Mind you, I knew it was you." Within a second she'd just cut the ground from underneath me!'

Sometimes the demarcation between the actor and the role he is playing can become blurred in the minds of the audience. For example, Rachel Kempson recalls that when she and her husband Sir Michael Redgrave were courting, they were appearing together as the love interest in *Miss Linley of Bath* at the Liverpool Playhouse, where the houses were packed every night because people thought that they were seeing the real romance unfolding. Barbara Leigh Hunt has two anecdotes that give further insight into how literally some members of the audience interpret what they see. First, she says, 'I went to Colwyn Bay, where I shared the leading parts with the director's wife, which meant that I'd play a small part one week and a much bigger part the following week. One day a woman stopped me in the street. She said, "Excuse me love, I thought it was you. Oh you are good in the play this week. I didn't like you in the play last week, but this week (in which I was playing the lead) you were so good. Mind you," she leant forward, "you've thought of more to say!" Later I thought, if she imagines we make it up every night, then she thinks we're a lot cleverer than we are.' Miss Leigh Hunt's second story shows an equal naïveté, but a typical loyalty as well. 'There was a girl in the company at Guildford called Berenice Baron, who was the juvenile lead. She had been there a long time so was given a week's holiday and another actress was brought in to take her part in *The Flowering Cherry*. They rehearsed the week she was away and when she returned *The Flowering Cherry* was playing at night. Rather than give up an evening to go and see the production, she decided to go to one matinée. During the interval she remained in her seat and there were two old girls sitting in front of her and one turned to the other and said, "That girl's very rude to her father, she's very outspoken. I don't think I like her." The other one said, "Yes, she's very rude, very outspoken." There was a pause, "And if our Berry had been playing that part, she wouldn't have spoken to her father like that."' A similar kind of allegiance is behind the remark made to Carmen Silvera in Warrington by a confused devotee of rep. 'I was in the market once doing some shopping and a little old lady came up to me and said, "You're from the theatre. Oh, I come every week, I never miss it, I haven't missed a single episode."'

Individual responses from members of the audience can be diverting, sobering and sometimes enlightening. They are flesh on the bones of the all-important relationship between the rep company and the community which it serves and in order for the theatre to flourish at both a regional and a national level it is crucial that this connection is kept alive, a point stressed by Richenda Carey. 'At Bristol there was a great feeling of ownership of the actors by the town. Theatre can't survive without a great sense of local pride and identification.' Some actors feel that this proprietorial attitude can be taken too far. Peter Bowles comments, 'You do build up a genuine audience following. In some places you're treated a bit like pet dogs,' but on balance performers seem to enjoy the sense of being part of the local town. Tim Pigott-Smith declares, 'You felt very strongly that the theatre was part of the community, you felt you were serving your city and if the play wasn't very good it didn't do very well, but generally speaking they were very good productions.'

Barbara Jefford describes the process by which actors were fostered by the local audience. 'There was a very close relationship between the town and the theatre at Dundee. I got to know many people who were regular visitors to the theatre. When you had been there for about four productions, you notched up a band of not so much admirers but people who were interested in what you were going to come on as next time.' John Nettles is clear that such attachments can be a positive benefit. 'The links with the community varied from town to town, but when they were strong, it didn't half help. You felt that you were actually providing a service that was appreciated. I worked at Alan Ayckbourn's theatre in Scarborough and that was wonderful. We stayed with people in the town, they came to see us, we went to see them, we visited each other's houses, it was terrific.' Another person who enjoyed being part of a community was Timothy West, although he discerns a shift in the dynamics of the inter-relationships. 'To become a sort of identifiable part of a community is a very nice thing. You get to know the shopkeepers and the people in the pubs and restaurants and people in the street come up to you. When I was in rep we all felt we were being rather nice to the Friends, letting them in on a secret. Now, you feel you must be nice to the Friends because they might drum up some business, and there's a slight difference.'

Not all performers were as lucky as Nettles and West in benefiting from the vitality of the connection between the town and the theatre, as Richard Bebb recalls, 'In Buxton there was absolutely no sense of a relationship between the theatre and the town,' but an experience like this seems to have been the exception which proves the rule; more common was the perception that Alison Steadman has of her time in Lincoln. 'It was a very good relationship between the town and the local community. Philip Hedley, the director, was very keen on getting the town involved. It was a living space, all day long there were people coming in and out. We had art exhibitions by local artists. It was not just, "We are the Rep, we are exclusive." ' Jonathan Church, who is now artistic director of the Playhouse in Salisbury, shares Philip Hedley's commitment to the general public. He says, 'I really like the fact that you do develop a relationship with the community. It's a strange job to be doing. What's its function? What's its point? Entertainment is valid, but I think there has to be more than that and what I enjoy is that we have a main house, a studio, an education department and a youth theatre and that's how you link with the community. It develops over time, you develop your taste together. I quite like the fact that theatre is a public service as well as entertainment and art.'

Francesca Ryan thinks that live theatre can have particular importance for local communities because as shared experience it helps to bond people together. 'I have quite an old-fashioned view of what a rep's role in the community is. I think they should provide good-quality classical plays, or large-cast plays of the kind that they won't see in touring theatres or on television. In the end you can't beat live theatre. It's a different experience. There's a communion between the people who come; though they're strangers to you, you do share an experience. In the cinema or watching television you don't have the same feeling of being in an audience. The cinema's a much more private experience. The theatre did have its roots in religious ritual and I don't think it's too fanciful to say that it still has a kind of ritual feeling – the lights go down and you're in communion with a lot of other people.'

In an ideal world local people would identify with their reps in the way that football supporters take the home team to their hearts. Christopher Luscombe saw this happen at Leatherhead. 'I saw every production at Leatherhead for six or seven years, all through my teens. During that time I remember that Leatherhead Football Club were doing very well in the FA Cup. I used to go and watch them as well and I remember them winning against an unlikely, successful, high-profile side, I think it was Leicester, and at the end of the match this great big bruiser stood up in front of us and saying, "This is the best thing to happen to Leatherhead since the Thorndike Theatre."' Sir Derek Jacobi agrees that the theatre can be a unifying factor in a town or region. 'Rep is a wonderful focal point in a local community and they get very proprietorial about it – they're proud of it, they will criticize it if they don't think it's doing well – it becomes a great cultural focal point as well as a learning centre for future actors.'

The relationship between a repertory company and its community has to be worked at and responsibility for doing this rests with the person in charge. When he was artistic director of the Lyceum Theatre in Edinburgh, Leslie Lawton was diligent in carrying out his duties. 'I went round and talked to Women's Institutes and clubs and I did lunches and dinners to make people more aware of the theatre. I think the more of that you do, the more chance you've got. You've got to go out to them if you want to build up a kind of regular audience, which is critical, you've got so much against you – television, football, etc. My approach was: I've come to see you, now you come to see me. I went out and brought the audience in, basically.' Reggie Salberg, who enjoyed successful decades running the theatre in Salisbury, was a past master of the art of outreach. 'You do everything you can, we always did, to foster a relationship with the community. When David Horlock was artistic director he would direct the amateurs, he was chairman of the orchestral society, and I sat on the festival committee. That's the way you foster it, by being part of the community. In addition, what we have developed is children's theatre, or young people's theatre. We have our own group, Stage Sixty Five, called that because it started in 1965, which has produced a few actors, amongst them Christopher Biggins.'

Jonathan Church is now in charge at Salisbury, but before his appointment the Playhouse was one of many theatres whose future was in grave doubt, indeed it closed for a time, as Church reports. 'When they decided to shut the theatre at Salisbury, the staff were made redundant, the board was changed, the funders put quite a lot of pressure on people to decide what they wanted to do with the theatre. They had a consultants' team in and they had several options, it didn't have to be a repertory theatre, it could have been a touring house, it could have been an arts centre, there were all these other options. The people of Salisbury chose very, very firmly that what they wanted was a theatre which produced its own productions. There is a large section of the audience who really care and want a theatre in their community.' In this case the spadework done over many years by Reggie Salberg and David Horlock paid off.

Bernard Hepton also adopted a policy of bringing theatre to young people when he was in charge of the Liverpool Playhouse, in spite of the short-sighted attitude of his board of directors. 'At Liverpool I inaugurated a Saturday morning for children, to open the theatre for children, and I did this in Birmingham as well. We did it every three weeks. We had a programme, the history of the theatre. It was well received but rather frowned on by the board because, "We've never done that kind of thing before and they don't pay."'

Jean Boht, who was in the company at the time, recognizes the wisdom of investing in new audiences, if only to counteract the spreading influence of television. 'There was to be a Theatre in Education programme with regular Saturday morning shows for school children free of charge . . . we were to introduce all aspects of theatre to young people, with excerpts from productions in rehearsal, poetry reading – it was the beginning of the realization that something had to be done to counteract the effects that television must have been having on the box office.' Anna Calder-Marshall also recognizes the advantages of this sort of extra-curricular activity. 'We did Saturday morning classes for the community, when we would do warm-ups and show them bits of rehearsal. I remember working with about two hundred children from a rather mixed-up school and I did *The Charge of the Light Brigade* accompanied by a football rattle. I asked them to bring weapons, some offered to bring guns, but most of them had sticks and saucepan lids. You really got to know them, then they'd come and see you do Juliet and come round and talk to you about it after. They were quite tough in their criticism. When they came to see the shows you knew who you were appearing to.'

This cross-fertilization is something which Harriet Walter values, 'It was a very young company and we did pub shows, late-night revues, pantomimes, old classics, Shakespeare, new plays written specifically for the company by David Pownall. There was a lot of feeding back into the local community – we'd take tape recorders to the pub and collect stories from them and use them for the late-night revue so there would be material the community could relate to. It was a very unusual situation; Stoke-on-Trent had something of the kind. I got the impression that most regional theatres were much more traditional, people came to see something that they expected theatre to be like, but we were making the rules up as we went along.'

The Liverpool Everyman was so convinced that theatre should be taken out into the community that it not only targeted schools and young people but also tried to reach other sectors of the city's inhabitants who would never normally go to a theatre, as Alison Steadman reveals. 'I did a year at the Liverpool Everyman. It was great, really ahead of its time. That was the first time I was aware of doing plays that were really political, that were saying something. The first thing we did was to go on a trip round the Ford Halewood factory, which seemed a bit odd, but then we realized – none of us was familiar with Liverpool and the director wanted a company who understood what the city was about, what the people were about. It was such an eye-opener. If you've never been in a factory, you have no idea what it's like. It was very good indeed to think about the city we were in and the people we were going to cater for. Later one of the factories in Liverpool, Fisher-Bendix, had a sit-in and we did a show for them, we went to the factory and did a show. When they won the strike action, they gave us all a little metal fish with the date of the industrial action and the result stamped on it. It meant a lot. That was in the early Seventies when theatres like the Everyman were very involved politically.'

Vigorous outreach work such as this helps to break down the preconceptions which Frank Middlemass found in Oldham. 'I think the ordinary working people from the mills were terrified of the theatre because it was a theatre club. I think they thought it was over their heads.' This account from Leslie Lawton gives an insight into how elitist the theatre can appear to certain parts of the community. 'I remember when I first went to Liverpool I was helping to put the posters up and two kids came by and one said, "What goes on in there?" And the other answered, "Oh, that's where the posh people go." I remember thinking that I'd got to fight that. That was the best thing I could have heard.'

One means that strategists within the repertory movement came up with to draw in the young and uninitiated was to accommodate them in a different auditorium, hence the rise of the studio theatre in the 1960s and 1970s, as Timothy West explains. 'What happened in the Sixties was a very sensible definition of the audience. Younger people were beginning to find that theatre was for their parents. That was partly why a lot of studio theatres were built, kind of deliberately dividing the audience. The younger people wouldn't be seen dead in the main house. It did mean that you were getting a good representative audience. When the cuts started to bite under a Conservative government, the first thing that was lopped off was the second auditorium, thus losing the younger audience so that it was not viable to do new plays. It started getting dull, it started getting middle aged and middle brow and middle income. It may have been a very clever ploy by the government to woo a particular audience into the theatre who were prepared to pay higher prices, then call it elitist and cut off the funding. A clever ploy.' In contrast to this point of view, Elizabeth Counsell is concerned that in reaching out to new audiences theatres run the risk of alienating their traditional supporters and warns that, 'We need more middle-class plays to keep the middle class audience on board.'

In the heyday of the repertory movement from the 1940s, to the 1960s, there was no need to woo audiences consciously because they came in their droves. Vilma Hollingbery recalls, 'In the Fifties not everyone had television.Because it was twice nightly, the queue for the second house started as soon as the first house was in. The galleries used to be full because you could get up there for one and six. They used to queue up quite literally right round the block. We didn't know what it was to play to empty houses.' Eileen Atkins shared this experience. 'People at Bristol were terribly proud of their rep. I don't ever remember playing to empty houses,' although Alison Steadman was not always so fortunate: 'From our base in Bolton we toured to the Little Theatre in Builth Wells in North Wales, which held a hundred people. We never had more than ten in the audience. We stayed for eight weeks and did three plays in repertoire – *Billy Liar*, *Dial M for Murder* and *Look Back in Anger*. It was a nightmare, you can imagine it. One night someone looked through the curtains and said, "Right, there's only three people in front, we're not doing it." There used to be an Equity rule, if there are more in the cast then there are in the audience then you don't have to do it. The three people in the audience were my sister, my brother-in-law and my niece and they'd travelled eighty miles to see the show. I said to the others, "Couldn't you do it? They've come all this way . . ." and in the end they said, "Oh, all right then," so we did it for those three.' Occasions like this are exceptions. Maurice Denham's recollection of his time in Hull is more typical. 'The town were very good, they were very, very proud of their theatre, we used to have very full audiences. The marvellous thing was the faithfulness of the audience, the same people used to come in the same seats to every show.'

Not only did people sit in the same seats for each play, crucially they liked to see the same actors cropping up in a variety of different parts, this being one of the factors which defines rep as opposed to other types of theatre. Derek Nimmo confirms that audiences used to enjoy seeing the same actors over and over again. 'Part of the fun of going to the rep theatre was seeing actors whom you knew well, who'd sort of become part of the family, playing a variety of parts.' Philip Voss believes, 'The audience wanted to be part of our lives.' Jonathan Cecil agrees: 'Even when I went to Salisbury in 1965, there was a great feeling which the local people had for their repertory company. They used to go there to see the same people. That was part of the fun really, week after week or fortnight after fortnight to see the same people in different roles. They had their special favourites.' Deborah Grant recalls how this bias manifested itself. 'The audience in Bristol had their favourites, their matinée idols, their *grandes dames*, who automatically got rounds of applause as soon as they walked on stage because everybody knew them. Frank Barry and Peggy Ann Wood – I think they were there for ever, they played everything.'

Stephanie Cole thinks that reps now would do well to tap into the wellspring of affection which communities develop for a particular group of performers. 'One thing I noticed when the reps were very, very well attended, the one thing the audience liked was seeing the same people week after week after week. They got to recognize them and they became part of their families. It's the same if you're constantly on television, you become part of people's families. I wonder if you were running a repertory theatre now and you had the same company for a whole year, if that would help with attendance levels?'

Members of the public often expressed the affection they felt by giving presents to the actors. Nancy Mansfield remembers, 'There was the most amazing audience in Preston, they just loved it, it was really a part of their community and their life. It was weekly rep and you got the same people coming to each play. When I was in the company there I got presents over the footlights every week, chocolates every week unfailingly and sometimes quite big presents.' Peggy Mount did not receive chocolate, but, 'While I was in Chester there was meat rationing and the butcher loved me. I couldn't go wrong, and he used to bring me steak, I used to get all this wonderful meat and I can't remember ever having to pay for it,' and Philip Voss says, 'We were so committed and the audience loved us. One Christmas someone sent me a cheque for ten pounds, which was an awful lot of money in those days.'

Similar levels of generosity from the audience in Barnsley are remembered by Barbara Lott. 'Our last week, we played *East Lynne* on Monday, Tuesday and Wednesday, *When Irish Eyes Are Smiling* Thursday and Friday and we did a variety bill on the Saturday night in which I sang and I can't sing at all really. And after the first house on our last night, it was the last night in season, members of the audience handed up presents and the management made us give them all back so that we could have double the amount in the evening. And the next day when all the company left to go back to their various homes, practically the whole town came to see us off. There was no television, there was radio and the rep. It was their lifeline.'

The giving vein was equally strong in Warrington, according to Carmen Silvera. 'Every week a father used to come in with his family and I'd get flowers handed up over the footlights. Another night the florist or the grocer would come and we'd be given fruit and vegetables. At the end of the season of thirty-two weeks, we were hip-deep in presents. They took you to their hearts, you belonged to them. Everybody in the town used to know you, it was wonderful, they used to protect you.'

This kind of bounty seems to have been almost universal. Vilma Hollingbery was another beneficiary. 'At the curtain call there would be flowers sent up and boxes of chocolates. One leading man always used to get these marvellous flowers every Friday, then we discovered he was sending them to himself. Human frailty! We used to take it in turns to make the curtain speech. We used to say, "Ladies and gentlemen thank you for coming this evening. Next week Harry Hanson's

Court Players are proud to present – whatever play it was – and when it was my turn a man who always sat in a box used to throw me down a cylindrical packet of chocolate-dipped pastilles, they were terribly expensive. It was all rather undignified, because in order for them not to hit me on the head, I had to anticipate them and make sure I caught them.'

This lavish response from the audience and their affectionate interest in the company could mean that actors became dependent on a certain level of praise, as Alec McCowen explains, 'The desire to please the audience was enormous. We were like tarts, we really longed to be loved. There was a lot of playing out front, very obvious placing of laugh lines, and an eagerness that the first entrance was somehow special.' If for some reason a performer felt that her work was not liked the effect could be devastating, as Diane Fletcher relates. 'I remember an actress leaving the stage in hysterics once and the stage manager panicking completely and coming rushing round and shaking her and shouting, "Get back on stage!" and she was going, "Oh I can't, I can't." I think that she was peeved that they'd started to laugh.'

Anyone involved in theatre of any sort must give some thought to what the expectations of an audience are. Gemma Jones reflects, 'It's this thing of what do the audiences want? Theatres have to cater for what seems to be the mean level, but I often think they are underestimating people's intelligence. Sometimes if I've toured with a play, people have said, "It's so nice to see something with meat on." I don't think we do actually have to aim for the lowest common denominator. When you're aware that it's happening, introducing people to very good theatre is tremendously exciting.' Introducing people to good theatre can also prove to be risky, as Estelle Kohler discovered recently. 'I did *Old Times* in Birmingham and we had to struggle for an audience. Pinter was too elitist, it's hard to know what rep audiences want, although they'll come to Shakespeare.'

It is difficult to know what the people of Birmingham would have made of the Glasgow Citizens' notorious *Hamlet*, which was staged in September 1970; Rupert Frazer gives an impression of what the production was like. 'We didn't really stick to the text of *Hamlet*, it was ruthlessly cut. There were no tabs [curtains], it was an open stage covered in black gauze that had been stretched across the space. When the front-of-house lights went down, light came up behind this gauze, which fluttered to the ground, where it stayed for the rest of the evening. There was a black cube ten foot by ten, with a man with shocking bright hair kneeling on it and two feet below him a black catafalque with the outline of a human body draped in black. There was complete quiet, with no music at all. The man on the cube was writhing and silently tearing his hair. Presumably this was Hamlet and below him was the body of his father. Then the shape of the human body underneath the black material began to fuck, both audibly and visually. Everybody in the audience was utterly appalled at this. We began speaking from inside the cube, "List, list, O list! If thou didst ever thy dear father love . . .". That gives you the flavour of how it started, it regressed from there.'

The production took Scotland by storm. Rupert Frazer continues, 'None of us had any idea of just how big the gamble was, we were young actors absolutely thrilled to be doing such unconventional, physical stuff. The myth is that Giles Havergal and Philip Prowse had bought single tickets to Euston. It did cause the most amazing scandal. Looking back cynically, you could say that Giles and Philip deliberately did this to put the Citizens on the map. I remember arriving in a cab at the stage door and the cabbie saying to me, "Are you in *Hamlet*?" and I said, "No, no, it's just that I'm visiting a friend . . ." I was so frightened of being done over by this guy that I couldn't even admit to being in the production. We were quite beleaguered, it was quite a scary time.'

The sensitivities of audiences at the People's Palace in the Mile End Road during the late 1930s are recalled by John McCallum. 'In a play called *Judgement Day* I played an anti-Nazi guard and I had to say something about "those bastards". The audience fell about, they'd never heard the word on stage before.'

No doubt the laughter that John McCallum heard came from embarrassment. To protect the sensibilities of local communities from potentially shocking material, Watch Committees were set up. Never mind what the audience wanted to see, the Watch Committee ordained what they were allowed to see and sometimes it took very little to spur them into action. Barbara Leslie remembers, 'When we tried *On Monday Next* out in Southsea, the Watch Committee came round because there were two words in it that the Lord Chamberlain's office was unsure about. There was an "arse" and "a pregnant fishwife". Honestly, it was so funny, the stage-door keeper said to me, "You've got to come round, the Watch Committee are here." There was an actor called Richard Goolden, he never wore any make-up, so he prided himself that he could get out of the theatre before the last bars of the King, he was there and I didn't know how to talk to the Watch Committee and Richard Goolden came off having quoted reams of the Old Testament at them and they skittered away.'

They may have been easily cowed in Southsea, but the committee in Exeter were made of more tenacious stuff, as Martin Duncan remembers. 'The local worthies at Exeter didn't like the choice of plays. One of the biggest scandals at Exeter was a production of *Measure for Measure* that Jane Howell commissioned and William Gaskill came to direct it. He got Howard Brenton to rework it. It came out as the two protagonists, the Duke and Angelo, being Enoch Powell and Harold Macmillan. It was all modernized, it was set in a police state, it was all about pornography. I was going through a phase of making Super 8 underground movies at the time and Bill Gaskill asked me to make a blue movie for one sequence, so I had to make this blue movie that had nothing blue about it at all, it was really rather harmless, a few close-ups of parts of the bodies, and eyes, it was very suggestive and really quite innocent and I was quite pleased with it. Downtown in Exeter word was out that a scandalous play was on and they did their best to make trouble and they managed to do it by saying that we didn't have the right to show a film. The local Watch Committee said we hadn't been licensed. I didn't understand this as we showed films on a Friday and Saturday night late on a regular basis. They said we didn't have the right to show this movie, that they'd have to pass it and they couldn't do that before the first night. I remember Jane having to go out front on the first night and say, "This has happened, we haven't got a licence, it's my decision whether the show goes on with the movie or without the movie and I have to say it will go on without the movie." Bill Gaskill left the production, he walked out. Jane was in a terribly difficult position.'

There is a fine line between being provocative to the point of alienating the public or playing safe and losing a potential audience. Bob Eaton is in favour of encompassing both ends of the spectrum. 'At the Sheffield Crucible there was a really broad church of stuff going on. At the more artistic end there were Stephen Pimlott, Tom Cairns and Martin Duncan, at the craft and graft end there were people like me,

Mike Kay and John Tams. There was a tour of *The Rocky Horror Show* in the main house and in the studio Mike was doing *American Buffalo* by David Mamet. They were just starting the show in the studio when the doors burst open and this bloke came flying in wearing full basque and suspenders, which is the kind of costume you dress up in to go and see *The Rocky Horror Show*. He sat down on the front row and the show started and Mike was watching him and he could see him thinking, "This isn't *The Rocky Horror Show* . . . !" and he sat through the first half of this Mamet play and he went out at the interval and Mike thought, "Well, at least he stayed." Then he came back in for the second half! That kind of cross-fertilization I think is very important and it has always happened in the best sort of way in rep. You had that cross-fertilization initially of the amateurs and the professionals and then you get the cross-fertilization of the commercial and the subsidized, then you get the cross-fertilization of the Art for Art's Sake and the community-minded and if all of them can be kept rubbing up against each other and producing sparks, then you have the chance of something happening.'

What Bob Eaton does not mention is the cross-fertilization between repertory theatre and television, which was pronounced in the early days of the latter when directors like Shaun Sutton moved to the BBC and took their repertory actors with them, lock, stock and barrel. However, the relationship between the two media operates on other planes as well, notably on the effect that they both have on their audiences. Joss Ackland says, 'Today audiences watch the same show – *Coronation Street*, *EastEnders* – week after week after week. People are lonely, they want to familiarize themselves with other people, but it comes to nothing, whereas in repertory the actors and the audience had to relate. They sort of grew up together, the audiences were able not to be lonely and to have a sort of communication but not to become stagnant.'

Now it has become an accepted fact that television has poached audiences away from the theatre. Ian Hogg believes television achieved this by taking over the kind of drama which was popular in reps. 'I was brought up in the north-east in the Fifties and the first theatre I saw was the local rep in Darlington. It was weekly rep, I've no idea what quality it was. My father was a doctor and it was a sign of kind of social cred to have a season ticket for the theatre. I'm sure that reps existed on that kind of patronage. I went once a week and the fare was Agatha Christie, *Quiet Weekend*, that sort of thing. A sort of endless acreage that has now been replaced by the soap opera. That's what gets me about the theatre – to see work portrayed by living people, ie drama, is bigger, greater than television. Television has taken the popular fare – domestic ongoing situations – away and put it into soap opera. That was what weekly rep provided for the public.' Having divined what was popular in live theatre, the television companies were able to give their own productions a gloss of realism with which most reps found it hard to compete. Timothy West notes, 'A lot of the kind of audience involvement that went with doing a different play each week has gone. It had to happen because the visual standard of weekly rep did not come up to the expectations of the telly viewer. Old parts being played by young people with terrible wigs and lines all over their faces; the same grandfather clock appearing on the set every two weeks, only two sets of curtains – the chintz curtains and the velvet curtains.'

Just as the expectations of the audience were influenced by the advent of television, Sir Peter Hall suggests that their tastes were altered too. 'There's been a fundamental shift in audience tastes. People wax romantic about the old days when you saw the young Laurence Olivier or the young Albert Finney, they wouldn't like it now. They don't want to see young actors playing parts that they're too young for.'

Audiences can be seduced away from their reps by the rival attractions of television, video, computer games, sport – the competition for their custom is endless and without them the theatre cannot function. This is why audiences were accorded such respect in the past by actors, but Paul Daneman fears this may no longer be the case. 'Nowadays you never hear actors talking about audiences, you never hear directors or writers talking about audiences, but all we ever talked about was the audience.' A similar concern is voiced by Joss Ackland, 'What happens nowadays is that audiences have become the least important people in the theatre, actors tend to work for their own enjoyment and that is fatal.' This lack of consideration for their public by performers is unwise. Eileen Atkins recognizes that the audience is important not only for the preservation of theatre, but for the actor in developing his talent. 'You can't really know how to act until you get in front of an audience. They will tell you what you can do. Sometimes you mustn't give way to them because they want you to be sentimental or something, but it's not until you get that relationship with an audience that you know your own power, you know how far you can take things.' Daniel Massey is passionate on the subject. 'If, when you start as an actor, you do not have consistent exposure to performing in front of an audience you cannot make decisions, you cannot come to an understanding of how the relationship with that audience works, not only on you and your nerves, but on you and the character you're playing and the characters you're playing with in the play. You cannot understand how to dominate them, how to provoke them, how to romance them. The audience is where you learn – in comedy, for instance, where the laughs are.' He goes further, 'In acting, alone among the interpretive arts, the audience is the fourth player, the fifth dimension in the actor's art. You can sit and talk about acting, you can do it in class, but until you hit the audience you do not begin to learn how to act. Most actors will tell you, if they have any intelligence, that the audience is the maker of the play.'

Although, in Fiona Shaw's opinion, 'Rep gave the community the habit of theatre-going', and she believes that once the habit had become less strong and theatres started to close, 'People mourned rep and tried hard to keep it going,' the theatres undoubtedly face an uphill task. There is no question that, as the century draws to a close, regional theatre is in serious decline, perhaps because the audience has not been sufficiently wooed away from other enticing diversions. The origins of repertory theatre lay within the community from which it sprang, and Patricia Hodge believes that it is with the local community that rep's future lies. 'Rep is a community thing. We have a problem in this country with extended families, we isolate ourselves too much. I think that people really want to live within a community and that rep will be part of that.'

19

The Decline of Rep

'It's been mooted all my life that theatre is dead.'

Phyllida Law

THE LINKS BETWEEN repertory companies and the communities they serve are close, so it is not surprising that the major events which affect society send reverberations through the theatre. An example of this is given by Jean Anderson, who recalls that on the death of King George V in 1936 the Court went into official mourning and all the reps were closed for one month. Leslie Lawton says that when the nation is plunged into recession then provincial theatres suffer heavy losses. 'Regional theatres are not independent of what is going on in their region. When you have terrific unemployment in Scotland and the north-west, that's going to show and there's nothing you can do to counteract that.'

According to many actors, the Second World War had the greatest effect on the closed and often inward-looking world of repertory theatre. Judy Campbell remembers the outbreak of hostilities with Germany. 'I was in Liverpool when the war broke out. On the eve of the declaration, we were in someone's digs and I remember singing Ivor Novello songs with Robert Helpmann. The next morning I woke up to find a message from William Armstrong, saying that he'd gone to stay in the Hebrides for the duration of the war and that the company was disbanded and a note from the landlady saying that she'd gone to stay with her sister and the whole building was deserted. I made myself some porridge and ate it in the bath, then I went along to the theatre, which was deserted, and a few of us got together and decided to buy a motorcar and we bought a Ford V8. You could get about five people in it and it was going for about ten quid, so we bought it. We dropped me first in Lincolnshire and the last man out took it to Sussex. The men were all going to join up. All I knew about was the First World War and I thought I would be driving an ambulance across France, but nobody asked me to drive an ambulance. What I did get was a postcard from William Armstrong saying, "We're starting up the rep again, but we're only doing plays with one set."'

The initial panic at the news spread as far as Ireland, where Jean Anderson was working. 'When we got the news of the outbreak of war we were playing Killarney. The night we heard we were playing *Wuthering Heights*. The leading man was so distraught about the war that he climbed up a sort of mountain where there was a colossal stream coming down and said he was going to commit suicide and I had to go up and talk him down to come and do the play that night.'

Among those who remember the sense of teetering on the brink of catastrophe all the time is Barbara Lott, who says that the sense of imminent disaster was particularly strong early on in the conflict. 'I worked at the Theatre Royal in Brighton in 1940 at the beginning of the London Blitz and at the time of the invasion scare. They thought that because Hitler had got as far as France and the coast of Holland that England was the next step. And there were all these rumours that you would see the flat-bottom barges coming over the horizon and so we were told we must always have a pound about our person, in our bra or somewhere, which was our "invasion pound" which would get us back to London. We were paid on Fridays in those days, and come Thursday there was a lot of, "Could you lend me the invasion pound?"'

As the nation settled down to war, the reps carved a strong role for themselves, entertaining the inhabitants of towns up and down the country and maintaining public morale. Some theatres restricted themselves to playing only matinées, but if there was a show on, then the houses were generally full. Among the different sectors of the population that the reps catered for, there was one unique to that period – the prisoners of war. Edward Jewesbury describes an occasion at the theatre in Colchester. 'There was one really sensational thing that happened there. The theatre was run by Robert Digby, who was a great philanthropist and enthusiast for the theatre. He was a friend of

Trevor Howard and they almost started Colchester Rep between them. There was a big prisoner-of-war camp just outside Colchester. We were doing *Hamlet* at the time and I was playing Hamlet and Bob suggested that we put on a special matinée for the German prisoners of war, which we did. They all marched in from their camp one afternoon and they were the most wonderful audience I have ever known in my life, you could hear a pin drop. They all knew their Shakespeare much better than most English people do.' Peter Copley recalls a similar contact, this time with some Russians, for whom the outcome of the war was tragic. 'During the autumn of 1944 Worthing was in a bad way because of the war. I went down to run the theatre and discovered that there were many Russian prisoners of war billeted in a hotel on the sea front. One day I saw them marching through the town and they were singing, quite beautifully. I arranged to give them complimentary tickets to the theatre in return for them singing ballads on stage after the show. They were repatriated after the war and shot.'

These anecdotes date from a time which heralded a boom in theatre throughout the regions of Great Britain. The companies were numerous. Alec McCowen remembered writing off for jobs in 1945 and sending letters to more than two hundred companies. Paul Daneman says, 'After the war almost every town of any size in the country had three theatres, a variety house, a touring house and a rep. And there were audiences to go to these, there really were,' a point which Derek Nimmo re-inforces, 'Every little mill town, Bury, Rochdale, Oldham, they all had their own rep theatres. In Bolton there was the Grand, which was the variety theatre, the Theatre Royal, which was the touring theatre, then there was the Hippodrome, which was the rep.'

Michael Bogdanov believes, 'There was a moment in postwar theatre when a lot of things came together: theatre in education, young people's theatre, community theatre.' These halcyon days outlived the war by little more than a decade, according to Michael Kilgarriff. 'By 1957 or 1958 rep was beginning very rapidly to die out, the old rep theatres were not very attractive, very old-fashioned and dusty, dingy and uncomfortable. In the summers before the war Harry Hanson had as many as fifteen or twenty companies, gradually he went down and down and down until when I joined him in Peterborough he only had about six. The Arts Council was still comparatively new, that formed out of the Council for the Encouragement of Music and the

Arts (CEMA) after the war. That didn't give money to weeklies, you had to be at least two weekly to get money from the Arts Council. By the end of the Fifties the decent actors were going into the better reps, they didn't want to do weekly. Harry Hanson started closing down companies, in Peterborough and Stockton-on-Tees.'

As Kilgarriff explains, some of the weekly reps not subsidized by the new Arts Council began to fall by the wayside, but for those lucky enough to secure public funding the golden age lasted well into the 1960s. Sir Peter Hall says, 'I laid the foundation stone for the theatre in Salisbury in the Sixties, it was a time of great hope for the future.' However, Sir Peter observes that this hope in the future proved to be rather short-lived. 'Things weren't too healthy in the Seventies because of the nervous breakdown the whole country went through. Once the Tories got in, it became the era of sponsorship. In real terms the grants to all the theatres have been reduced over the last twenty years.' Looking back to her time in Lincoln in 1969, Alison Steadman says, 'The theatre was supported by the Arts Council, but we were always in trouble, we were always on a very tight budget, there was never any extra money, the theatre was always under the threat of closure even then.' The decline which started in the 1970s had become something resembling wholesale destruction by the 1980s in John Nettles's view. 'It's deeply depressing, the whole of the last decade seems to have been devoted to destroying what was left of the repertory system. Fewer plays are put on and now all you get is four-handers. Actors are cast from production to production and it's all very hand to mouth.'

Francesca Ryan pinpoints the moment of sharpest decline as occurring when the Arts Council published its report on regional theatre, *The Glory of the Garden*, in 1985. '*The Glory of the Garden*, that infamous Arts Council document, started the rot, I think. It held up centres of excellence so that the bigger theatres got more and the little theatres got less. Which means smaller production budgets, less actor weeks, staff leave and don't get replaced. There's a general feeling of being run down, then the publicity budget gets cut and you can't attract people.' Peter Bowles accounts for the general public's failure to fight the cuts which the report called for in the following way. 'Rep is in decline because on the one hand councils started to withdraw money from the repertory companies, but also television. A lot of young actors want to get into television series. I also think that many of the new plays that were being written didn't appeal to the people in the provinces so they stopped going to the theatre and when the Arts Council said we've got to cut back, people didn't take to the streets.'

For Dorothy Tutin, the blight which afflicts the provinces is infecting the profession as a whole. 'Of course regional theatre is in serious trouble, but acting is in serious trouble.' William Franklyn believes one cause of this is the diminished status of actors. 'Why should actors go and beat themselves to death somewhere like Birmingham to do plays and find that there's no posters up? Or, if the poster is up, it will say the name of the writer, the director, the art director, the lighting man, but not one mention of an actor. Actors have been so devalued.' Maria Charles is frank in her assessment of the current situation. 'The difference between rep now and rep then? It's just an engagement now, they call it rep, but it's not weekly rep, it's not repertory theatre any more, there is no repertory theatre.' If this is the case, then Derek Nimmo believes that a new term must be found for what passes as regional theatre in the 1990s. 'A lot of ones that call themselves repertory companies now, like Windsor, aren't really. A word hasn't really been coined for theatres that put on eight plays a year that don't progress beyond that theatre.'

In searching for reasons why rep has come to grief, Fiona Shaw suggests, 'Failure in rep wasn't ideological or aesthetic, it was circumstantial.' Many circumstances have contributed to the problems faced by regional theatre. Ian Mullins also believes that the Arts Council is significantly culpable. 'I think the Arts Council is a lot to blame because to a great extent they encouraged changes of policy. They said that theatres should not think of themselves as being so local and they wanted them run much too expensively. They encouraged theatres to upgrade and upmarket their entire administration and as a result theatres became top-heavy, they had top-heavy economies with a rather overloaded staff. We did twice as many plays because we had shorter runs, we did them all the year round, we had half the staff and we did larger cast plays.'

Cuts in Arts Council funding meant that many companies closed their Theatre in Education teams, which in turn drained lifeblood from the repertory movement, something which Harriet Walter mourns. 'I think the really regrettable change in theatre is the cutting of funds to TIE. It's really important work, it builds an audience for the future. Young people get something of an experience of drama inter-action, which is slightly different from what I mean by theatre; theatre is associated with a building, and many people still feel it's something posh and it's a big occasion and you dress up; drama is what really should happen in a theatre, but it can happen in a room or a pub or a school. If you have that experience young then it sets up an expecta-tion. A form of TIE still exists in some places, but in a very slimmed-down way. It used to be part of the institution.'

Just as the erosion of Theatre in Education had a detrimental effect on reps, Belinda Lang believes that when permanent companies were faded out an equal amount of damage was done. 'Managements stopped using companies that would stay for a year or so and started using individual actors to come and go who were more suitable, cast per play. I think that's probably a more expensive and a much more difficult way to run a theatre. There were certain theatres, Birmingham Rep was one of them, where they got well-known actors to come in and play big parts and they tried to cast the other parts more carefully per play, then it began to creep into the whole system so that it was no longer acceptable for companies to come together for a whole year. I think it stopped audiences going in the end. One of the reasons people went was that it wasn't very expensive and they saw the same actors playing very different parts each week and maybe it wasn't entirely successful, but that was part of the night out.'

Patricia Hodge shares Leslie Lawton's view that the state of the national economy inevitably influences the health of regional theatre. 'I think that the reason rep is in decline is economics. Things are often affected by the economy and you get a downward spiral. Repertory companies have not got the money to do things the way they would like, the quality of the plays being produced is on a smaller and smaller scale – companies these days survive by doing two-, three- and four-handers. They can't present their audiences with the spectacle and range that they would like, the audiences think that it's not as inter-esting as it used to be and they don't come and it goes on from there. That kind of economic decline is very difficult to do anything about.'

A tangible example of this vicious circle is provided by Christopher Luscombe. 'I went to work in Leatherhead, which I knew very well because as a theatregoer I went there as a child. That was just desper-ate, we did a Bernard Shaw play, which sold very badly. The scenery was very spartan compared to what I'd been used to seeing there. When I used to go there it would all be beautifully dressed with wonderful box sets, but this production of *You Never Can Tell* was just two-dimensional flats which had been painted, nothing three-dimensional, it was shocking. The designer made a virtue of it but it was not what it should have been.' The stark nature of this production is not calculated to attract people who can find more lavish alternatives elsewhere. For Luscombe, realization that rep was in serious trouble came early on in his career and was crystallized in a single moment, 'My first rep job was at Windsor. It was the end of an era because John Counsell was very ill and he had run that theatre for such a long time, it was his kingdom. It had been a very good rep, but I think it was going off slightly. I remember standing in the wings with a much older actor and he said, "I think we're looking at the end of an era here." We were conscious that the audiences weren't as full, the play was a bit of an old pot-boiler, it all seemed a bit sad. It made me think, "Perhaps I've just caught the end of something." '

For Belinda Lang, realization only came in retrospect. 'I suppose one didn't realize it was going to end. One thought, "Oh well, this is OK, but I prefer to play that part, I don't want to be the old lady in this play," and later you think, "Oh what a fool, I was there when it was all ending and there aren't going to be those opportunities now. It would be unthinkable for me to turn up at a theatre now and play an old lady. We didn't know at the time how lucky we were.'

One of the principal reasons which actors believe has caused the decline in regional theatre has already been referred to by Sir Peter Hall, namely the erosion of grants. Many feel strongly about this issue, among them Lynn Farleigh, who declares, 'I'd stand on my soap box and shout about theatre funding, I think it's disgraceful.' Stephanie Cole gives a comprehensive analysis of what she sees as the problems bedevilling repertory theatres. 'I don't have a lot of hope for the future of rep, to be honest, partly because we're wildly under-subsidized and I know everybody says it and everybody is tired of hearing it. We are underfunded to a degree that is an absolute joke. It is true that British theatre is the best theatre in the world, it produces the best actors, a lot of the best writers, a lot of the best directors and designers, to say nothing of wonderful stage management. Drama school gives them a basis which is wonderful, but if you don't have the place to start those young muscles, where are we going to be in twenty-five years' time? We're going to have a lot of young people who can say five lines on television and do bugger all else. There really is a very strong danger. Repertory theatres do need much more funding, but they do need to look at themselves, for instance look at their publicity departments. It's no good getting somebody just out of college to ring up the odd local paper and think that that will do. You've got to have people with dynamic ideas who are going to get out there and sell your product, because we're all in the marketplace now. I went on tour with *A Passionate Woman*, which was tremendously successful in the West End. The theatre we started the tour at was basically a repertory theatre – a lot of repertory theatres are becoming feeder houses, they make the set, the play will start there and it helps them financially – but this particular theatre had about as much idea about publicity as my carpet. It was absolutely ridiculous and you wanted to shake them. You don't deserve to succeed if you don't do your job properly. So there are two sides to it, but I do feel that under-funding is the main problem.'

The shortcomings of certain theatres, compounded by a lack of balanced and comprehensive funding for the arts from the government, has provoked a crisis in the repertory movement, which has seen companies closed on a temporary or even permanent basis. Amongst those under threat in recent years have been the once mighty Liverpool Playhouse, bastion of the rep tradition, Farnham, Leatherhead, Salisbury, Guildford, Windsor – the list is frighteningly long and, as Timothy West points out, 'It is the "safe" Home County reps that are going to the wall. At one time in the late Sixties when the Bristol Old Vic also had the Little Theatre, twenty-seven plays were staged each year in three auditoria, now eight plays are done in one.' Christopher Luscombe perceives a downward spiral in operation. 'I think the decline is to do with a fall in subsidy, it's a vicious circle – the less money there is, the more standards of production go down and the quality of personnel you can attract to work there goes down. I don't think audiences have a particular loyalty to the idea of rep or theatre, I think they go if they enjoy themselves. I think too often the standard has become low, it's become tatty. So the audience stays away, the box office drops. To compete with cinema, television and video we've got to be better than we were and we're not, we're worse.'

Sir Peter Hall agrees, 'I do think people expect the theatre to be better at the very moment when it is turning for the worse. That's the double bind.' Sir Peter makes several further points. He claims that, 'In the past, though the cinema was important, the theatre was where most actors were going to spend their lives, but that isn't the case now. If they work in the theatre now they subsidize it, because theatre pay is frightful.' He also says, 'The trouble is reps can't afford to pay actors, they get one or two people in leads who are good, then not very good actors for the other roles, then the standard drops and the audience drops with it. Unless we pour money into the regional theatres to raise their standards and their audiences, I think the theatre is really threatened. The reps not only breed the next generation of actors, they also breed the next audience.' He emphasizes that the theatre has done all that can be expected of it to face out the current crisis. 'The profession has done more than it should do to sustain itself. If you allowed market forces to operate there wouldn't be any theatre at all.' He adds, by way of conclusion, 'If anyone said to me you can go and run a theatre in Sheffield and you will have proper resources, I'd go and do it. But pigs might fly.'

In certain rep theatres it is whispered that the creation of the National Theatre on London's South Bank is partly to blame for the shortage of grant support for theatre in the regions. Leslie Lawton suggests that, 'A lot of the rot set in when the National moved to the South Bank and there was a quite definite feeling then that there was going to be less money for the regions. No matter how much Peter Hall assured us that it wouldn't be so, it was so. There was a big white elephant on the South Bank which Richard Eyre turned round and he did that through his experience of running Notthingham.' Sir Derek Jacobi supports the notion that funding for the theatre is top-heavy, with the lions' share going to the two main companies at the expense of regional theatre as a whole. 'Money is wasted in the theatre. The huge subsidies they give the National and the RSC are way over the top. I've worked in both and I've seen it thrown away, just thrown away – never on actors, but on everything else – absolutely wasted, then other places are deprived of it. I think more even distribution of whatever wealth there is around would help enormously to provide opportunities for those who want to work in theatre.'

Daniel Massey is certain where the blame lies. 'The solution requires vision. A lot of the problems, some of them, have been generated by government philistinism, lack of vision and proper subsidy so that theatres are not able to plan. In fact the provincial theatres have had their horns blunted by having money taken away. Ten years ago I did a survey and I found that the average cast in the provincial theatre was six and a half people – there goes Shaw, there goes Shakespeare, the Ibsens and Chekhovs are out of the window, nobody can do them.' To counter this, Mark Piper, who has been instrumental in helping the rep at Windsor to struggle back from the brink, thinks that Windsor's lack of subsidy has in some ways been an advantage. 'If you haven't got subsidy then it can't be taken away and you're not living under a permanent sword of Damocles.'

Patricia Hodge is convinced that extra funding for reps would benefit the profession as a whole. 'There is a demand for people to see theatre, but they're not fools, they don't want to see something that is not as good as they can watch at home on the television. If there were funds available they should be poured into the repertory theatres because then they would come alive again. There is no doubt that would feed the profession and everything would benefit as a result.'

Reviving the repertory theatres and by inference live drama as well may be a way of addressing what Timothy West believes is becoming a major issue. 'The leisure problem is not going to go away and you have to provide some sort of alternative to television and videos, amusement arcades – and drugs. They have to start thinking seriously about the problem now, before it gets any worse. There has got to be money for the regional theatres to say to exciting people who might write plays for them, appear in them, direct, design . . . "Look, in two years' time we want you to do such and such," because the people who they want have things pencilled in their diaries two years ahead.'

Sir Derek Jacobi is another who feels that increasing leisure needs to be taken into account. 'People nowadays have more leisure, they diversify their leisure, there are more opportunities to do so many other things, apart from movies and television. Because there is so much on offer, because so much of it is instant and quick and forgotten and throw-away, the theatre is in danger of becoming a place where you have to concentrate. It takes effort and expense to go to the theatre.' He believes that, 'To revitalize the reps, the audiences in a sense have got to be re-educated. It's all got to be bigger these days, if it's big and brash and primary colours they'll go for it, but anything delicate is another matter – it's like comparing polyester to lace, but polyester is very popular and lace is a bit expensive and unusual.'

Jacobi's analogy between the theatre and lace suggests that drama is a luxurious commodity, a point with which Daniel Massey agrees, while maintaining that it still has a justifiable importance to the individual. 'Theatre is a luxury now, but the fact that it is a luxury doesn't mean that we can't do it, the fact that it is a luxury, as with the touch of suede leather, silk, gold or silver – that feeds you, actually. The greatest experiences in my life have been in the theatre. I love the cinema, love it, but the theatre is something else – unrepeatable and totally galvanizing.' Michael Bogdanov is more forthright, 'You've got to have a public infrastructure for the arts, they are part of education, they are a service, they are not a luxury. It should be the inalienable right of every man, woman and child to participate in or be present at events which enrich or develop their lives. That involves an approach to the arts that links it inexorably with education and the social fabric. You have to have a public base for funding that is linked to education.'

The educational benefit which can be derived from theatre is documented by Lynn Farleigh. 'You can talk about so many social problems in a non-po-faced way through the theatre. As part of a community project, I did a week in a school in Catford. You can talk about listening to each other and caring for each other and respecting each other in acting terms, and you feel that you can get through to them. It's very exciting. That's the kind of work that local theatres can do, going into schools and hospitals. I think that community and schools theatre is the route to go to keep theatre alive.'

Tim Pigott-Smith is convinced that reps can provide a civilizing focus for the increasingly fractured communities which they serve. 'The real problem is to do with society; community has been killed in the last eighteen years. You look at young people and they don't know how to sit in an audience, they don't attend church in the same way that we were obliged to, they haven't learnt to be with a group of people. What function does the theatre serve? What psychological nerve did it come out of? What is it there for? I think it's a kind of laboratory of the spirit and the soul, where as a group of people you get together and say, "I don't think it's a good idea to kill your father and sleep with your mother, do you? I wonder what would happen if somebody did that?" And something that is profound within the psyche, as one knows that particular story was, is dramatized for you as a group to share and then you can share your sense of moral identity, which is what is so tangibly missing from society now, where the only thing that matters is money.' Because the collectively civilizing experience of being in an audience together is less available, Pigott-Smith believes that society suffers the consequence. 'There is a connection between social dysfunction and the death of live theatre. There is a link between being purged and civilized by the collective experience.'

Collective experience is no longer a dominant feature of modern entertainment, since the advent of television has put the focus of amusement and diversion firmly within the home. Stephen Moore says, 'Regional theatre is most certainly in decline. There is no remedy, unless electricity were to become so rare or expensive that no one would watch television.' Derek Nimmo is among many who date the changing trend to 1953, when the coronation of the Queen was televised, prompting the nation to rush out and buy television sets in a way that they had not done previously. It can also be argued that the first blow struck against rep was delivered by the cinema. Jean Anderson recalls, 'No one had any idea that talkies would be a success. We used to hang out of the dressing-room window and see queues around the cinema and none around our theatre. Most of the theatres we were playing were converted to talkie houses.' Although regional theatre sustained a blow during the 1930s, it rallied during the war years and its serious degeneration can be attributed to the spread of television. As Eileen Atkins says, 'I think it is sad but inevitable that rep is in decline. On TV you can get a polished, well-thought-out performance, although even on TV they aren't doing single plays any more.' Paul Daneman explains, 'The rep movement supplied what the television now supplies, it supplied the equivalent of the sit-com and the soap operas. There was a whole sort of community feeling about it. But when the television got a grip – why should they go to the bloody theatre?'

Audiences are not unique in preferring the delights of television to those offered by the theatre. Gemma Jones believes that actors have similar inclinations. 'It seems to me that the standard has dropped in rep because the good actors are staying in London in case a telly comes up and people with less aptitude are ending up going to the smaller reps.' Bernard Hepton agrees, 'Actors nowadays look on going into the provinces as a penance. One of the results of TV and the opportunities it offers, and one of the results of the reps closing, is that the youngsters at theatre school are no longer looking to the theatre. Their eyes are directed towards television and film and all their energy is focused there. Consequently we're going to get a whole lot of actors who cannot work on a stage. They can work in front of a camera, but not on a stage, and it shows. Unless something's done about it, our theatre's going to flop. It really is going to go. It's no good wonderful directors coming up with bright ideas if the actors can't do it. Most times the actors can't do it, even if you can hear them.'

Some people believe that actors' predilection for television is encouraged by their agents, among them Sir Peter Hall, who says, 'The current situation is that actors are frightened by their agents into keeping themselves free for the mythical television series that will never arrive,' a thought echoed by Timothy West, 'I've done quite a bit of directing in the regions and I do find that some agents will say to their clients, "You don't really want to go and do *Uncle Vanya* in Sheffield do you? There might be an episode of *The Bill* coming up."' Jonathan Church, currently director in Salisbury, frequently finds himself faced with this resistance. 'Actors and agents don't have any respect for repertory theatre any more. Because there's no stability in funding terms, there are no companies any more and as actors aren't getting the grounding in theatre any more, their agents are far more willing to keep them free for television.'

While actors and directors are able to point a finger towards television for offering rival temptations to both performers and audiences and thus weakening the theatre's position, some believe that there is an elitism inherent in the experience of going to the theatre which deters a large part of the population from attending. Michael Kilgarriff believes the buildings themselves can be daunting. 'Those huge old theatres were very class orientated, the hoi polloi in the gallery had to go in by a separate entrance well away from the carriage trade and there was no carpet on the stairs. I remember doing pantomime at the Pavilion Theatre in Liverpool and you could smell the decaying plaster, the secondary lighting was gas jets still, it was very depressing to be in that one.'

Michael Bogdanov thinks, 'Theatre in Britain has reached crisis point, it is splitting into a number of directions. My fear is that mainstream theatre will disappear into an even more elitist foxhole. The small theatres close and the big ones dig in and call themselves "centres of excellence". So we get theatre that is exclusively upper middle class, whereas once upon a time there was a chink in the armour and the proles were clambering through, but they've been excluded now.' He believes that even the drama schools are contributing to the creation of a theatre which is socially exclusive. 'People can't afford drama school fees so you have an elitist group of people being trained for an elitist job.' Ian Hogg is broadly in support of this standpoint, saying, 'Round about the Thirties the theatre was captured by the middle class and it's never been released. There aren't any groundlings at all. Of course, by the time Thatcher arrived the whole of society said it is a middle-class thing and the middle classes are earning good salaries so they should pay for it. That immediately knocks out the kind of people that my generation were reaching for.'

Whether regional theatre has become too elitist and is 'knocking out' whole sectors of the community, or whether the rival attractions of the cinema and television are culpable for the loss of audiences, some actors are of the opinion that the administrations of the companies themselves are partly responsible for the current crisis. Malcolm Farquhar and Leslie Lawton both identify over-manning as a factor in the decline of reps, the former suggesting with a certain amount of trepidation, 'It's awful to say, but I think you could get rid of fifty per cent of the people who run a theatre. I don't see why a publicity department needs three people when my general manager used to do it on his own. One would see some justification if it brought in a hundred per cent, but it doesn't. The boards for theatres are all voluntary. I think a lot of people on the boards for theatres are useless, they're there for the prestige, they're somebody in the town. There should be people on each board who are artistic, who have been in the theatre and who know where the money is going.'

Lawton talks at length about what he perceives to be top-heavy administrations within regional companies. 'If you go to any regional theatre now and open your programme, you will see a cast of about ten and a staff of about fifty, if you look back at a programme from about twenty or thirty years ago, you will see there were more actors than anything else. What happened with all the new buildings and the new formations of companies is that they are top-heavy on administration

– we're talking about the malaise of this country anyway. We've handed over the theatre generally in this country to the amateurs – there is far too much administration and not enough work for actors. They say they can't afford to do big-cast plays and no, they can't – they're all in the bloody offices working nine to five. What do you need a publicity department for in a regional theatre? That could be something done by the associate director. I used to do all the publicity and printing stuff myself with the help of my assistant director. Alan Bleasdale was the permanent writer at the Playhouse in Liverpool and he used to help writing the programme notes. When I was at Folkestone we had a scenic designer who also built the sets, he was a carpenter; we had a front-of-house manager who did everything – he was theatre manager and he paid the salaries. We had a secretary who came in part-time to do the typing. We had a stage manager and two ASMs who were always actors and that was it. We did a play a week. We're all still alive, it didn't kill us.'

William Franklyn is equally adamant that bureaucracy is choking the theatre to death and he too proposes radical surgery. 'Don't let reps be run by the council, don't let them be run by funders and committee people because they are death. I believe in the SAS – who dares wins, there are only three of us involved, I'm the governor and it will be run like this. You appoint a director of productions and an assistant director so that you have a young director being trained up. You need an administrator who has been trained in theatre administration, most of them these days don't know a cleat line from OP.'

There is a universal feeling that the fate of repertory theatre is closely linked to the survival of the profession as a whole. Robin Herford comments, 'Under the Tory government, theatres have been dying like flies and there's no sense of "Look what you're doing to the theatrical heritage." We still win Oscars, Tony Awards, Olivier Awards, but none of this would have happened if it weren't for the fact that we had a thriving regional theatre which provides the plays and the players, the directors and the technicians,' while John Moffatt is fervent in his belief that, 'Rep was the lifeblood of British theatre.' For John Nettles there is no question that, 'The decline of rep has a hellish knock-on effect for the rest of the theatre. The major subsidized companies now have to do all the training inhouse themselves because the actors they have to work with have no background in repertory. The standard of acting will tend to decline because of the demise of provincial theatre,' and Jenny Seagrove says, 'Tony Hopkins came from the rep system, Dan Day-Lewis came from the rep system. All our best actors have come up through the reps and we are very proud of our exports of international actors and our theatre is the finest in the world and yet we do everything we can to destroy that which actually feeds them, which is the rep system. And if you are not careful there will be nothing left.'

Miss Seagrove makes the point that regional theatre is uniquely placed to give emerging talent the experience and training that it needs. While agreeing with this, Sir Peter Hall laments, 'One couldn't have imagined that Bristol would ever be in trouble. About fifteen or eighteen years ago there was an assistant to the director doing plays in the studio there called Adrian Noble. Now the studio is shut. Who's breeding up the new director of the RSC?' His concern is shared by Daniel Massey. 'Repertory is vital, it's like a blood transfusion and it's required now. There is no vision in my business at the moment. It takes at least ten years to build a Shakespearean actor and I'm glad to see critics picking up on the paucity of both directing and acting in contemporary Shakespeare. It's very sad to me but it's no surprise because people aren't trained. The whole system of creating assistant directors who become house directors has gone, which is a great pity.' Annette Crosbie poses a similar question. 'When the big companies like the RSC and the National are looking for actors in the future I'm not sure where they'll find them. I have seen plays here already where some of the cast simply couldn't breathe properly and sustain a length of dialogue in a period play. I'm sixty-three and I think my generation had the last of it and the best of it.'

That rep is uniquely qualified to round out the talents of young performers is made clear by Francesca Ryan. 'I honestly believe that the government has starved the roots of the profession and for a while we'll still get the flowers, because we're trading on what has been in the past, but they're starving it at the roots by cutting off repertory theatre and it will only take a couple of generations for there not to be a tradition of stage acting any more. Working in rep is a craft apprenticeship. If you've got an open heart and an open throat and some intelligence, those are the three things that make a good actor, but there's a whole grammar of being on stage which is to do with the necessity of reaching the people at the back, making your physical and vocal instrument flexible enough.'

Derek Fowlds has a suggestion for novices who want to become proficient in the grammar of being on stage, 'When they leave drama school now, where do the kids go to train? They have to go to the pubs and the co-ops and the fringe – at least we were paid a wage in weekly rep.' Fowlds is among several to speak disparagingly about the lack of payment in fringe theatre, even though many concede that fringe is now taking over where rep left off, among them Richenda Carey. 'Fringe theatre has largely taken the place of rep, which is bad because the actors don't get paid for it.' Sir Peter Hall is in agreement. 'I don't really like all that, the fact that people aren't paid for what they're doing. The theatre would be much poorer if actors didn't do this, though.'

On the other hand, Cate Fowler maintains that the fringe makes the plays of Shakespeare available in a way that rep no longer can. 'The fringe is now what rep was, it's the training ground. The fringe does a lot of Shakespeare now, no one else can afford to do it. I wrote off for a job in which Portia was doubled with Old Gobbo. I've always wanted to play Old Gobbo and I wouldn't mind having a go at Portia too!' Leslie Lawton is another who is able to find a positive benefit in the rise of the fringe. 'I think that a very good thing which has happened is the way people go out and do things for themselves – all this fringe stuff, which has really taken over from rep. They know they must keep their costs down, they know they must go round and put the posters up themselves, one hopes that will now spread back into the regional theatre.'

Although the fringe may be a way of re-igniting the flame of live theatre for local communities, many actors are profoundly gloomy about future prospects. Paul Daneman declares, 'I can't see a revival in rep any more than I can see a revival in the horse as a means of transport,' and Russell Dixon is equally unequivocal. 'I'm not too fussed whether rep survives or not – nobody wants it.' There is a note of genuine regret in Jan Francis's comment, 'I think rep is in terminal decline. I think there may be a few companies who still do seasons but I don't think it will ever be what it was. It's very sad.'

While the fringe may provide a solution which to mainstream actors is of questionable legitimacy, there are those who put their faith in new writing, which they hope might invigorate the ailing regional theatres. Tim Pigott-Smith thinks that this may be possible. 'Doing new writing is the best way to keep theatre vital. The public aren't sympathetic to it, but the best way to preserve the link between the people who go to the theatre and the people who perform for the public good is through new and relevant writing.' Fiona Shaw goes even further, 'Experimentation is synonymous with theatre, if you keep playing the same old tune you are catapulted into oblivion.' William Franklyn is aware of the importance of new writing in avoiding this fate and says, 'Now that I'm on the board of the Basingstoke theatre what I'm interested in is looking for new playwrights to try and create interest in writing plays for the theatre, entertainment, plays. There are plenty of plays about important issues, but we want to try and entertain them and that is what we are really very short of. Television and film writers think there's no money in the theatre, but if you write a play that's even a quarter successful, let alone very, it has a ten-year life, it goes on and on, then it could be rediscovered later and have a revival. They should never think that it's wasted time, it's just very hard to do. A fixed set, five or six people, it's a wonderful challenge.' Franklyn elaborates, 'We have to say to playwrights, "We will give you a stage to put your plays on if you will write them." We can't just rely on people like Terry Johnson and David Hare. New writing will bring in new young audiences. We can't just do *Trainspotting* every week, but when I was twenty-four or twenty-five I used to go and see plays which I thoroughly enjoyed. Where are the equivalent of those plays today?' Sir Peter Hall believes that there are people ready to rise to the challenge, 'There's an enormous amount of young playwrights out there and a lot of them are very good, so that's the hope.'

Martin Duncan sounds a note of caution, 'It's very hard finding good new work that will fill a seven-hundred-seat theatre. Too many people write television plays to put on stage and they are not theatrical enough.' Paul Daneman shares his reservations, agreeing that, 'New writing favours film and television before the theatre,' while Daniel Massey believes that the classics are a more tried and tested restorative, 'I don't think it's true to say that new writing is going to regenerate the actor and his art. That is going to be most easily apprehended through classic writing rather than new writing because the imagination is forced to work a great deal harder.'

Injections of fresh blood from the fringe or from new writing on their own will be insufficient to reverse the decline from which repertory theatre is suffering. Charles Simon identifies the need for radical rethinking. 'I think the whole system wants overhauling completely: the system of grants and subsidies, the relationship between the artistic element and the business element. The system wants completely rehashing before it can stand a chance. One side can be unscrupulous in the same way as the other side. We'll spend money if we're given it, and ask for more. There's got to be some scheme invented whereby each side acts as a check upon the other. How you do it, goodness only knows.'

One solution, unarguably radical, is provided by Jonathan Church, who advocates a cull of regional companies. 'With Nottingham, Leicester, Derby, Sheffield, West Yorkshire Playhouse and Manchester, there is a huge number of producing theatres. They would probably all say that they were thriving, but my hunch is, particularly with what is happening to Sheffield, that there could be one too many producing theatres and you need to think strategically and some difficult decisions need to be made. While I love the infrastructure of theatres, if they're not working, if the community doesn't need them, then hanging on to them I feel a bit odd about. I think just hanging on is dangerous because I don't think it's very creative. I'm convinced that theatre will continue to thrive, but I don't think it will continue to thrive everywhere.'

Mark Piper thinks that reps need to rise to the challenge offered by other sources of entertainment, such as multiplex cinemas, 'To bring people back, the theatre has to give them the complete night out – proper heating, air-conditioning, parking and eating facilities.'

The scenario is not unrelievedly bleak. Christopher Honer points to the fact that 'In 1993 Manchester City Council considered stopping money for the Library Theatre, but an effective campaign, led by the company itself, saved the situation.' This has been repeated across the country, with theatres in Salisbury, Leatherhead, Windsor, Liverpool and Farnham all being pulled back from the brink by individual benefactors like Bill Kenwright, or by the companies or the communities themselves. Honer admits, 'Regional theatre has shrunk, but pockets of energy remain, especially in the Midlands and the north,' and according to David Tennant, who as a relative newcomer has worked with the

RSC but not extensively in rep, 'My personal experience has been very positive, it has been about theatres discovering new audiences.'

Ian Mullins is a hardened campaigner for the repertory movement and his credo is as follows, 'The fundamental philosophy of repertory theatre is that it belongs to the community and is part of the community and the community share in it and very often take part in it. It belongs to the community and the community belongs to it. Therefore you create a situation in a town where you have a local, enthusiastic audience and you create an essential rapport between them and a semi-permanent company of repertory players. You can give a company a wider perspective by using a lot of actors who come frequently, so that over the years they become quite well known in the town. The right choice of plays is important and this does not mean that you have to choose rather poor old-fashioned plays. You can do progressive seasons and include adventurous pieces. The criticism often comes back – "Oh you just want to go back to the old pot-boilers!" but you don't. Occasionally you throw in the so-called pot-boiler, but that is just part of a balanced programme. I think what is staged in a repertory season should be a kind of microcosm of what goes on in the West End. In the West End you have classical companies, you have places like the Royal Court doing new work, you have all sorts of commercial managements doing new popular plays or old popular plays and if you put all that lot together, that's the sort of thing we should be doing. Experienced actors would give their eye teeth to get into that sort of repertory company.'

There are those who remain convinced that a revival on this scale can be accomplished. Stephen Hancock is adamant, 'I'm not pessimistic about the future, nobody is ever going to kill the theatre. There's nothing like it, it's unique.' Mark Piper agrees. 'I'm optimistic about the future simply because theatres have a very good history of surviving.' And Phyllida Law comments, 'I'm suspicious about the notion that rep is in decline because the same thoughts were voiced when I was young. It's been mooted all my life that theatre is dead,' a point resoundingly endorsed by Francesca Ryan, who declares, 'I think subsidized theatre is the real glory of British theatre, it's generally acknowledged that our theatre tradition is very good. It's probably been a perennial cry through the ages that theatre is dying and it never will because there's always young blood.'

Epilogue

'ONE CARED ABOUT the work to such an extent. One thing I remember from weekly rep which took me a long time to get over, particularly if you had been on the stage management and you had to stay for the strike on a Saturday night, was seeing it all taken down and all the bits taken away. Thinking, "That was the wall that was beautifully lit, that was the sofa we did the last scene on," and you'd stand there almost crying and think, "It's all over, that play is all over." '

Donald Pickering

Cast List

In Alphabetical Order

Joss Ackland: Joss Ackland worked with the Old Vic company and at the Mermaid early in his career and achieved success in many West End productions, including *A Little Night Music, Evita, Peter Pan* and *Jean Seberg*. Among his film credits are *White Mischief, The Sicilian* and *Lethal Weapon 2*.

Jean Anderson: Jean Anderson is best known for the portrayal of Joycelyn Holbroke in the television series *Tenko*, Mrs Fortesque in *Keeping Up Appearances* and for roles in *The Brothers, GBH* and *Upstairs Downstairs*.

Doreen Andrew: Doreen Andrew has recently been a member of the RSC and has also worked with the English Touring Theatre, in many of London's fringe venues and in the West End in Alan Ayckbourn's *Revengers' Comedies*. She played Sylvia in *Nice Town* for the BBC and the Grandmother in *Dodgem* for children's television.

Eileen Atkins: Eileen Atkins appeared with the Old Vic Company in 1962, then at the Royal Court before scoring a huge personal success in *The Killing of Sister George*, which was later filmed. Since then she has worked in film and television, as well as with the RSC and the Royal National Theatre, winning acclaim in the latter's production of *John Gabriel Borkman* with Paul Scofield. Her recent appearance in Edward Albee's *A Delicate Balance* was widely praised.

Howard Attfield: Howard Attfield has worked in rep at Harrogate and Salisbury and on television in *Cream in My Coffee* by Dennis Potter, *Minder* and *Great Expectations*.

Alan Ayckbourn: Alan Ayckbourn has written and directed more than fifty-two plays for the Stephen Joseph Theatre in Scarborough, of which he has been Artistic Director since 1971. More than half of these plays have been produced in the West End. Among the best known are *Relatively Speaking, Absurd Person Singular, The Norman Conquests, Bedroom Farce, Just Between Ourselves, A Chorus of Disapproval, Woman in Mind, A Small Family*

Business and *Man of Moment*. He has been knighted for his services to the theatre.

Robin Bailey: Robin Bailey's early days in rep were interrupted by four years of active service during the war. By the late 1940s he was at the Birmingham Rep. Seasons at the Old Vic followed, which were succeeded by productions in the West End, Australia and the United States. He has worked extensively in the theatre; his film credits include *Catch Us If You Can* and *Blind Terror* and he appeared in *The Pallisers* and as Charters in *Charters and Caldicott* on television.

Evangeline Banks: Evangeline Banks is the daughter of Leslie Banks, a pillar of the British film industry who appeared in more than twenty movies between 1932 and 1950. She worked extensively in rep until her marriage to the actor Tenniel Evans. Their son Matthew Evans is now a television director and their daughter Serena Evans is currently starring opposite Rowan Atkinson in *The Thin Blue Line*.

Richard Bebb: Richard Bebb has wide-ranging experience of the theatre and his recent television credits include *Melissa, The Prince and the Pauper, Poirot – Murder on the Links, A Question of Attribution, Jeeves and Wooster* and *The Lawlords*. He was married to the late actress Gwen Watford, whom he met when they were both in rep at Buxton.

Alan Bennion: a stalwart of many reps, Alan Bennion has appeared in productions at the West Yorkshire Playhouse, the Chichester Festival Theatre, the Bristol Old Vic and the Vienna English Theatre.

Suzanne Bertish: Suzanne Bertish has appeared in feature films which include *Thin Ice* and *Venice, Venice*; on television in *Madame Blavatsky* and in numerous stage productions both here and in the United States.

Caroline Blakiston: Caroline Blakiston has spent the last few years with the Royal Shakespeare Company, appearing in *The Learned Ladies, The White Devil* and *Coriolanus*. Before that, she played Charlotta in a Russian version of *The Cherry Orchard* at the Moscow Arts Theatre. On television she played Lady Patience Hardacre in *Brass*.

Michael Bogdanov: Michael Bogdanov has directed productions with several major companies, including the English Shakespeare Company and the RSC, where his recent work includes *The Taming of the Shrew, The Shadow of a Gunman, The Knight of the Burning Pestle, Romeo and Juliet, The Venetian Twins, The Hostage* and *Faust, Parts One and Two*.

Jean Boht: Jean Boht has worked in rep, on tour and in the West End on many occasions. She is remembered by millions of television viewers for her portrayals of Josephine in *Brighton Belles* and Nellie Boswell in *Bread*.

Peter Bowles: Peter Bowles is best known for his work on television, which numbers successes such as *Rumpole of the Bailey, To the Manor Born,*

The Irish RM, *Lytton's Diary* and *Perfect Scoundrels*. He has made many appearances in the West End, including *Present Laughter* and *School of Wives*.

Stephen Boxer: Stephen Boxer's theatre work encompasses seasons with the National, the RSC and Cheek by Jowl. On television he has appeared in *The Politician's Wife*, *Under the Hammer* and as DCI Thorndyke in three of the *Prime Suspect* series. His film credits include *Mary Reilly*.

Elizabeth Bradley: Elizabeth Bradley has had a varied career, comprising extensive experience in rep, together with appearances at the Royal Court and in the West End and culminating in her current portrayal of Maud Grimes in *Coronation Street*.

Paul Bradley: known to *EastEnders'* fans for his portrayal of Nigel, Paul Bradley has also worked in a number of reps including the Royal Exchange and Contact in Manchester, Lancaster and Southampton.

Patricia Brake: Patricia Brake played Ingrid in *Porridge* and Gwen Lockhead in *Eldorado* on television. Her many theatre credits include seasons at the Little Theatre in Bristol and at Salisbury and Chichester.

Richard Briers: Richard Briers has enjoyed a fruitful association with Kenneth Branagh, for whose Renaissance Theatre he played King Lear, Malvolio and Uncle Vanya, and in whose films of *Henry V*, *Much Ado About Nothing* and *Swansong* he has appeared. He is widely known for his television work in *The Marriage Lines*, *The Norman Conquests*, *The Good Life* and *Ever Decreasing Circles*.

Faith Brook: Faith Brook has made film appearances in *Elgar's Tenth Muse* and *North Sea Hijack*. She played Lady Knox in *The Irish RM* on television and has worked extensively with the National and the RSC.

Mark Buffery: Mark Buffery has worked in several reps, amongst them the Bristol Old Vic, the Salisbury Playhouse and the Windsor Theatre Royal. He has appeared in *Casualty* on BBC 1.

Jean Byam: having worked at the Oxford Playhouse before leaving the theatre to do war work, Jean Byam now serves on the board of the Everyman Theatre in Cheltenham.

Anna Calder-Marshall: Anna Calder-Marshall has worked with both the Royal National Theatre and the Royal Shakespeare Company, in addition to playing Lavinia in the BBC TV production of *Titus Andronicus*. She has made other television appearances in *Heartbeat* and *Lovejoy* and has worked on films, including *Wuthering Heights*, *Anna Karenina* and *Witness Against Hitler*.

Judy Campbell: Judy Campbell has made numerous starring appearances in the West End over many decades and created the parts of Joanna in *Present Laughter* and Ethel in *This Happy Breed* for Noël Coward. In recent years she has played roles in *Downwardly Mobile* and *The House of Eliott* on television.

Richenda Carey: Richenda Carey worked in rep at Derby, Coventry, Wolverhampton and the Bristol Old Vic. She has made television appearances in *The Choir*, *The Darling Buds of May* and *Wycliffe* and played Lady Pembroke in the original production of *The Madness of King George* at the Royal National Theatre.

Ian Carmichael: Ian Carmichael began his career at the People's Palace in Mile End Road and much of his early work in the theatre was in revue. He made his first television appearance in *New Faces* in 1947 and his portrayals of both Bertie Wooster and Lord Peter Wimsey have won him much affection.

Belinda Carroll: Belinda Carroll comes from the fifth generation of a theatrical family, which includes her sister Kate O'Mara. She scored an early success in *There's a Girl in My Soup*, followed by appearances in theatres across the country and in *A Question of Guilt* and *Lovejoy* on television.

Anna Carteret: known to the general public for her portrayal of the eponymous heroine in *Juliet Bravo*, Anna Carteret has more recently appeared in *The Shell Seekers* on ITV and in the West End in *An Ideal Husband* and *On Approval*, both directed by Sir Peter Hall. In rep she worked at Butlin's in Skegness, as well as at Lincoln and Bristol.

Jonathan Cecil: Jonathan Cecil has appeared in rep at Northampton, Dundee, Hornchurch and Salisbury, as well as in numerous West End and television productions and more than twenty films, including *Barry Lyndon* and *Little Dorritt*.

Julia Chambers: Julia Chambers's many television credits include *The Mallens*, *Fanny by Gaslight*, *Sense and Sensibility*, *Beau Geste*, *Triangle*, *Emmerdale Farm*, *The Bill* and *Casualty*. She also has a wide-ranging experience of rep in Bristol, Salisbury, Farnham and Newcastle.

Maria Charles: Maria Charles starred in the original production of *The Boyfriend* and recently directed its anniversary revival at the Players Theatre. She has appeared on television in *Agony* and *Agony Again* and in the film *Savage Hearts*. She was in rep at Oldham and Buxton.

Jonathan Church: currently artistic director at the Salisbury Playhouse, Jonathan Church has worked his way up through the ranks backstage and into direction at a number of reps, including Lancaster, Sheffield, Nottingham, Derby, Liverpool and the West Yorkshire Playhouse.

Michael Cochrane: as well as working a great deal on radio, Michael Cochrane has a number of television appearances to his credit, including *Wings*, *The Chief*, *Sharpe's Sword* and *Sharpe's Regiment*, *Ruth Rendell's Simisola* and *Out of Sight*. He also has a wide experience of theatre work.

Stephanie Cole: Stephanie Cole's innumerable television appearances include *Tenko, In the Cold Light of Day, Memento Mori* and *Waiting for God*, culminating in *Keeping Mum*. Her most recent theatrical success was in *A Passionate Woman*.

Tom Conti: Tom Conti has been acclaimed for his work in the theatre – he won a Tony for his appearance on Broadway in *Whose Life Is It Anyway?* He is probably more widely known for his television appearances in *The Glittering Prizes, The Norman Conquests* and Dennis Potter's *Blade on the Feather*. He has starred in a number of films, amongst them *Reuben Reuben, Merry Christmas, Mr Lawrence, Beyond Therapy* and *Shirley Valentine*.

Beryl Cooke: since the 1920s Beryl Cooke has appeared in rep companies across the country. Now well into her eighties, she has worked extensively on television, appearing in *Fortunes of War, Waiting for God, Only Fools and Horses* and *Love Hurts*.

Ray Cooney: Ray Cooney is a talented farceur as well as writer and director of his own plays, which include *Chase Me Comrade, Run for Your Wife, Two into One, Move Over Mrs Markham* and *Wife Begins at Forty*.

Peter Copley: Peter Copley's theatre career has so far spanned sixty-six years and encompasses work in rep, at the Old Vic, the Gate in Dublin, the RSC and the West End. His television credits include *Brother Cadfael, Lovejoy, Ruth Rendell's An Unwanted Woman* and *A Dangerous Man*.

Elizabeth Counsell: the daughter of Mary Kerridge and John Counsell, who ran the rep company at Windsor for many decades, Elizabeth Counsell was bred into the theatre tradition. She has worked in regional theatres both as part of a resident company and on tour, appeared on the radio and at the Royal National Theatre. Her television credits include playing Jackie Spicer in *Nelson's Column*.

Brian Cox: Brian Cox has served a thorough apprenticeship in the theatre, where he worked at the Birmingham Rep, the Nottingham Playhouse, the Royal Exchange, the Royal Court and the National, but in recent years his career has been centred in the cinema, where he has appeared in *Desperate Measures, The Boxer, Kiss the Girls, Chain Reaction, The Glimmer Man, The Long Kiss Goodnight, Braveheart, Rob Roy* and *Secret Weapon*. He has not entirely abandoned his theatrical roots, since he appeared in *The Masterbuilder* when the newly refurbished Lyceum Theatre opened in London.

Wendy Craig: Wendy Craig began her career in rep at Ipswich, before moving on to work at the Royal Court Theatre and in the West End in plays such as *A Resounding Tinkle, Sport of My Mad Mother, A Doll's House*, and *The Bed Before Yesterday*. Her television career was launched by *Not in Front of the Children*, which was followed by a string of hits including *And*

Mother Makes Five, *Nanny* and *Butterflies*. Among the films she has appeared in are *Room at the Top*, *The Servant* and *Just Like a Woman*.

Bernard Cribbins: Bernard Cribbins started in the theatre when he was fourteen and has worked in the West End, at the National Theatre and in the United States. For a time he had his own television series, *Cribbins*, and he has appeared in many films, most notably *The Railway Children*.

Annette Crosbie: Annette Crosbie's television career spans an early appearance as Catherine of Aragon to Keith Michell's King in *The Six Wives of Henry the Eighth* to starring opposite Richard Wilson in *One Foot in the Grave*. In between she played Queen Victoria in *Edward the Seventh*, Janet in the Revival of *Dr Finlay* and appeared in *Paradise Postponed*. She has worked in rep in Glasgow and Bristol.

Liz Crowther: Liz Crowther's work in the theatre includes appearances in many rep companies, notably in *Communicating Doors* for Sir Alan Ayckbourn. On television she has been seen in *Growing Pains* and *Ghosts* and is currently playing Annie Hart in the Channel Five series *Family Affairs*.

Paul Daneman: Paul Daneman worked at the Bristol Old Vic, the Birmingham Rep, the Nottingham Playhouse, the Royal Court, the Lyric Hammersmith, the Old Vic and in the West End. On television he has been seen in *Corrigan Blake*, *Not in Front of the Children*, *Never a Cross Word* and *Spy Trap*.

Geoffrey Davies: best known for his portrayal of Dr Stuart-Clark in the *Doctor in the House* series, which ran for more than ten years, Geoffrey Davies has recently been seen in *Woof* and *Stick with Me Kid*, *The Labours of Erica* and *Bergerac*. He has worked in rep in Harrogate, Southwold, Derby and Sheffield.

Maurice Denham: Maurice Denham first worked in rep at Hull in 1934. He was on active service during the Second World War, was associated with the famous radio programme *ITMA* and from 1946 to 1949 could be heard regularly in *Much Binding in the Marsh*. He worked at the Old Vic, the Royal Court and in the West End. Among his many television credits are *Talking to a Stranger*, *The Lotus Eaters*, *Fall of Eagles*, *The Old Men at the Zoo*, *The Bill* and *Pie in the Sky*. His films include *The Chain* and *84 Charing Cross Road*.

Russell Dixon: Russell Dixon has worked in many reps, most recently in Derby and Leicester, as well as at the RSC and the Royal Exchange. His television work includes *Kavanah QC* and *Heartbeat*.

Gabrielle Drake: Gabrielle Drake played Nicola Freeman in *Crossroads*, Diana in *Medics* and also appeared for five years in *Kelly Monteith*. Her many West End appearances have been interspersed with work in rep at

Nottingham and Manchester, where in 1997 she scored a notable success in *Lady Windermere's Fan*.

Keith Drinkel: Keith Drinkel has worked in rep in Birmingham, Salisbury, Ipswich and Westcliff-on-Sea, as well as in the Radio Rep for the BBC. His television work includes *A Family at War*, *Country Matters* and two separate portrayals of John Major in *Scott and the Arms Antics* and *Thatcher – The Final Days*.

Martin Duncan: Martin Duncan has worked both as an actor and a director in rep at Lincoln, the Midland Arts Centre, Exeter and Sheffield. He is currently artistic director at the Nottingham Playhouse.

Bob Eaton: Bob Eaton is artistic director at the Belgrade Theatre, Coventry, having worked previously in rep at Stoke-on-Trent, Scarborough, Contact and the Liverpool Everyman.

Robin Ellis: Robin Ellis is best known for his portrayal of Ross in *Poldark*. Among his other television credits are *Blue Remembered Hills*, *Elizabeth R*, *The Guardians* and *Bright Eyes*. He was in rep at Cheltenham and in Salisbury.

Tenniel Evans: as well as working in rep at Farnham and Huddersfield, Tenniel Evans has appeared at the Royal National and Royal Court Theatres. He has been seen on television in *Wycliffe*, *Giving Tongue*, *Moving Story*, *September Song*, *Casualty* and *The Bill*. He is married to Evangeline Banks.

Lynn Farleigh: Lynn Farleigh has worked at the Royal National Theatre and Theatre Clwyd in recent years and her television credits include playing Mrs Philips in the BBC's acclaimed *Pride and Prejudice*, Helen Wycliffe in *Wycliffe*, as well as roles in *Castles* and *The Bill*.

Malcolm Farquhar: Malcolm Farquhar started his career as an actor at the Rapier Players in Bristol's Little Theatre and has worked extensively in reps including Salisbury, Leatherhead and the Alex in Birmingham as a performer and latterly as a director; he was artistic director of the Everyman in Cheltenham.

Julian Fellowes: Julian Fellowes has been involved in rep seasons at Frinton, Northampton and Harrogate as well as working in the West End. His television credits include *Kavanagh QC*, *Our Friends in the North*, *Martin Chuzzlewit*, *All Quiet on the Preston Front*, *Love Hurts*, *Rumpole*, *Pie in the Sky* and *Sharpe's Rifles*. Among his films are *Jane Eyre*, *Shadowlands* and *Damage*.

Lucy Fleming: Lucy Fleming's stage work includes appearances at the Chichester Festival Theatre and the West End, most recently in *Our Song* with Peter O'Toole. She has worked widely in television, where her credits include parts in *Smiley's People*, *Wycliffe* and *A Dance to the Music of Time*.

Diane Fletcher: best known for her portrayal of Elizabeth Urquart in *The House of Cards*, Diane Fletcher has also appeared in *Poirot* and as Angela in *Coronation Street*. Latterly she has been under contract to the RSC and has worked at the Palace Theatre in Watford.

Oliver Ford Davies: Oliver Ford Davies won acclaim for his performances in David Hare's plays, *The Absence of War* and *Racing Demon*, at the Royal National Theatre. On television he has appeared in *A Dance to the Music of Time*, *Kavanagh QC*, *Anglo-Saxon Attitudes*, *Inspector Morse* and *A Taste For Death*. He has been in the films *Scandal* and *Mrs Dalloway*.

Barry Foster: Barry Foster's distinguished career encompasses work in the theatre at Nottingham, the Royal Court and the West End; on television as the eponymous hero in *Van der Valk*, *Divorce His; Divorce Hers*, with Richard Burton and Elizabeth Taylor, *Fall of Eagles* and *The Three Hostages*. Among his many films are *King and Country*, *The Family Way*, *Twisted Nerve*, *Ryan's Daughter* and *Frenzy*.

Derek Fowlds: currently entertaining television viewers with his portrayal of Sergeant Oscar Blaketon in *Heartbeat*, Derek Fowlds is also fondly remembered by millions as Bernard Woolley in *Yes, Minister* and *Yes, Prime Minister*. His other television work includes *Firm Friends*, *Darling Buds of May*, *Chancer*, *They Never Slept* and *Setting of the Sun*.

Cate Fowler: trained as a dancer, Cate Fowler switched to working in the theatre and has appeared in several rep companies. In 1996 she was in the film *Young Poisoners' Handbook* and her television experience includes parts in *EastEnders*, *Border*, *Small Zones* and the role of Princess Anne in *Charles and Diana – Unhappily Ever After* for ABC television in the United States.

Clive Francis: recent television work includes *The 10%ers*, *Sharpe's Company*, *The Plant*, *Lipstick on Your Collar* and *The Piglet Files*, but Clive Francis has also worked extensively in the West End and for the RSC. He was in rep with the Penguin Players at Bexhill-on-Sea.

Jan Francis: probably best known for her performance in *Just Good Friends*, Jan Francis has worked prolifically in television and among her film credits are *Champion*, in which she played opposite John Hurt, and *The Corvini Inheritance*. She has done rep seasons at Cheltenham and Bristol.

William Franklyn: William Franklyn has worked in rep and in the West End; his loyalty to the former is demonstrated by the fact that he now sits on the board of the Haymarket Theatre in Basingstoke. He has been seen on television in *London Suite*, *Lovejoy*, *Young Indy* and *GBH*. Among his films are *Robert Ryland's Last Journey*.

Rupert Frazer: Rupert Frazer received his theatrical blooding at the Glasgow Citizens and has also worked at the Royal Court and the Royal National

Theatre. On television he has been see in *Testament of Youth*, *The Importance of Being Earnest*, *The House of Eliott* and *The Prince and the Pauper*. His films include *The Shooting Party* and *Empire of the Sun*.

Jill Freud: Jill Freud took leave of absence from her theatre career to raise her family and on returning to the business, as well as appearing in television series such as *Maigret*, has devoted her time to establishing a rep company at Southwold, where she works both as producer and actress.

Jill Gascoine: Jill Gascoine spent seven years playing Maggie Forbes in *The Gentle Touch* and *CATS*. Her other major television work includes *Northern Exposure* and she starred in *42nd Street* in the West End. Her rep experience consists of seasons in Leicester, Nottingham, Bexhill-on-Sea, Dundee, Glasgow and Worthing.

Liza Goddard: Liza Goddard came to fame playing Victoria in the BBC's *Take Three Girls* and again in *Take Three Women*. She also appeared in *Yes – Honestly*, *Bergerac*, *Pig in the Middle* and *Roll Over Beethoven*; her theatre credits include *Arms and the Man*, *See How They Run*, *Wife Begins at Forty* and *No Sex Please, We're British*.

Jennie Goossens: Jennie Goossens has worked with the RSC and was seen on tour in *My Fair Lady*, directed by Simon Callow. Her television credits number *Grange Hill*, *Just William*, *Murder in the Family*, *The Wimbledon Poisoner* and *EastEnders*.

Nickolas Grace: Nickolas Grace's theatre work includes seasons at Frinton, Theatre 69 and the RSC. On television he has appeared in *Brideshead Revisited*, *Robin of Sherwood* and *The Final Cut*. His films include *The Hunchback of Notre Dame*, *Shooting Fish*, *Two Deaths*, *Tom and Viv*, *Salome's Last Dance* and *Heat and Dust*.

Deborah Grant: for ten years Deborah Grant played Debbie Bergerac in *Bergerac* for the BBC. She also appeared as Leonora in *Bread* on television. In the theatre she has appeared in *A Little Night Music* at the Theatre Royal in Plymouth and more recently opposite Tom Conti in *Present Laughter* in the West End. She was in rep at Bristol, Coventry and Liverpool.

Dulcie Gray: Dulcie Gray's theatre career has spanned almost sixty years, encompassing work in rep, the West End, on film and television, often with her husband, the actor Michael Denison. In the late 1980s she appeared for five years as Kate Harvey in *Howard's Way* and her most recent theatre work has been in Sir Peter Hall's theatre company in productions of *Tartuffe* and *An Ideal Husband*. She is also a prolific author.

Elspet Gray: Elspet Gray appeared in many of her husband Brian Rix's farces both in the West End and later on television. Her TV work includes *The Wingless Bird*, *The Ruth Rendell Mysteries – Heartstones*, *Murder Most Horrid* and as Mrs Finlay in Scottish Television's remake of *Dr Finlay*. Recent among her many films is *Four Weddings and a Funeral*. She was in rep at Worthing and Bridlington.

Paul Greenwood: Paul Greenwood has worked in reps in Chesterfield, Tynemouth, Birmingham, Windsor, Hornchurch and Harrogate, as well as doing many seasons with the RSC. On television he played the title role in *The Growing Pains of PC Penrose* and its sequel, *Rosie*.

Peter Hall: Peter Hall began his directing career in rep at Windsor and then the Oxford Playhouse. He became artistic director of the Arts Theatre in London, after which he worked at the Shakespeare Memorial Theatre in Stratford-upon-Avon and supervised its transformation into the RSC, which he ran from 1960 until 1968. Five years later he was in charge of the National Theatre and directed inaugural productions at its new home on the South Bank in London. He has directed opera at Covent Garden and Glyndebourne and after leaving the National mounted productions with his own company at the Haymarket in the West End. His most recent venture has been the establishment of a company run along repertory lines at the Old Vic. He has been knighted for his services to the theatre.

Stephen Hancock: Stephen Hancock is probably best remembered for his role as Ernie Bishop in *Coronation Street* and in recent times has been heard by millions as the theatre director Laurence Lovell in *The Archers*. He still works in rep and was involved in the RSC's hugely successful *Two Gentlemen of Verona* as musical director.

Chris Harris: Chris Harris has worked largely in rep as an actor, director and occasionally as a writer. In all these capacities he has been responsible for a dazzling string of pantomimes at the Bristol Old Vic. He also performs a highly successful one-man show about Will Kempe, who was the comedian in Shakespeare's company.

M.C. Hart: M.C. Hart started his career with the Butlin's rep and went on to become a television director; among his credits is *Waugh on Crime*.

Bernard Hepton: Bernard Hepton's career has been divided between acting and directing. In the theatre he was the last artistic director employed by Barry Jackson at the Birmingham Rep and he had the same position at the Liverpool Playhouse. On television he worked as a producer of shows like *Naked Island* and *The Wednesday Thriller* and is widely remembered for his performances as the Kommandant in *Colditz*, and in *United!*, *Secret Army*, *Tinker, Tailor, Soldier, Spy* and *The Charmer*.

Robin Herford: Robin Herford has enjoyed a long association with Alan Ayckbourn at the Stephen Joseph Theatre in Scarborough, where he began as an actor and finished up as associate director. He has appeared in Ayckbourn's plays *Henceforward, Intimate Exchanges, Tons of Money, Absent Friends* and *Way Upstream*. On television he has been seen in *The Secret Diary of Adrian Mole* and *The Growing Pains of Adrian Mole*.

Patricia Hodge: Patricia Hodge's theatre work in the West End and at out-of-town venues such as the Chichester Festival has been complemented by her appearances on television, which began with *The Naked Civil Servant* and went on to include *The One and Only Phyllis Dixie*, Phyllida in *Rumpole of the Bailey*, the eponymous heroine in *Jemima Shore Investigates* and *The Life and Loves of a She Devil*. She was in rep at Chester and Edinburgh.

Ian Hogg: Ian Hogg's career has encompassed work at the Royal National Theatre, the RSC, the Donmar Warehouse and with Sir Alan Ayckbourn's company in Scarborough. On television he is best known for his portrayal of Rockliffe in *Rockliffe's Folly* and *Rockliffe's Babies*. His other television credits include *Expert Witness, The Blood That's in You* and *Death of a Salesman*.

Vilma Hollingbery: Vilma Hollingbery has worked with both the Royal National Theatre and the RSC and has both appeared in and adapted plays for the Royal Theatre, Northampton, where her husband Michael Napier Brown is the artistic director. Her television credits include *The Bill, A Touch of Frost* and *Do the Right Thing*.

Christopher Honer: Christopher Honer has pursued a career as a director in rep at theatres in Frinton, Coventry, Birmingham, Chester and Derby and he is now artistic director at the Library Theatre in Manchester.

David Horovitch: David Horovitch has worked in rep at Cheltenham, Newcastle and the Royal Exchange in Manchester. He has appeared in several productions at the Royal National Theatre, notably in David Hare's *Racing Demon*. On television he played Mr Brown for two years in *Just William* and has also been seen in *Drop the Dead Donkey, Ivanhoe* and *Miss Marple*.

Bernard Horsfall: Bernard Horsfall has worked in rep at Dundee, Leatherhead, Nottingham and recently in Birmingham. His television credits include *Heroes and Villains, Nice Town* and *Casualty* and he has appeared in the films *The Seekers* and *Braveheart*.

Peter Howell: Peter Howell has a wide experience of rep in Oxford, Guildford, High Wycombe, Dundee and Bristol. He has been heard often on the radio and on television has been seen in *Jeeves and Wooster, The 10%ers, Emma* and *Rory Bremner – Who Else?* His films include *Shadowlands*.

Derek Jacobi: Derek Jacobi started his career at the Birmingham Rep, after which he joined the National Theatre when it was based at the Old Vic in London. Here he stayed for eight years and was in illustrious productions such as Laurence Olivier's *Othello*. His subsequent work in the theatre has included seasons with Prospect, the RSC and at Chichester. He shot to fame when he played the title role in *I, Claudius* on television and has recently gained equally wide recognition for playing the eponymous hero in *Cadfael*. He has been knighted for his services to the theatre.

Barbara Jefford: Barbara Jefford came to prominence when she worked at the Shakespeare Memorial Theatre at Stratford-upon-Avon during the 1950s. She went on to appear with the Old Vic Company and later the Royal National Theatre and the RSC and has worked often in the West End and on Broadway, as well as in Russia, South America, Australia and Europe. She did rep seasons at the 'Q' Theatre, in Brighton and at Dundee.

Peter Jeffrey: Peter Jeffrey has worked with a number of rep companies including Chorlton, Grange-over-Sands, Weston-Super-Mare and Bristol. He has also done seasons with both the Royal National Theatre and the RSC. On television he has been seen in *The Moonstone, The Prince and the Pauper, The Treasure Seekers, Our Friends in the North* and *Middlemarch*.

Lionel Jeffries: Lionel Jeffries is a much-loved figure on television, stage and in films. He made 110 films in twenty-six years. Best remembered are *Two Way Stretch, The Wrong Arm of the Law, Camelot, Chitty Chitty Bang Bang, The Trials of Oscar Wilde, Baxter, The Amazing Mr Blunden, Ménage à Trois, The Prisoner of Zenda, Royal Flash* and *The Railway Children*, which he directed from his own screenplay. He began his career with a season of rep in Lichfield.

Edward Jewesbury: Edward Jewesbury has worked in rep in Birmingham, Colchester and Coventry, as well as doing seasons with Kenneth Branagh's Renaissance Theatre Company, the RSC and at Chichester. On television he has recently been seen in *Kavanagh QC* and *Hildegard* and his films include *Peter's Friends* and *Much Ado About Nothing*.

Richard Johnson: Richard Johnson has a distinguished career in classical theatre at the Bristol Old Vic and the RSC. He played Laertes in Peter Brook's production of *Hamlet* and has worked in the West End and on Broadway. His recent television work includes *Breaking the Code, Heavy Weather, Anglo-Saxon Attitudes* and *The Camomile Lawn*. Among his film credits are *Captain Horatio Hornblower, The Pumpkin Eaters* and *The Beloved*. He has appeared in rep at Dundee, Perth and Bristol.

Gemma Jones: best known on television for playing the title role in *The Duchess of Duke Street*, which was shown in more than thirty episodes on BBC 1, Gemma Jones has a wide-ranging experience of theatre as well. In 1965 she won the Clarence Derwent Award for her portrayal of Adèle in *The*

Cavern and she has also worked at the Birmingham Rep, the Nottingham Playhouse, the RSC and the Royal National Theatre.

Rachel Kempson: Rachel Kempson started her career at the Liverpool Playhouse, where she met her husband Michael Redgrave and with him is founder of a theatrical dynasty which includes Vanessa, Lynn, Corin and Jemma Redgrave, and Natasha and Joely Richardson. She appeared in one of the earliest productions for the BBC in *The Case of the Frightened Lady* in 1938 and went on to play roles in *Tales of Unease, Elizabeth R, Jennie* and *The Jewel in the Crown*. She has worked extensively at Stratford and in the West End and her film work includes *Georgy Girl, The Charge of the Light Brigade* and *The Virgin Soldiers*.

Mary Kenton: Mary Kenton was the leading lady at the Theatre Royal in Northampton for many seasons and has considerable experience of rep. In 1964 she appeared in *The Sullavan Brothers* for ATV and between 1965 and 1967 she played a central role in *The Newcomers* for the BBC.

Michael Kilgarriff: Michael Kilgarriff has worked in rep on Jersey and in Peterborough, Stockton-on-Tees, York, Harrogate and Bristol. He can often be heard on the radio. His television work includes appearances in *Growing Pains, A Curse on the House of Windsor* and *Tales from the Map Room*.

Estelle Kohler: Estelle Kohler has pursued a career in the classics, which she started when she played Ophelia in Peter Hall's production of *Hamlet* for the RSC in 1964. Other Shakespearean roles include Juliet, Titania and Adriana, all for the RSC and the New Shakespeare Company. Her West End appearances include *An Inspector Calls*.

Mark Lambert: Mark Lambert's theatre experience encompasses appearances at the Gate in Dublin, the Almeida, the Bristol Old Vic, the Royal Court and in the West End. He has been seen on television in *Boon, Bottom* and *Time After Time* and the cinema in *A Prayer for the Dying*.

Belinda Lang: famous for her portrayal of Bill in *Two Point Four Children* for the BBC, Belinda Lang's other television work includes *The Inspector Alleyn Mysteries, Second Thoughts* and *To Serve Them All My Days*. She has appeared in *Antigone* and *Mrs Klein* at the Royal National Theatre. Her rep experience includes seasons at Frinton, Manchester, Bristol, Leicester, Oxford and Exeter.

Phyllida Law: Phyllida Law has extended a career, which began largely in the theatre, with a number of performances in film and television in recent years. Among her credits are the films *Peter's Friends, Much Ado About Nothing, Emma* and the *The Winter Guest*. She was married to Eric Thompson, who created *The Magic Roundabout*, and is the mother of actresses Emma and Sophie Thompson.

Leslie Lawton: Leslie Lawton has been artistic director of reps in Westcliff-on-Sea, the Playhouse in Liverpool and the Lyceum in Edinburgh. He started as a child actor and has worked widely in theatre and television.

Roger Leach: Roger Leach is known to millions for his portrayal of Sergeant Penny in *The Bill* over a seven-year period. He has also been in *Perfect Scoundrels* on television and has worked extensively in rep.

Rosemary Leach: Rosemary Leach has worked widely in the theatre and her television credits include *No – That's Me Over Here*, *The Roads to Freedom*, *Brief Encounter*, *Second Verdict*, *Now Look Here*, *The Jewel in the Crown*, *The Charmer* and *The Buccaneers*. She has starred in many films, not least *A Room with a View*.

Barbara Leigh Hunt: Barbara Leigh Hunt has a distinguished career in the theatre, which includes many seasons with both the RSC, where she now sits on the board of governors, and the Royal National Theatre, where she has lately appeared to great acclaim in *Absence of War* and as Lady Bracknell in *The Importance of Being Earnest*. She is married to the actor Richard Pasco.

Maureen Lipman: much-loved actress, comedienne and columnist, Maureen Lipman has appeared in numerous television successes, amongst them *Rogue Male*, *Outside Edge*, *Agony* and, recently, a reprise of the last, *Agony Again*. She has won both a Laurence Olivier award and a Variety Club award for her work on stage and has recently been acclaimed for her one-woman show about Joyce Grenfell, *Re Joyce*.

Philip Locke: Philip Locke's career has centred mainly on the classics and he has worked with both the Royal National Theatre and the RSC, where he played Quince in Peter Brook's legendary production of *A Midsummer Night's Dream*. He has been in the films *Jacob – The Old Testament* and *And the Ship Sails On*. He was in rep at Oldham and Dundee.

Barbara Lott: Barbara Lott is best known for her portrayal over seven years of Ronnie Corbett's mother in *Sorry*. Her other television work includes roles in *Daisies in December*, *Law and Disorder*, *Woof* and *Two Point Four Children*. She has appeared in the films *Electric Door* and Peter Greenaway's *The Pillow Book*.

Christopher Luscombe: Christopher Luscombe's extensive experience in rep in companies at Windsor, Harrogate, Leatherhead, Basingstoke, Coventry, Bristol and Northampton has been followed by several seasons with the RSC. He has devised and appeared in *The Shakespeare Revue* and *Half Time* and was seen in *A Dance to the Music of Time* on television.

Richard McCabe: Richard McCabe has appeared in rep in Leeds, Sheffield,

Manchester, Oldham and Birmingham, as well as in productions at the Royal National Theatre and the RSC, where he is a rising star. His television credits include *Between the Lines* and *Persuasion*.

Joanna McCallum: Joanna McCallum has appeared in the feature films *The Eligible Bachelor*, *The Mysterious Affair at Styles* and *Tom and Viv*; her television work includes *Class Act* and *Moving Story* and she has done several seasons at the RSC and in Chichester. She is the daughters of actors Googie Withers and John McCallum.

John McCallum: John McCallum began his career at the People's Palace in Mile End Road and went on to work at the Old Vic, the Shakespeare Memorial Theatre and on frequent occasions in the West End. His twenty-six films include *It Always Rains on Sunday*, *The Loves of Joanna Godden* and *Valley of Eagles*. In his native Australia he has worked as an actor, director and producer (in this last capacity he was responsible for the long-running children's television series *Skippy, the Bush Kangaroo*).

Alec McCowen: Alec McCowen began his career in rep, but soon moved on to the West End and Broadway. He has done seasons with the Old Vic and the RSC, for whom he toured the USSR as the Fool in Peter Brook's *King Lear*. He has twice won the Evening Standard Best Actor Award and once the Variety Club Award for Best Actor. Among his films are *The Cruel Sea*, *Frenzy*, *Travels with My Aunt* and *The Age of Innocence*.

Peter McEnery: an early start in rep on the Palace Pier at Brighton and with Harry Hanson's Court Players soon led Peter McEnery on to the RSC, the West End and many film and television roles. His movies include *Tunes of Glory*, *Negatives*, *The Atlantic Wall* and *Entertaining Mr Sloane* and among his television credits are *Candida*, *Progress to the Park* and *Clayhanger*.

Juliette Mander: Juliette Mander has worked in the stage management of the Leicester Phoenix and other companies across the country.

Nancy Mansfield: Nancy Mansfield started her career in rep soon after the war, but after working in Dundee and Ipswich took leave of absence for thirty years to raise her family. On her return to the profession she has been a regular member of the *Bergerac* cast, as well as appearing in *Grange Hill* and *The Gruesome Grannies of Gobshoot Hall* on television and she has been back to Ipswich to play many leading parts there.

Patricia Marmont: Patricia Marmont started out as an actress and worked in the theatre both here and in the United States. She gave up performing in favour of becoming a theatrical agent and her company Marmont Management is now one of the foremost in its field, with an impressive list of loyal clients.

Hilary Mason: Hilary Mason's considerable work in the theatre has been complemented by a list of television credits comprising *An Independent Man, Casualty, One Foot in the Grave, Nelson's Column* and *Love Hurts*. In films she played Heather in *Don't Look Now* and the medium in *Haunted*.

Daniel Massey: Daniel Massey appeared in several films, including *Girls at Sea, The Entertainer, Star* and *In the Name of the Father*. On television he was seen in *On Approval, War and Peace, Back of Beyond, The Roads to Freedom* and *The Golden Bowl*. His first love was the theatre and in particular the classics and he worked on many occasions with the RSC, as well as in London and on Broadway. He maintained a strong commitment to rep, as demonstrated in the work he did at Worthing, Coventry, Stratford East, Nottingham and Guildford.

Peter Meakin: Peter Meakin has worked mainly in rep, at Contact in Manchester, Coventry and the Derby Playhouse, where he is now associate director with special responsibility for community theatre.

Frank Middlemass: Frank Middlemass worked in Harry Hanson's companies at Stockton-on-Tees, Chester and Bradford and was also in rep at Penzance, Oldham, Canterbury and Bristol. He has worked both in the West End and with the RSC and his television work includes *Crime and Punishment, As Time Goes By, King Lear, To Serve Them All My Days* and *War and Peace*.

John Moffatt: John Moffatt's career was grounded in rep at Perth, Oxford, the Bristol Old Vic and Windsor before he went on to work at the Royal Court, the Old Vic in London, the West End and on Broadway.

Stephen Moore: Stephen Moore's work in rep encompasses seasons at Windsor, Colchester, Bristol and Birmingham. As well as working for the RSC, he has appeared at the Old Vic, the Mermaid and in the West End of London and also on tour in the United States and Hong Kong. To television audiences he is known for playing Danny in *Solo*, the father in *The Secret Diary of Adrian Mole* and for his appearances in *Three Men in a Boat* and *Rock Follies*.

Cherry Morris: Cherry Morris has recently been involved in several productions for the RSC, the culmination of many years' work in theatres across the country, including reps in Guildford, Sheffield, Bromley, Exter, Edinburgh and York. She has also appeared at the Royal Court and in the West End. Her television work includes *Mapp and Lucia, Lovejoy, The Prime of Miss Jean Brodie, Little Lord Fauntleroy, Worzel Gummidge, Poldark, Softly, Softly* and *Tales of the Unexpected*.

Peggy Mount: after working in rep for fifteen years, Peggy Mount shot to stardom in *Sailor Beware*, which ran for years in the West End and was also filmed. Her stage work includes seasons at the Old Vic, the

National and the RSC and among her films are *The Naked Truth*, *Hotel Paradiso*, *Inn for Trouble*, *One Way Pendulum* and *Ladies Who Do*.

Ian Mullins: throughout his career in the theatre Ian Mullins has dedicated himself to the repertory movement, working as artistic director in Cheltenham, Farnham, Basingstoke and Auckland in New Zealand over several decades.

Brian Murphy: early in his career Brian Murphy worked with the renowned Joan Littlewood and her company at Stratford East; his other rep experience includes seasons at Canterbury, Nottingham and Coventry. His television work consists of *Man About the House*, which spawned the popular series *George and Mildred*, in which he played opposite Yootha Joyce. Recent television work has been centred on the children's series *The Famous Five* and *Wizadora*.

John Nettles: for ten years John Nettles played the title role in the successful series *Bergerac*, which has perhaps eclipsed his work in the theatre, which includes seasons with the RSC and, during his early days, at Scarborough, Exeter and Bristol. He has recently been seen again on television in *Midsomer Murders*.

John Newman: John Newman's early experience in rep at Colwyn Bay, Rhyl, York and Cheltenham culminated in him forming his own production company, Newpalm Productions, with his wife Daphne Palmer. Newpalm sends out many national tours, but also stages a rep season in Chelmsford every year.

Derek Nimmo: Derek Nimmo started his theatrical career with rep seasons in Bolton, Worcester and Crewe before going on to make many appearances in the West End. He is known to millions for his television successes, which number *All Gas and Gaiters*, *Oh Brother*, *Oh Father*, *If It's Saturday It Must Be Nimmo* and *Just a Nimmo*. He has appeared in many films, among them *Casino Royale*, *Joey Boy* and *One of Our Dinosaurs is Missing*. His appearances on *Just a Minute* have earned him a wide radio following.

Tony O'Callaghan: Tony O'Callaghan started out in rep, appearing in theatres in Cheltenham, Northampton, Worthing, Greenwich and Keswick, before a sustained stint as Sergeant Boyden in *The Bill*.

Roger Ostime: Roger Ostime began his career in fit-up with the Garrick Players, who were based in Newton Poppleford. He worked extensively in rep and has made several television appearances, in *Stolen*, *Countdown to War*, *Capital City* and *Lovejoy*. He is married to the actress Hilary Mason.

Jocelyne Page: Jocelyne Page began her career in rep with seasons at Nottingham and the Oxford Playhouse, where she was directed by the novice Peter Hall. She gave up the profession to devote herself to the family she has raised with her husband, the actor Stephen Hancock.

Nicola Pagett: Nicola Pagett came to prominence when she starred as Elizabeth in *Upstairs Downstairs*. Her other television appearances include *The Caesars* and *A Woman of Substance*; among her films are *Privates on Parade*, *Oliver's Story*, *Operation Daybreak*, *The Price of Freedom* and *There's a Girl in my Soup*.

Daphne Palmer: having started out in rep working for other managements, with her partner John Newman Daphne Palmer founded the company Newpalm, which stages a repertory season in Chelmsford every year and produces shorter seasons and tours elsewhere in the country.

Bridget Panet: Bridge Panet has an encyclopaedic knowledge of rep, having worked in theatres at Salisbury, Liverpool, Chesterfield, Guildford and Ipswich.

Richard Pasco: Richard Pasco's first job was at the 'Q' Theatre near Kew Bridge in London. Seasons at the Old Vic in London, the Birmingham Rep, the Royal Court, the Bristol Old Vic and the RSC followed, enabling him to develop into one of our finest classical actors. On television he has been seen in *Julius Caesar* and recently in *A Dance to the Music of Time*.

Peter Penry-Jones: Peter Penry-Jones has worked in rep at Perth, Sheffield, York and Paignton. On television he has been seen in *Genghis Cohen*, *The Cold Light of Day*, *The Silent Twins*, *Colditz*, *Strike It Rich* and *To the Manor Born*. His films include *Dance of Death* and *Unbroken Arrow*.

Donald Pickering: Donald Pickering has worked in rep at Oldham, Canterbury, Derby and with the Penguin Players at Bexhill-on-Sea. He has appeared many times in the West End and on television, notably in *Yes, Prime Minister*.

Tim Pigott-Smith: Tim Pigott-Smith began as an acting ASM at the Bristol Old Vic and has also worked at the Birmingham Rep. His work on television includes *Antony and Cleopatra*, *Measure for Measure*, *I Remember Nelson* and *Life Story*, but he is probably best known for his portrayals of Ronald Merrick in *The Jewel in the Crown* and the title role in *The Chief*.

Mark Piper: Mark Piper has worked as a director in rep at Kirkcaldy, Dundee, Edinburgh and Harrogate and is currently artistic director at Windsor.

Angela Pleasence: Angela Pleasence followed her father, the actor Donald Pleasence, into the profession and scored an early success playing Jane Seymour in the BBC's acclaimed series *The Six Wives of Henry the Eighth* opposite Keith Michell. Her theatre experience includes repertory seasons in Birmingham, Nottingham and the Edinburgh Lyceum.

Nyree Dawn Porter: Nyree Dawn Porter's recent theatre roles include *Sunday in the Park with George* at the Royal National Theatre, *Beyond Reasonable Doubt*, *The Winslow Boy* and *Great Expectations*. On television she was in *Six Shades of Black*, *The Liars* and *The Protectors*, but is probably best remembered for her portrayal of Irene in the BBC's *The Forsyte Saga*.

Dennis Ramsden: Dennis Ramsden has worked as an actor at Dundee rep and a director at Aberdeen. During his five decades in the profession he has become a noted farceur, working many times in the West End as well as on Broadway, in South Africa and Canada. He has been seen most recently on television in *As Time Goes By*.

Amanda Redman: with theatre work at the Royal Court and the National to her credit, Amanda Redman has also made numerous appearances on television, most notably playing Joanna in *Dangerfield*, the eponymous heroine in *Beck*, *The Secret House of Death* and *Demob*. Her films include *Body and Soul*, *For Queen and Country* and *Richard's Things*. The celebrated production of *King Lear* starring Ian Holm at the Royal National Theatre, in which she played Regan, has just been broadcast on television.

Sheila Reid: Sheila Reid has recently been seen in *Martin Guerre* in the West End, where she was also in the hit production *When I Was a Girl I Used to Scream and Shout*. She appeared in *Taggart* on television and her films are *American Friends*, *Brazil* and *Five Days One Summer*.

Brian Rix: Brian Rix worked in rep at Harrogate before setting up his own companies at Ilkley, Bridlington and Margate. He subsequently embarked upon a series of farces at the Whitehall Theatre and then the Aldwych Theatre, in which he was both leading man and producer. Many of his farces were presented on television, among them *Reluctant Heroes*, *High Temperature*, *All for Mary*, *Women Aren't Angels* and *Six of Rix*. During the last two decades much of his time and energy has been devoted to the charity Mencap, in recognition of which he was made a life peer.

Francesca Ryan: Francesca Ryan has worked in reps in Birmingham, Manchester and Bolton, with the RSC and the English Shakespeare Company, and she appeared in the West End production of Arthur Miller's *Broken Glass*. In television she has worked on *Prime Suspect* and *Trust Me* and played Dr Claire Armstrong in *Medics*.

Patrick Ryecart: Patrick Ryecart started his theatrical career in rep at Hornchurch and, after making an early appearance on television in *General Hospital*, went on to star in the BBC's production of *Romeo and Juliet* and later in the series *The High Life*.

Reggie Salberg: part of the Salberg theatrical dynasty, Reggie ran a number of rep companies at Kettering, Penge and Hull before settling at Salisbury, where his Arts Theatre was one of the first regional concerns to receive funding when the Arts Council was established.

Jenny Seagrove: Jenny Seagrove first made her mark playing Emma in the television adaptation of Barbara Taylor Bradford's *A Woman of Substance*. She went on to carve a career for herself in films, which include *Local Hero, Miss Beatty's Children, The Guardian* and *A Chorus of Disapproval*. In recent years she has played Jane in *Jane Eyre* at Chichester and made numerous West End appearances.

Fiona Shaw: Fiona Shaw is acknowledged to be one of the most distinguished classical actors of her generation, a reputation which has been forged by the work she has done both with the Royal National Theatre and the RSC, culminating in her recent mould-breaking rendering of the King in *Richard II*. Among the films in which she has appeared are *Anna Karenina, Jane Eyre, Persuasion* and *My Left Foot*.

Carmen Silvera: Carmen Silvera is best known for her portrayal of Edith in the popular television series *Allo Allo*. Among her recent stage work are roles in *The School for Wives, Two of a Kind, The Cemetery Club, The Importance of Being Earnest, Habeas Corpus* and *Rebecca*.

Charles Simon: Charles Simon has worked in the theatre as an actor, director and in management for more than seventy years, starting with his early days running a company in Darlington right through to a recent appearance at the Royal National Theatre. He has been seen in many television programmes and his film credits include *Stiff Upper Lips, Turning World, Shadowlands* and *American Friends*.

Michael Simpkin: Michael Simpkin started his theatrical career at Hornchurch and went on to work in Scarborough, where he appeared in many of Alan Ayckbourn's productions. He is best known for his portrayal of Philip Castle in the BBC series *Castles*.

Alison Steadman: one of our foremost television actresses, Alison Steadman has given unforgettable performances in *Abigail's Party, Nuts in May, The Singing Detective* and *Pride and Prejudice*. Her film credits include *Shirley Valentine, Clockwise* and *Life Is Sweet*.

Virginia Stride: Virginia Stride has recently worked in rep in both Bristol and Vienna. With wide experience on the stage, she has also been in *A Touch of Spice* on television and the film *London Suite*.

Michael Stroud: Michael Stroud has worked in Salisbury, Dundee, Bristol and Coventry reps as both a performer and a director and has also been in seasons at the Royal National Theatre.

Shaun Sutton: Shaun Sutton was well grounded in the repertory tradition after working at the 'Q' Theatre, the Embassy Swiss Cottage, Croydon,

Buxton, Ipswich, Eastbourne and Hayes. He joined the BBC as a director in the 1950s and became the corporation's Head of Television Drama.

David Tennant: David Tennant has worked at the Dundee rep and the Royal Exchange in Manchester, as well as at the Young Vic, the Royal National Theatre and the RSC. His television appearances include *A Mug's Game*, *Takin' Over the Asylum*, *Tales of the Para Handy* and *Rab C Nesbitt*.

Josephine Tewson: Josephine Tewson has worked widely in the theatre, notably with Alan Ayckbourn in *Woman in Mind*. Her television appearances include *Keeping Up Appearances* and playing Peggy Philips in *Coronation Street*. She was in the film *Wilt*.

Angela Thorne: Angela Thorne is one of many stars who have been drawn to appear at Islington's Almeida Theatre in London, where she recently appeared as Titania in *A Midsummer Night's Dream*. She is better known for her work on television, which comprises the role of Marjorie in *To the Manor Born* and Daphne in *Three Up Two Down*.

Anthony Tuckey: during his career in rep Anthony Tuckey has worked in many theatres, starting at Perth and progressing to become director in Liverpool and Ipswich.

Dorothy Tutin: Dorothy Tutin has worked with many renowned theatre companies, including the Old Vic, the Shakespeare Memorial Theatre and then its reincarnation as the RSC, the Royal Court, Chichester, Prospect and on Broadway. She is known to television audiences for her work in *The Six Wives of Henry the Eighth* and *South Riding*. Her films include *The Importance of Being Earnest*, *The Beggar's Opera*, *A Tale of Two Cities*, *Cromwell* and *Savage Messiah*.

Philip Voss: Philip Voss started his career on the pier at Bognor Regis and went on to work in rep at Colchester, Ipswich, Birmingham, Cheltenham, Hornchurch, Oxford and Salisbury. In recent years he has been in a number of productions for the RSC. His television credits include *Bad Company*, *The Dwelling Place*, *A Royal Scandal* and *A Village Affair* and among the films he has appeared in are *Indian Summer* and *Four Weddings and a Funeral*.

April Walker: April Walker has worked both in rep and the West End. Among her television credits are *Honey for Tea*, *Inspector Wycliffe* and *Never the Twain*.

Eileen Walsh: Eileen Walsh worked in the theatre until she gave up her career in order to raise her children with her husband Lionel Jeffries.

Harriet Walter: Harriet Walter played Harriet Vane to Edward Petherbridge's *Lord Peter Wimsey* on television and was also in *The Men's Room*. She appeared in the hit film *Sense and Sensibility* and has a string of theatre successes behind her, including *Children's Hour* and *Arcadia* at the National.

John Warner: in the early part of his career John Warner worked at the Little Theatre and the Old Vic in Bristol, and at Colchester, the Liverpool Playhouse and the Glasgow Citizens theatre. More recently he has been in seasons at Chichester, Nottingham and with the RSC. His television credits include *Mr Bean's Christmas Special, Desmond's* and *Lovejoy*.

Moray Watson: Moray Watson has worked in rep in Whitley Bay, Nottingham, Leatherhead, Reading, Canterbury, Liverpool, Brighton and High Wycombe as well as in many West End productions. His recent television credits include *Lovejoy* and *Medics*.

Clare Welch: Clare Welch has a considerable amount of experience in rep in companies at Northampton, Exeter and elsewhere in the country. She was recently seen in television in *Our Friends in the North*.

Timothy West: Timothy West started his career in various reps, among them Wimbledon, Salisbury, Hull and Northampton. He then went on to work in the West End, at the RSC, with Prospect and the Bristol Old Vic. On television he has been seen in *Edward VII, Henry VIII, Framed, Hard Times, Brass* and *A Very Peculiar Practice*. His films include *The Deadly Affair* and *Nicholas and Alexandra*.

Janet Whiteside: Janet Whiteside has worked a great deal in rep at Northampton and Chichester and on many occasions with both the RSC and the Royal National Theatre, where she was in recent productions of *The Shaughruan, The Voysey Inheritance* and *The Winter's Tale*.

June Whitfield: decades of splendid performances on television have made June Whitfield known to everybody. Highlights in her career include *The Arthur Askey Show, Hancock's, A Show Called Fred, Seven Faces of Jim, Baxter on Travel, Beggar My Neighbour, The Fossett Saga, Scott on . . ., Happy Ever After* and most recently *Absolutely Fabulous*.

Simon Williams: Simon Williams began his career in Worthing and then made a considerable impact as Major Bellamy in *Upstairs Downstairs*. He has also been seen in *Agony, Agony Again, Law and Disorder* and *A Respectable Trade*. He appears frequently on stage and has written two novels and two plays.

Paul Williamson: Paul Williamson has worked extensively in rep in Hull, Preston, Dundee, Richmond, Birmingham and at the Stables Theatre in Manchester. Among his television credits are *Thorndyke, The Jewel in the Crown, Keeping up Appearances* and *Hello, Girls*.

Tim Woodward: Tim Woodward has worked in rep at the Citizens Theatre in Glasgow. He has been seen on television in *Wings* and *Piece of Cake*.

Marjorie Yates: Marjorie Yates has appeared in rep in Liverpool and at the

Bristol Old Vic and has worked with the RSC and the Royal National Theatre. Her television experience includes parts in *It's a Lovely Day Tomorrow* and *The Ruth Rendell Mysteries*. She became known to a wider audience, playing the title role in Lynda La Plante's *The Governor*.

Pauline Yates: Pauline Yates gained fame playing Leonard Rossiter's long-suffering wife in *The Fall and Rise of Reginald Perrin*. This was the culmination of a varied career, which began with seasons in rep at Chorley, Bolton, Wakefield, Dewsbury, Oldham and Richmond.

Repertory Theatres in Great Britain

ALEC MCCOWEN SAID that when he was writing round to reps in an attempt to find a job in theatre in 1945 he was able to send letters to more than two hundred companies. There are now approximately seventy-five left and the future of a number of these is uncertain.

I am indebted to John Elsom, *Theatre Outside London* (Macmillan, 1971) and to Ian Mackintosh, *Curtains* (John Offard, 1982) for some of the details in the following list, which is an inventory of theatres which at some time housed repertory companies, although, given the transitory nature of the profession, in some cases it has been impossible to find any information about the companies concerned other than the fact that they once existed.

Aberdeen: His Majesty's Theatre, built in 1906 by Frank Matcham.

Amersham: for ten years, between 1936 and 1946, Caryl Jenner and Sally Latimer ran a weekly rep company at the Playhouse in Amersham.

Ayr: the Civic Theatre, a converted church hall which seats 352 people, is still active as a rep.

Barnsley: Charles Denville ran a twice-nightly, twice-weekly rep at the Alhambra, which was built in 1915.

Barrow-in-Furness: His Majesty's Theatre.

Basingstoke: the Haymarket Theatre continues to survive in a difficult climate.

Belfast: the Arts Theatre.

Bexhill-on-Sea: the De La Warr Pavilion, seats 1,150, for many years the home of the Penguin Players, run by Richard Burnett and Peggy Paige.

Billingham: the Rex. Michael Gambon made an early appearance in rep here, although the theatre is now a receiving house for tours.

Birmingham: the Alexandra Theatre ('the Alex'). Derek Salberg ran a rep company to rival Barry Jackson's here, but the plays were of a more popular kind and the pay was better. The Alex is struggling to survive even as a touring date.

Birmingham: the Repertory Theatre was situated from 1913 to 1971 in Station Street, seating 450. In 1971 the New Rep opened in Centenary Square; it seats 900 and is still functioning.

Bognor Regis: the Esplanade.

Bolton: in the 1950s the Lawrence Williamson Players were established as a weekly rep company in Bolton and Derek Nimmo began his career with them. In 1967 the Octagon Theatre was built, seating 427 maximum, at a cost of £97,000, which was raised by public subscription in less than a year. Rep seasons are still presented here.

The Boltons: weekly rep theatre in South Kensington.

Bradford: Harry Hanson had a rep company in the city.

Bridgend: no details available.

Bridlington: at the start of his career Brian Rix ran a company at the Grand Pavilion.

Brighton: the Dolphin Theatre operated as a rep in the 1940s, when it was run by H.M. Tennant's and launched the career of Barbara Jefford among others. There was also the Palace Theatre on the Palace Pier, which was built in 1901 and closed in 1973 after being hit by a barge. A theatre, built in 1893, was situated on the West Pier as well and the actress Jean Anderson has done repertory seasons in both.

Bristol: Theatre Royal, built in 1766 at a cost of £5,000, which was raised by public subscription, seats 681. The Old Vic Comapny was founded in 1946 with help from the Council for the Encouragement of Music and the Arts (CEMA), making it the first publicly funded rep in the country. The theatre was redeveloped in 1971, when it produced twenty-seven plays a year on its three stages. It now produces considerably fewer.

Bromley: the New Theatre, originally a Victorian swimming pool, seating 902, replaced by the Churchill Theatre, which is used for touring, although a few productions originate there.

Butlin's: the holiday camps at Skegness, Pwllheli and Barry Island all had resident rep companies in the 1950s.

Buxton: the Playhouse. Anthony Hawtrey produced plays in the late 1940s and early 1950s under the direction of Shaun Sutton. It is now used as a discothèque.

Cambridge: Terence Grey ran the Festival Theatre in the 1920s. The city now has the Arts Theatre, which is used largely for touring.

Canterbury: the Marlowe Theatre, a converted cinema seating 645, founded in 1951 by Christopher Hassall and Peter Carpenter. Is now used for touring productions.

Cardiff: the Sherman Theatre still functions as a rep.

Chelmsford: the Civic Theatre is used by Newpalm Production to present rep seasons.

Cheltenham: the Everyman, a Victorian touring theatre designed by Frank Matcham, who also designed the London Palladium and the London Coliseum, seats 750, was opened by Lillie Langtry in 1891. Served as a rep for many decades, but has recently reverted to receiving touring productions.

Chester: Harry Hanson ran a rep company here in the 1950s. The Gateway, built in 1968, seats 500 and also has a studio theatre, which is still presenting seasons.

Chesterfield: the Civic Theatre was built in 1879 and reconstructed in 1948.

Chichester: the Festival Theatre, built in 1962, seats 1,360. The Minerva Studio was added in the early 1990s.

Chorley: the Royal, at one time home to the Richard Lyons Adams Company, demolished in 1960.

Chorlton cum Hardy: Bernard Cribbins helped to construct the theatre that housed the Piccolo Players, which was a breeding ground for the actors who went on ultimately to work at the Royal Exchange. It was opened by Peggy Ashcroft.

Clacton: the Operetta House was built in 1894 and is now a bingo hall.

Clapham: the Grand Theatre was built in 1900 and opened by Dan Leno. By 1912 it could hold 2,500; it operated as a rep in the 1940s and is now a bingo hall.

Colchester: the original rep was converted from an art gallery in 1937 by Robert Digby, who ran a company there for many years. In 1972 the existing Mercury Theatre was built and continues to stage rep seasons.

Colwyn Bay: the Prince of Wales Theatre, seats 518.

Coventry: the Belgrade, seats 900, built in 1958, the first new theatre constructed after the war, named to acknowledge a gift of timber for the auditorium, which was given by the government of Yugoslavia. Has recently survived a threatened closure.

Crewe: home of the Lyceum Theatre, which was built in 1911 and seats 850; also the New Theatre, in which Frank H. Fortescue ran a weekly rep company.

Croydon: the Ashcroft Theatre has become a receiving house for touring companies.

Darlington: the Civic Theatre was built in 1901 as an Edwardian touring theatre and converted into a smaller theatre in 1966, seats 601.

Derby: the Playhouse replaced the old Playhouse, which seated 396, and continues to present rep seasons.

Dewsbury: the Empire was demolished in 1960.

Dundee: the Repertory Theatre replaced the old rep, which was a converted church hall, when it burnt down in 1963. It is still functioning as a rep.

Eastbourne: the Devonshire Park Theatre, built in 1884, seats 1,008.

East Grinstead: the Adeline Genée Theatre, originally served as the theatre for the ballet school in the town, but sometimes operated as a rep, seats 330.

Edinburgh: the Royal Lyceum, built in 1883 and named after Henry Irving's London Lyceum, seats 1,292. Richard Eyre was associate director there. The theatre is still presenting rep seasons.

Edinburgh: the Traverse Theatre supplements its rep work with productions by visiting companies.

Exeter: the Northcott Theatre, built in 1968, seats a maximum of 580 and continues to present rep seasons.

Farnham: the Castle Theatre, a medieval granary, was converted to a theatre in 1939, it seated 167 and was replaced in the early 1970s by the Redgrave Theatre, seating 350. It is one of many reps in the Home Counties whose future hangs in the balance.

Folkestone: the Leas Pavilion was converted from a restaurant in 1902 into a hall for concert parties and for forty years from 1929 was home to the Arthur Brough Players, but in 1969 the Penguin Players took over management of the theatre, which seats 460.

Frinton: Frinton Summer Theatre still presents an annual eight-week season.

Glasgow: the Citizens Theatre was built in 1878 as a touring theatre, which seated 1,004 but in 1943 the Princess, as it was then called, was leased to James Bridie's rep company. The 'Citz' underwent extensive renovation in 1978 and continues to present rep seasons.

Grange-over-Sands: the town once housed a weekly rep company at the Victoria Hall.

Grantham: the Empire Theatre was demolished in 1954.

Greenwich: Greenwich Theatre. In 1969 the new theatre was constructed in the shell of a Victorian music hall, which dated from before 1869 and is currently under serious threat of closure.

Guildford: the Yvonne Arnaud Theatre, built in 1965, seats 568 and manages to survive by mounting productions destined for the West End.

Guernsey: the Hippodrome started life in 1880 as a skating rink, was a cinema from 1912 to 1929 and for ten years after that housed a rep company.

Hammersmith: the King's Theatre was built in 1902 and demolished in 1955.

Harrogate: Harrogate Theatre, a Victorian touring theatre seating 850, originally called the Opera House, built in 1900, for many years home to the White Rose Theatre Company which faced a chequered history during the 1950s and 1960s. The council bought it in 1965 and ran it as a fortnightly rep from then. It now operates on a three- to four-weekly basis.

Hastings: the Hippodrome was built in 1899 and is now a bingo hall.

Hayes: various managements tried to succeed with weekly rep at the Regent Theatre, where Joss Ackland made appearances early in his career.

High Wycombe: I understand that the Tower Theatre was converted from a swimming pool and ran as a weekly rep in 1950s.

Hornchurch: the original Queen's Theatre was a converted cinema, seating 379, which opened in 1953, has since been replaced by the new Queen's Theatre, which is still mounting rep seasons.

Hull: the Little Theatre had a rep company, which launched the careers of Maurice Denham and Margaretta Scott in the 1930s. There also appears to have been a rep at the New Theatre. Its function was taken over by the University Theatre, but the city's theatre needs are now provided by the Hull Truck Theatre Company.

Ilkley: Brian Rix ran a rep company in the King's Hall in the 1940s.

Ipswich: the Arts Theatre was a converted hall, seating 345, which was replaced by the Wolsey Theatre, which is still active in the rep movement.

Jersey: Marjorie Denville ran a rep company at the Opera House, which was built in 1900, opened by Lillie Langtry and reconstructed in 1921. It seats 709.

Keighley: the Queen's Theatre was demolished in 1956.

Keswick: the Century Theatre is still staging rep seasons.

Kettering: Reggie Salberg ran a company in Kettering at the Victoria Theatre in the 1940s, but in 1970 the building was demolished.

Kirkcaldy: the King's Theatre was opened in 1904 and is now a cinema.

Lancaster: the Duke's Theatre has recently had problems, but continues to survive.

Leatherhead: Leatherhead Rep was founded in 1951 by Hazel Vincent Wallace. The current Thorndike Theatre was built in the shell of an existing building and seats 530. Its prospects for survival have recently been under question.

Leeds: Harry Hanson ran a rep company at the Theatre Royal, but when that closed Leeds became the largest city in Western Europe without a rep, until 1970, when a temporary theatre was built on a site given by the university. This was, in its turn, superseded by the flourishing West Yorkshire Playhouse.

Leicester: the Phoenix Theatre was built in 1963 and seated 274. It has been replaced by the Haymarket, which also has a studio theatre and continues to present rep seasons.

Lichfield: the David Garrick Memorial Theatre was built in 1872 and named after the famous actor, who was born in the city. Lionel Jeffries started out here when it was functioning as a rep in 1949. It is now a spare-parts workshop.

Lincoln: Theatre Royal, a Victorian touring theatre built in 1893, which was partly converted for rep in 1930 and seats a total of 448. After the resident company went bankrupt in the 1970s, it reverted to use as a touring theatre.

Liverpool: the Everyman, a converted cinema seating 450, the company was founded in 1964 by Terry Hands and Peter James, with an emphasis on community and educational theatre.

Liverpool: the Pavilion was built in 1908 and was the home to a rep company run by Charles Denville. It is now a bingo hall.

Liverpool: the Playhouse started life as the Star Music Hall in 1866; in 1911 it was set up as a rep to rival Annie Horniman's Gaiety Theatre in Manchester. The legendary director Basil Dean was involved in the early days. In 1968 it was renovated and in recent years has been saved from closure by the support of Bill Kenwright.

Llandudno: the Grand Theatre was built in 1899.

Lowestoft: the Hippodrome originally had a circus ring as well as a stage, but in 1948 it was converted for purely theatrical use.

Lytham St Anne's: the Pavilion was built in 1904 and destroyed by fire seventy years later.

Macclesfield: the Theatre Royal was where Alec McCowen began his career.

Malvern: the Festival Theatre has occasionally housed a rep company.

Manchester: Contact Theatre evolved from the Theatre '69 company, which in its turn grew out of the Theatre '59 company, both of which were run by Michael Elliot. The university theatre at Contact is now under major reconstruction.

Manchester: the Gaiety Theatre was founded by Miss Horniman in 1908 and was home to the first rep company in mainland Britain. Early company members included Sybil Thorndike and Lewis Casson.

Manchester: the Library Theatre, converted from a lecture hall in the basement of the City Library, seats 308. The Library also operates the Forum Theatre in Wythenshawe and is managing to survive.

Manchester: the Royal Exchange, built in 1976 inside the shell of the old Corn Exchange. Michael Elliot, Casper Wrede and Braham Murray piloted it into existence; it was virtually destroyed when the IRA bombed Manchester and is currently being rebuilt.

Manchester: the Stables, run as a theatre club by Granada TV in the 1960s with a view to developing experimental work in the theatre which might lend itself to being televised.

Margate: the Hippodrome; my grandfather, the actor Hugh Williams, began his career in rep here in 1921 and was paid £4 a week. In the late 1940s the Hippodrome accommodated a rep company established by Brian Rix. It was demolished in 1974.

Milford Haven: the Torch Theatre continues to present rep seasons.

Mold: Theatre Clywd is currently enjoying a renaissance under former RSC director Terry Hands.

Morecambe: the Royalty Theatre was demolished in 1957.

Musselburgh: the Brunton Theatre runs a rep season from April to September.

Newbury: the Watermill Theatre, seats 115, a pioneer of the Dinner Theatre movement, in which the audience is offered dinner before the show to enhance their evening out.

Newcastle upon Tyne: the University Theatre, built in 1970, seats 450 and is still engaged in the production of rep seasons.

Newquay: Timothy West worked in a rep company in Newquay in the early stages of his career.

Newton Poppleford: provided a base for a fit-up company called the Garrick Players.

Northampton: the Theatre Royal, a Victorian touring theatre which converted to rep in the 1920s, seats a maximum of 630, in 1983–4 it was incorporated into the Derngate centre and is still presenting rep seasons.

Norwich: the Hippodrome was home to a rep company run by Douglas Quayle. It was demolished in 1960.

Nottingham: the Playhouse, built in 1963 and during the 1960s home to John Neville's famous company, seats 756. Under Martin Duncan's direction it is gaining an international reputation for its work.

Oldham: the Coliseum, founded as a private theatre club in 1938, was renovated in 1966 and three years later became a public theatre, which is still presenting rep seasons. In the early days Harold G. Roberts ran a rival rep company at the Theatre Royal, which was demolished in 1967.

Oxford: the Playhouse, seating 700, was converted from a museum and run by J.B. Fagan from 1923 to 1929, and then Sir Ben Greet in the 1930s. Sir Peter Hall launched his directing career here, but the theatre is now a receiving house for touring productions.

Palmer's Green: the Intimate Theatre, run as a rep in the 1930s by John Clements, still functioning in the 1950s. Richard Attenborough started his career here.

Penge: the Empire Theatre, operated as a rep during the 1950s by Reggie Salberg.

Penzance: the Pavilion was built in 1911.

Perranporth: Peter Bull ran a rep company in a converted hall during the summer season and a later company included Eileen Atkins.

Perth: a Victorian touring theatre, which turned to rep in 1935 under the ownership of Marjorie Dence and David Steuart. It was the first rep in Scotland and when Dence died she left it in her will to the Scottish Arts Council, who sold it to Perth Council. It seats 606 and is still active as a rep.

Peterborough: Harry Hanson ran a company at the Theatre Royal, which was originally built as a skating rink in 1872 and became a theatre in 1899. This was demolished in 1961 and now the only theatre in the town is the Key Theatre, which is mainly a touring theatre but occasionally runs its own rep seasons.

Pitlochry: the Festival Theatre; originally the festival was held in a tent, but a theatre seating 502 has been built (with a tent-shaped auditorium).

Plymouth: the Theatre Royal and its studio, the Drum Theatre; pre-London productions are often mounted here.

Preston: the Hippodrome was home to a rep company run by Reggie Salberg in the 1950s.

'Q' Theatre: Kew Bridge. Dirk Bogarde had his first job here.

Richmond: the Richmond Theatre was designed by Frank Matcham as a touring theatre in the late Victorian age, in the 1960s it housed a fortnightly rep company, but soon reverted to touring productions only.

Rhyl: the Pavilion was built in 1871 and demolished in 1974.

Ryde: the Theatre Royal was built in 1871 and ninety years later was destroyed by fire.

St Andrew's: the Byre Theatre, built in 1970, seats 128 and still offers four-weekly seasons.

Salisbury: the Arts Theatre was converted from a church hall and seated 406, one of the first reps to receive funding from the Arts Council. It was replaced by the Playhouse Theatre, which under the late David Horlock became the best-attended rep in the country. It was threatened with closure during the early 1990s, but is now holding its own.

Scarborough: the Royal Opera House started out as a circus in 1876 and became a theatre in 1900, seating 970. The Stephen Joseph Theatre in the Round was built and is run by its artistic director, Alan Ayckbourn.

Shanklin: the Pier Theatre on the Esplanade.

Sheffield: the Playhouse was replaced in 1971 by the Crucible. The original theatre was converted from a British Legion hall seating 546. In 1923 Herbert Prentice transformed his amateur company into a professional one. In the twenty-five years after 1923 it produced 711 plays. The Crucible is partially dependent on its televising of the snooker championships to remain viable.

Southampton: the Nuffield Theatre still presents rep seasons.

Southsea: there was once a rep company on the pier at Southsea.

Southwold: Jill Freud runs a summer season of weekly rep.

Stockton-on-Tees: the Grand Theatre was a venue for one of Harry Hanson's many rep companies.

Stoke-on-Trent: the Victoria Theatre, director Peter Cheeseman, has been a great exponent of theatre in the round and all productions at the Victoria are staged in this form, with audience members seated on every side. The Victoria still presents rep seasons.

Stratford East: for many years Joan Littlewood's famous company was based at the Theatre Royal, which was built in 1884 and seats 499. It was run as a rep by Philip Hedley.

Swiss Cottage: the Embassy Theatre, in the 1930s run by rep legend A.R. Whatmore; Sybil Thorndike started her career here.

Tunbridge Wells: the Opera House was built in 1902 and is now a bingo hall.

Wakefield: the Opera House was built in 1894, seats 600, and is now a bingo hall.

Walham Green: the Granville Theatre briefly housed a weekly rep company.

Warrington: Harry Hanson ran a rep company in Warrington.

Watford: the Palace Theatre was built in 1908, seats 640, and is still running as a rep.

Westcliff-on-Sea: the Palace Theatre was built in 1912, seats 520 and is still actively staging rep seasons.

Weston-super-Mare: the Opera House was built in 1900 and seats 650.

Whitley Bay: the Playhouse was built in 1911 and became a theatre and cinema complex. It hosted a couple of seasons of rep in the early 1950s.

Wimbledon: the Wimbledon Theatre was once a rep, but is now a touring theatre.

Windsor: the Theatre Royal was run for decades by John Counsell without any subsidy. Without Counsell, the theatre began to run into trouble, but has recently been rescued by Bill Kenwright.

Wolverhampton: the Grand was built in 1894 and seats 1,410. When it was run as a rep, it launched the career of Peggy Mount, but now functions as a touring theatre.

Worcester: the Swan, built in 1965, seats 353 and continues to serve its local community as a rep.

Worthing: the Connaught was converted from a cinema and run as a rep from 1933; during the war the Rank film organization took it over. Worthing is one of the reps which has closed in the last few years.

York: Theatre Royal, building started in 1765, but the theatre was rebuilt in the nineteenth century and renovated in 1967. It seats 927 and is still in business as a rep.

Examples of Weekly Repertory Seasons from the Early 1950s

This information is provided by Richard Foulkes in his book *Repertory at the Royal: Sixty-five Years of Theatre in Northampton, 1927–92*, and by Shaun Sutton and Paul Williamson.

The Royal Theatre, Northampton, July–December 1950, Director, Alex Reeve

French Without Tears, Terence Rattigan
The Foolish Gentlewoman, Margery Sharp
The Damask Cheek, John van Druten and Lloyd Morris
Master of Arts, William Douglas-Home
The Years Between, Daphne du Maurier
The Mill on the Floss, David Tearle (from George Eliot)
Young Wives' Tale, Ronald Jeans
Top Secret, Alan Melville
Max, Denis Cannan
The River and the Sea, Noël Scott (première)
Don't Listen, Ladies, Stephen Powys and Guy Bolton
Devonshire Cream, Eden Phillpotts
Mr Gillie, James Bridie
Mansfield Park, Constance Cox (from Jane Austen)
If This Be Error, Rachel Grieve
A Wind on the Heath, Ronald Adam
The Perfect Woman, Wallace Geoffrey and Basil Mitchell
The Eleventh Hour, Heath MacGregor
Summer in December, James Liggat
Background, Warren Chetham-Strode
Wishing Well, E. Eynon Evans
The Snow Princess, Alex Reeve and Dorothy Carr (première)

The Playhouse, Buxton, May–October 1951, Director, Shaun Sutton

Castle in the Air, Alan Melville
If This Be Error, Rachel Grieve
The Good Young Man, Kenneth Horne
Murder at the Vicarage, Agatha Christie
High Temperature, Avery Hopwood and Wilson Collison
Bonaventure, Charlotte Hastings
The Ghost Train, Arnold Ridley

Traveller's Joy, Arthur Macrae
A Murder Has Been Arranged, Emlyn Williams
The Holly and the Ivy, Wynyard Browne
Queen Elizabeth Slept Here, Talbot Rothwell
Pick-Up Girl, Elsa Shelley
Charley's Aunt, Brandon Thomas
Mr Bowling Buys a Newspaper, Donald Henderson
Tovarich, Robert E. Sherwood
Deliver My Darling, Joan Temple
Poison in Jest, Val Gielgud
School for Spinsters, Roland Pertwee
Fresh Fields, Ivor Novello
Black Chiffon, Lesley Storm
Rope, Patrick Hamilton
Captain Carvallo, Dennis Cannan
See How They Run, Philip King

The New Theatre, Hull, 1952, Directors Oliver Gordon and Herbert Wise

The Seventh Veil, Muriel and Sydney Box
French Without Tears, Terence Rattigan
Johnny Belinda, Elmer Harris
The Holly and the Ivy, Wynyard Browne
Peg O' My Heart, J. Hartley Manners
She Stoops to Conquer, Oliver Goldsmith
The First Mrs Fraser, St John Ervine
It Won't Be a Stylish Marriage, A.P. Dearsley
The Importance of Being Earnest, Oscar Wilde
Night Must Fall, Emlyn Williams
Traveller's Joy, Arthur Macrae
The Young in Heart, revue by Ross Parker, Bryan Blackburn and Greatrex
    Newman
Busman's Honeymoon, Dorothy L. Sayers
Saloon Bar, Frank Harvey

Bibliography

J. Keith Angus, *A Scotch Playhouse, Being the Records of the Old Theatre Royal, Marischal Street, Aberdeen* (D. Wyllie & Sons, Edinburgh, 1878).

'Britain's Reps: How Are They Making Out?', *Quarterly Theatre Review* (Autumn 1982).

James Carter, *The Oldham Coliseum Theatre – the First Hundred Years* (Oldham Coliseum Theatre, n.d.).

John Counsell, *Counsell's Opinion* (Barrie & Rockliff, London, 1963).

Michael Coveney, *The Citz – 121 Years of the Glasgow Citizens Theatre*, (Nick Hern Books, London, 1990).

John Elsom, *Theatre Outside London* (Macmillan, London, 1971).

Richard Foulkes, *Repertory at the Royal: Sixty-five Years of Theatre in Northampton, 1927–92* (Northampton Repertory Players Ltd, 1992).

Freda Gaye (ed.), *Who's Who in the Theatre*, Fourteenth and Jubilee Edition (Pitman, London, 1967).

Phyllis Hartnoll (ed.), *The Oxford Companion to the Theatre*, Second Edition (Oxford University Press, London, 1957).

Ian Herbert (ed.), *Who's Who in the Theatre*, Concise Sixteenth Edition (Pitman, London, 1978).

John Hodgson, *Repertory in Britain, A Survey* (Leeds Playhouse Souvenir Brochure, September 1970).

Richard Jerrams, *Weekly Rep* (Peter Andrew, Droitwich, 1991).

Alec McCowen, *Young Gemini* (Elm Tree Books, London, 1979).

Iain Mackintosh, *Curtains* (John Offard, 1982).

Not in the Script: Bristol Old Vic Anecdotes on Stage and Off (Redcliffe Press, Bristol, 1992).

Harold Pinter, *Mac* (Emanuel Wax for Pendragon Press, 1968).

George Rowell and Anthony Jackson, *The Repertory Movement: A History of Regional Theatre in Britain* (Cambridge University Press, 1984).

The Peggy Ann Wood Archive, Theatre Collection, University of Bristol.

The Walter Potter Archive, Theatre Collection, University of Bristol.

Index

Index